THE ILLUSTRATED CORVETTE SERIES

A History of the Corvette from 1953 to 2010

K. Scott Teeters

*Every Production Corvette From 1953 to 2010,
Plus Every Important Corvette Show Car, Prototype,
Engineering Study, & Many Significant Corvette Race Cars*

CarTech®

CarTech®

CarTech®, Inc.
39966 Grand Avenue
North Branch, MN 55056
Phone: 651-277-1200 or 800-551-4754
Fax: 651-277-1203
www.cartechbooks.com

© 2010 by K. Scott Teeters

All rights reserved. No part of this publication may be reproduced or utilized in any form or by any means, electronic or mechanical, including photocopying, recording, or by any information storage and retrieval system, without prior permission from the Author. All text, photographs, and artwork are the property of the Author unless otherwise noted or credited.

The information in this work is true and complete to the best of our knowledge. However, all information is presented without any guarantee on the part of the Author or Publisher, who also disclaim any liability incurred in connection with the use of the information.

All trademarks, trade names, model names and numbers, and other product designations referred to herein are the property of their respective owners and are used solely for identification purposes. This work is a publication of CarTech, Inc., and has not been licensed, approved, sponsored, or endorsed by any other person or entity.

ISBN 978-1-61325-024-2
Item No. CT494P

Library of Congress Cataloging-in-Publication Data

Teeters, K. Scott.
  Illustrated corvette series / by K. Scott Teeters.
    p. cm.
  ISBN 978-1-934709-46-7
  1. Corvette automobile--Pictorial works. I. Title.

TL215.C6T47 2010
629.222'2--dc22

                    2010020791

Printed in USA

Back Cover Photos

Top:
1953 Corvette–The Beginning of a Legend.

Bottom:
C7 Corvette–Return of the Split-Window Coupe Sting Ray?

CONTENTS

Foreword by Marty L. Schorr 4

Preface by K. Scott Teeters 4

Chapter 1: Production Corvettes 5

Chapter 2: Experimental and Prototype Corvettes 67

Chapter 3: Corvette Show Cars 81

Chapter 4: Racing Corvettes 90

Chapter 5: Special Editions and Tuner Corvettes 115

The Future of the Corvette 141

Foreword by Marty L. Schorr - Founding Editor of *VETTE* magazine

It was on a bitterly cold day in New York City in January 1953 when I fell in love with the Corvette! All I could think about was owning a Corvette. But my fantasy affair would have to wait for some 25 years.

After starting college I joined the Draggin Wheels hot rod club. Since I wasn't much good at turning wrenches, I became the club's publicity director. With a cheap camera, I starting writing stories for *Custom Rodder* and *Car Speed & Style* magazines. In 1961 I was hired as Editor of those magazines. After a couple of years I took over the publisher's flagship publication, *CARS* magazine, and all the company's automotive publications.

In 1967 I teamed with Joel Rosen, Baldwin Chevrolet, and Motion Performance. Rosen and I worked together to build the Baldwin-Motion Supercar brand. We started with 427 Camaros and in 1969 we unleashed SS-427 and Phase III 427 Corvettes. Baldwin-Motion Corvettes were built through 1974 and are documented in my book, *MOTION Performance: Tales of a Muscle Car Builder.*

Two years after launching *VETTE* magazine in '76, I bought a matching-number, Marlborough Maroon, 1967 big-block Sting Ray convertible with side exhausts and two tops. (Two decades later, while planning a move from New Jersey to Florida, I suffered major brain fade and sold my dream ride.)

My relationship with GM started when I was an editor and, in 1982, I began an 18-year relationship as a public relations consultant to Buick. I had access to GM Design, watched the C5 Corvette come to be, and previewed the C6. Then I fell in love all over again! In 2007 I took delivery of a Monterey Red convertible. What a car!

I was thrilled when Scott asked me to write a Foreword for this wonderful book. Scott and I go back to my early days at *VETTE* when I gave him his first assignment: a feature on "Stingray Styling" for the fourth issue (Volume 1, Number 4) in 1977. An extremely talented artist and a great storyteller, Scott is also, I am proud to say, a good friend. His unique style has been gracing the pages of *VETTE* and has been showcased in many Corvette collections for more than 30 years. Enjoy his latest creation!

(Marty Schorr is now the editor of www.CarGuyChronicles.com)

Preface by K. Scott Teeters - Artist & Author

When I was 10 years old, I went with my older brother to the local Chevy dealer to get his car serviced. While waiting for Bob, I saw the most stunning car—a '65 Corvette Coupe. My interest must have been obvious because a salesman said, "Here, kid, have a brochure." That was it, I was a young "car guy!" Three years later at a newsstand, an issue of *CARS* magazine grabbed my attention because there was a screaming yellow 1968 Baldwin-Motion Phase III 427 Corvette on the cover. WOW! Motion Performance Corvettes were TOPS in my book.

I started my working career as a technical illustrator and a weekend announcer at Cecil County Drag-o-Way. In '73 I bought a very rough '67 Corvette roadster with a 396 big-block for just $1,200. It was loud, fast, and needed everything. So in '75 I got a very nice '65 327, 4-speed, silver coupe with a black interior. A good-looker and FUN car to drive! But at night, I was still drawing cars. In '75 I had my first illustration published in *Drag Racing USA* magazine—a two-page, pen-and-ink drawing of what I though Bill Jenkins' new Pro Stock Monza might look like. Now I had the magazine art bug.

In the summer of '76 I discovered Marty Schorr's *VETTE* magazine. I thought it was great, but could use some art. So I sent a samples package off to Mr. Schorr. A week later, I got a phone call, "Scott, this is Marty Schorr. Got your samples; very nice. What would you like to do for *VETTE*?" I was "in" and I'm still with *VETTE*.

Through the '80s, and '90s, I mostly did column filler art. In the winter of '97, I pitched then-editor Richard Lentenello on a long-term series titled, "The Illustrated Corvette Series." Richard liked the idea, but didn't have an open page for another editorial, so that was that. A week later, he called me, "Still want to do that column we talked about?" That is how the series got started! At first, I thought it might last, maybe, 50 installments. But a few months into the series, I saw that I needed to branch off and cover the important show cars, prototypes, engineering studies, and racing Corvettes. As of this date, June 2010, the series has 161 installments.

This has been a longer and more gratifying ride than I ever expected way back in '76 when I had my first conversation with Marty. I suppose there will come a time when this great gig will come to an end. But between now and then, I still have LOTS of great cars to illustrate, and stories to tell.

(Scott's collection of more than 500 Corvette art prints can be found at www.IllustratedCorvetteSeries.com. His Corvette news and commentary blog is www.CorvetteReport.com.)

Chapter 1
Production Corvettes

In the mid-'50s, very few inside General Motors believed in Chevrolet's little Corvette sports car. Little did anyone know that the sedan-based, fiberglass-bodied car would one day become a world-class sports car and the longest-running automobile marque in Detroit history. This chapter covers Corvettes from 1953 to 2010.

1953 Corvette
"The Beginning of a Legend"

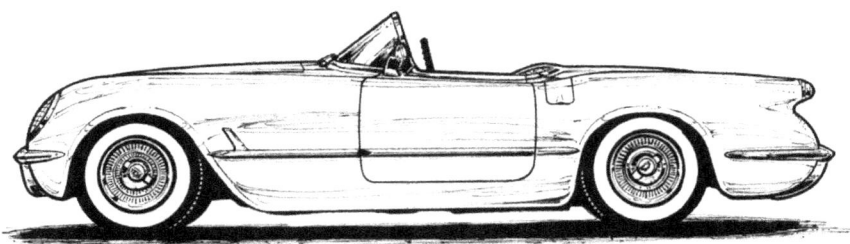

It was possibly one of the most outrageous car proposals in Detroit history. GM's legendary chief of design, Harley Earl was a visionary designer. As a lifelong car guy, Earl was drawn to the exciting new vehicles being built in postwar Europe - sports cars. Cars such as Jaguar and MG captured his imagination. Being well aware of what they were up to, Earl wanted GM to start making reasonably priced, American sports cars.

Harley was the creator of the GM Motorama and the concept of "the dream car." One of his first shots at an American sports car was his two-seater, '51 Le Sabre show car. The looks of the car were totally deceiving, as it looked huge, until you saw someone standing next to the car. Earl was also one of the pioneers of the American small car, as well as women's rights within the auto industry. Modeling of new designs in clay was another of Earl's innovations. So he started dreaming up a small American sports car on paper and in clay.

The original show car went from full size clay model in April 1952 to a complete running car, ready for the January 17, 1953 GM Motorama. Along the way, a bootlegged photo was shown to Ford's styling studio. While they were already working on a sports car, this kicked them into overdrive. By 1953 standards, the Corvette show car was drop dead gorgeous. Almost four million people saw the two show cars that toured America and Canada. The two Corvette show cars only cost Chevrolet $55,000 to $60,000 to build.

The response was so overwhelming, the order was given, and the Corvette was rushed into production as a 1953 model.

The only really new technology there was time for on the Corvette was the use of fiberglass as the body material. And for a very brief time, the decision was made to make the body in steel, but obviously, the decision was quickly changed. Although it was lighter than steel, the main reason for using the new material was the low cost of manufacturing the body parts.

Everything else on the car was directly out of the Chevrolet parts bin. Because of this, the car was essentially a "regular" 1953 Chevy that looked like a million bucks - a point that would dog the Corvette until 1956. Even though the standard Chevy inline six engine was juiced up with solid lifters, a new cam shaft, and three horizontal Carter carbs, power was way off the mark. The softest part of the running gear was the two-speed Powerglide automatic transmission.

The design group gave it a good try, they really did. However, none of them had any experience building or designing high performance cars or lessons learned from racing. The Corvette concept had two major elements already going for it. The car was low-slung, sleek, and looked like a Hollywood movie star. Plus, the car had the might and resources of one of the world's most profitable companies, GM. What it desperately needed was a trainer, someone to take Earl's show car and turn it into a street fighter, tough guy.

Because of the huge public support for the Corvette show car, Chevrolet pressed the Corvette into production almost "as is." GM had decided that the '53 models be considered test cars, but orders could be placed. Once word got around about the average-to-poor performance, sales went flat. Of the 300 cars produced, only 183 were sold. Those that weren't sold were used for various tests - ice test, shake test, fire test, etc. V.I.P.s and famous people were given Corvettes to show off. Actor John Wayne was given a '53 Corvette. The car must have looked even smaller than it really is, next to the Duke.

When Zora Arkus Duntov saw the original Corvette show car, he called it the most beautiful car he'd ever seen! Fortunately for all of us, Chevrolet chief engineer and Corvette supporter, Ed Cole hired Duntov on May, 1 1953. By July, Zora started working his golden hands on the car he lusted for, improving the suspension of a Corvette prototype. Over the next year and a half, Duntov was asked to solve various other problems, including looking into fuel injection. By October '55, Zora started making racing Corvettes. Thus, the third part of the Corvette formula fell into place. Although it was a very bumpy ride for several years, thanks the the Corvette's three wise-men, the Corvette was destined for greatness.

THE ILLUSTRATED CORVETTE SERIES

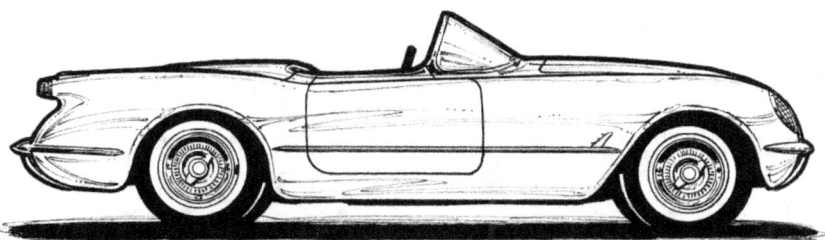

1954 Corvette
"A Rocky Start"

The 1953 Corvette was literally jammed into production. Most of the '53 Corvettes were either given or sold to prominent sports and entertainment people. Even though the '54 Corvette had many mechanical improvements, there was still the problem of price/value. By the end of the year, half of the 3,640 Corvettes produced were not sold, and rumors started that the Corvette would be axed!

Sports car purists were turned off by the mandatory automatic transmission and the

simulated knock-off hubcaps. The boulevard crowd didn't like the side curtains and manual fold-up top. A minor face-lift was proposed by Harley Earl's design group, but since sales were so slow, styling was unchanged.

Due to such poor sales, Earl's "reasonably priced, simply built," American sports car was in serious trouble. They needed and expected sales of at least 20,000 units. Needless to say, 3,640 units fell far short. But the right people at Chevrolet were committed to the Corvette, and minor mechanical and cosmetic improvements were made to fix numerious shortcomings.

A whole host of small details were corrected and improved for the '54 model. The starter motor was improved and brake lines were moved to the insides of the frame rails. Radios were improved and the hood latch mechanism was reduced to just one latch. The engine's camshaft was improved for performance, and the exhaust tips were lengthened to 6-inches to

reduce body discoloration from the exhaust. Color choice was expanded from just white the year before, to blue, red, copper, gold, and white.

Beginning in January '55, engineering started testing the fit of a prototype 265 small-block Chevy. The heat got turned up in the following month when Ford announced that its Thunderbird show car was going into production as a '55 model. But not as a sports car, as a "personal car." Stylists had already started designing the next look for the Corvette. A new design was shown in March and rejected. And the Corvette was getting help from outside. McCulloch Motors started offering a supercharger kit for the Vette's Blue flame-Six, claiming an 87 to 117-hp increase over the stock engine. The Corvette started getting some much needed PR help from Chevrolet National Sales promotion Manager, Joe Pike when he launched the first Corvette club in June '54. And it wasn't until September that the first V-8 '54 Corvettes were built. But things got ugly when the first Thunderbirds hit the Ford showrooms in October and Ford scooped up 4,000 orders the very first day!

1954 is arguably the darkest year in the Corvette's history. In September '54, Duntov was told by a GM executive that the Corvette was going to be canceled. A few weeks later, Zora wrote a letter to chief engineer, Ed Cole and director of R&D, Maurice Olley, suggesting that to drop the Corvette so soon would be an admission of failure. He went on to make various suggestions, urging GM to keep the car and create a separate department exclusively for the Corvette. Obviously, the Corvette made it into '55, with a lot more involvement from Duntov to come.

Management determined that since the Corvette was basically a '54 Chevy, its inherent reliability was an asset. The car wasn't temperamental like a Jaguar, MG or Ferrari. By the time the magazines got Corvettes to test the '54 model, they sincerely liked the car. *Road & Track* said, "Frankly, we like the Corvette very much ... it's really a good combination of ride and handling qualities." *Motor Trend* said, "Chevrolet has produced a bucket seat roadster that will hold its own with Europe's best, short of actual competition and a few imports that cost 3 times as much." Publicity like this was like gold for the floundering Corvette. But soon, the race track would be the Corvette's new publicity arena!

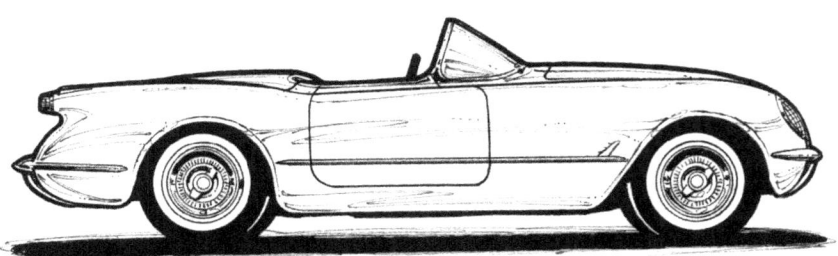

1955 Corvette
"Enter the Small-Block Corvette"

It was actually because of Ford that the Corvette survived! According to Zora Arkus-Duntov, "There were conversations in the hallways of GM about the Corvette being dropped. Then the Thunderbird came out, and all of a sudden GM was keeping the Corvette. I think that Ford had brought out the competitive spirit in Ed Cole." Although Ed Cole wasn't a racer, like Zora, he liked fast cars was a very competitive man. It was Cole who first recognized Duntov's potential and hired him. One could say that he was Duntov's "angel" inside GM.

Indeed, the '55 Corvette was on the slippery slope to oblivion. From a financial standpoint, there was no reason to keep the Corvette since it was losing money. GMs decision to make the body from fiberglass was to avoid the creation of expensive steel stamping tools. Fiberglass, and wooden bucks cost a lot less than steel. So, if the car failed, GM would not have that much invested.

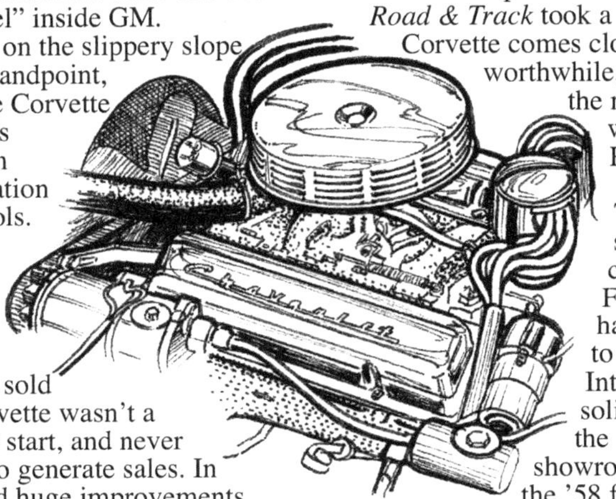

Sales for the '55 model were only 700 units, while Ford had sold 16,155 Thunderbirds! The Corvette wasn't a bad car, it just got off to a poor start, and never generated enough excitement to generate sales. In fact, the 1955 Corvette featured huge improvements.

Most exciting was the replacement of the Blue Flame Six with Chevy's all-new small-block 265 V-8. It was Ed Cole and Harry Barr that co-developed the '49 Cadillac V-8 engine that the small-block Chevy design was based upon. Right from the beginning of the small-block Chevy's life, there was a hot version. The Corvette setup ran a special camshaft, a Carter four-barrel carburetor, and a low-restriction air cleaner that raised horsepower to 195-hp. With only 8:1-compression, there was a lot more power left inside the new engine. Predictively, the extra 40-hp gave a nice performance bump, with 0-60 mph in 8.5-seconds and the quarter-mile times of 16.5. Top speed was close to 120 mph. The new, lighter engine also got better gas mileage, some 2-to-3-mpg better than the Six.

But the biggest sports car no-no was still with the '55 Vette - the 2-speed Powerglide automatic transmission. It's estimated that as few as 75 to 80 '55 Corvettes were equipped with the new 3-speed manual gearbox. Unfortunately, it was too late for magazine tests with the 3-speed manual 265 small-block '55 Corvette. *Road & Track* took a chill to the Corvette, stating, "The Corvette comes close to being a really interesting, worthwhile, and genuine sports car, yet misses the mark almost entirely." Yes, the car was still just a beauty queen as far as R&T was concerned.

With the arrival of the '55 Thunderbird and its astonishing sales, Chevrolet realized they'd been caught with their britches down. Fortunately, the right people in GM had fire in the belly and weren't ready to give up on the Corvette. Interestingly, Ford wasn't really solidly behind their sports car either. As the '55 T-Bird was hitting the showroom floors, Ford was busy designing the '58 four-seater Thunderbird. They were walking away from the concept as it was just coming out. The 1956 Corvette would finally shake off all the limitations of the Motorama show car and begin the process of making the Corvette America's only true sports car. There were even plans for racing the Corvette. Things were about to get very interesting.

Meanwhile, at the Phoenix, Arizona, GM test track, Duntov was blasting the course with a speciallly prepared '54 promotion Corvette, fitted with the hottest 265 V-8 engine he could build for the day. He clocked the track at 163 mph -- on stock tires!

THE ILLUSTRATED CORVETTE SERIES

1956 Corvette
"The First Revision"

This time they got it right and everyone noticed! The '56 Corvette was truly a pivotal model. At Chevrolet, every car has to pay its way or die. The 1955 Corvette hit an all-time low sales volume of only 700 units. It was put-up, or shut-up for the struggling Corvette. It's important to remember that when the Corvette first arrived in '53, the only engine Chevy had to work with the Stovebolt-Six. The lackluster performance of the '53 and '54 Corvette was as much of an anchor as the heavy Blue Flame Six engine was. Had the small-block Chevy engine been available in '53, the Corvette would have had a very different beginning.

The expensive, undeveloped car was off to a bad start and even the arrival of the new 265 small-block engine in '55 wasn't enough to grab the attention of the public. In an odd twist of fate, the Corvette got its second chance, thanks to the arrival of the '55 Thunderbird. Chevrolet certainly wasn't a performance icon yet, but they weren't about to let Ford have the sports car market all to themselves. So, defying all corporate logic, GM granted the Corvette one more chance. Stylists took their inspiration from two main sources: first was the '55 Cadillac LaSalle II roadster and second was the '54 Mercedes-Benz 300SL. What was to become the Corvette's signature side coves was taken from the LaSalle II and the twin bulges on the hood came from the Mercedes-Benz. The stylists did a wonderful job in taking those queues and making a unique design. The end result was a new American classic.

When the restyled Corvette arrived, the public noticed, in a big way. Although not "big" numbers by GM standards, Chevrolet sold 3,467 Corvettes in 1956, nearly a 500-percent increase from '55 sales, more than enough to buy a future for the fiberglass car that many wanted to see die!

The mechanicals of the '56 model are essentially the same as the '55 car. For some odd reason, perhaps due to time restraints, the dash was the same as the '55 car. Aside from the dash, all of the '50s comforts were finally included: roll-up glass windows with optional power assist, external door handles with door locks, bucket seats, an optional hardtop, and a quality AM radio. The side coves allowed for a stylish optional two-tone paint combination.

By far, the best part was under the hood. The 265 V-8 came in two versions. The base engine, single four-barrel was rated at 210 hp, and the optional $172.20 dual four-barrel engine was rated at 255 hp. The optional version had high compression 9.25:1 pistons, a special camshaft, and a cast aluminum intake manifold. With the close ratio 3-speed manual transmission, the '56 Corvette would go 0-60 mph in just 7.3 seconds. Quarter-mile times were 15.9 seconds at 91 mph. Gas mileage averaged 12 miles per gallon. With the right stuff in the '56 Vette, Zora Arkus-Duntov set out to prove the Corvette on the race track.

At the 1956 Daytona Speed Week, the car made an impressive two-way run of 150.583 mph, with Zora himself at the wheel! With John Fitch driving during competition, a Corvette was fastest in the Modified class with an average of 145.54 mph. Even Carroll Shelby was quoted as saying, "Racing was the thing that actually saved the

Corvette." At the Sebring 12 Hour race, Corvettes placed ninth overall and first in-class. From here on, racing would forever define the Corvette.

With a fresh, new look, and newfound grunt under the hood, the Corvette finally had a fighting chance. *Road & Track* blessed the '56 Corvette by saying, "The new Corvette is as good to excellent compared to other dual purpose sports cars." Little did they know that things would get even better in '57!

CHAPTER 1: PRODUCTION CORVETTES

1957 Corvette
"Zora Arkus-Duntov Delivers Fuel Injection"

The '57 Corvette looked just like the '56 model, but all the difference in the world was hidden under the sexy-looking fiberglass. What had originally started out as a show car sweetheart had become a fire-breathing, world-class sports car.

What got the automotive world's attention was the Corvette's newfound performance ability. In 1957, Zora Arkus-Duntov was promoted to "Director of High Performance Vehicle Design and Development." Zora made sure that everything but the racing gas was either already in the car or just a check mark and a few dollars away, on the order form of every local Chevrolet dealer.

The biggest performance item was not only the enlargement of the new 265 small-block Chevy engine to a 283-ci, but the addition of the new Rochester "Ramjet Fuel Injection" option. Fuel injection was already common on exotic European sports cars, but the Chevrolet Fuelie was the first American-made mass-production car to offer fuel injection. This was truly exotic stuff for 1957. And for its day, the Fuelie was a real stump-puller, developing 283-hp at a screaming 6,200-rpm. While not the first American engine to develop one-horsepower-per-cubic-inch (that accolade went to the '56 Chrysler 354 Hemi) the 283 Fuel Injected Corvette was the fastest machine in Detroit.

There are three basic parts to the Rochester fuel injection unit. Based on the vacuum in the aluminum intake manifold, the air meter sends a signal to the fuel meter, which sends a signal that regulates the fuel flow to the injector nozzles. The intake manifold, then provides the distribution of the air/fuel mixture into the cylinders. Fuel injection is superior to standard carburetors because the pressurized system eliminates fuel starvation as a sports car accelerates hard through curves. The last thing a driver wants is for his car to sputter due to a lack of fuel as he's exiting a fast, hard curve. The fuel injection system provides continuous fuel flow and superior performance - at least in theory.

The rest of the 283 engine was stout, featuring 10.5:1 compression, the Duntov high-lift cam, solid-lifters, and a special exhaust system that used a crossover pipe for better exhaust flow. There were only two drawbacks: first was the price. The street version, RPO 579B, cost $484.20 and the racing version cost $726.30, on top of the car's $3,176 base price. Combined with the $780.10 RPO 684 Heavy Duty Racing Suspension, the RPO 685 4-speed transmission, and the $48.44 Positraction rear axle, a '57 Corvette could be bought, almost ready for battle, for around $5,000 - a LOT of money in 1957. There were four different Fuelies, two of each rated at 250-hp and 283-hp respectively. The downside to the Fuelie was that they could be very tricky to setup and to keep running smoothly. Many frustrated customers had their Fuelies retrofitted with carburetors - hard to imagine.

Performance for its day was simply amazing. *Road & Track* magazine managed a 0-60 in just 5.7-seconds, with a quarter-mile time of 14.3 seconds, and a top speed of 132-mph. They called the Fuelie, "An absolute jewel... docile when driven gently, yet instantly transformable into a roaring brute when pushed hard." A total of 1,040 out of 6,339 Corvettes (16-percent) were Fuelies in '57.

Nearly everything else was a carry over from '56, and no one cared. Fuel Injection cars wore badges on the side coves and over the round trunk lid Corvette insignia. The previously mentioned racing extras were the first of Duntov's famous "racer kits" that helped many a Corvette racer to victory. In 1957, Dr. Dick Thompson won the SCCA B/Production Championship in one of Duntov's racer kit Fuelies. From here through to '62, Corvettes were the dominating force in SCCA class racing. Chevy's fledgling sports car had arrived!

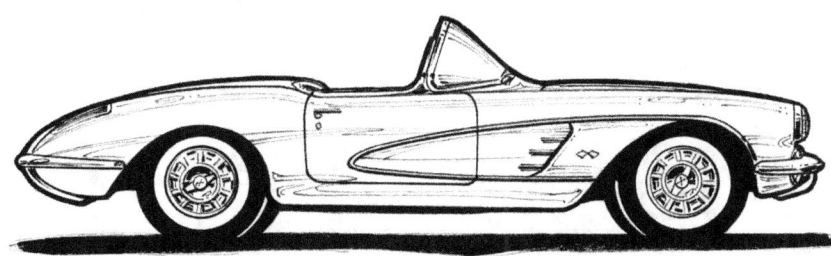

1958 Corvette
"The Second Restyling"

For better or worse, Chevrolet changed everything in 1958. The classic '57 Chevy Bel Air was gone after one year, along with the simple and elegant '57 Corvette. Chevrolet and the rest of GM's car lines were on a roll and styling was getting overdone.

From a business standpoint, the '58 Corvette was a huge success. Sales were up from 6,339 in '57 to 9,168 in '58. So, with a 41-percent increase in sales, no one at Chevrolet wanted to hear about styling excesses on the Corvette. With the lion's share of the work for '58 having gone into the new body, there were only slight improvements under the hood also. The top-of-the-line fuelie was up 7-hp to 290-hp, while the base 283 4-barrel, was up 10-hp to 230-hp. The drivetrain and brakes were all carryovers from the '57 model. The Corvette had finally shaken off its Motorama/European roots and was truly a high performance American classic.

Where the 1958 Corvette took flak from the critics was in its styling. But of course, customers vastly outnumbered critics. The 1956-57 design was simple yet elegant, while the '58 design seemed overdone, with too many add-ons. The most obvious addition was the extra set of headlights. This was a styling look that was applied to most of GM's line for 1958 - part of the "bigger is better" approach to styling. Under each headlight was a large simulated air duct. This was a styling look that came from the Oldsmobile Golden Rocket show car. The bumpers were larger and there was a chrome accent atop each fender. The hood had 18 fake louvers, similar to the SR-2. On the trunk lid there were two strips of chrome from the bumpers to the top edge of the trunk. The rear bumpers were also larger. And the side coves now had extra chrome trim.

All of these extra styling elements added 9 inches to the overall length and 2.3 inches to the width. Worst of all, the weight went up by 200 pounds to 3,080. The inside joke was how "Cadillac-like" the new Corvette had become. The interior did get good reviews. The instruments were in front of the driver and a console was added, along with new door panels. But the seats lacked side support and were uncomfortable on long rides.

Of course, Chevrolet was "officially" out of racing, thanks to the 1957 AMA factory ban on racing. But Zora Arkus-Duntov made sure that the Corvette order forms were loaded with almost everything needed to build a competitive Corvette. There were still those fortunate few who enjoyed a back-door friendship with Chevrolet. The most successful of these privateers was Dr. Dick Thompson, the "Flying Dentist." Thompson and his factory supported Corvettes dominated SCCA class racing in the late '50s and early '60s.

Numerous unusual things happened to the Corvette in 1958. On June 11 the 39 millionth Chevrolet rolled off the assemble line and it was a Corvette. The same month, a Corvette scored a first class win at the Pike's Peak Hill Climb event, then at the Bonneville speed event, racer Glen Minder's '57 Corvette hit 153.327-mph on the salt. And here's a quirky one - NASCAR abandoned the concept of building a sports car oval circuit. Yes, "go fast and turn left" for sports cars. Just as well it died. And Joie Chitwood started jumping ramps in a '58 Corvette.

The styling excesses lasted only one year, but the Chevrolet marketing and sales department was really hyping the new styling. One ad proclaimed, "Corvette Does America Proud" and described the car's handling as "silk-smooth." Another ad featured a white Corvette with a blue background and red stripes, described the car as, "... a dual-purpose machine... As American as the Fourth of July... a comfortable tourer, rally car, trials car... at one and the same time." It must have worked, sales of the '58 Corvette was more than double that of the '56 Vettes. The '59 Corvette was a much cleaner car. Best of all, the Corvette was now a performance icon.

1959 Corvette
"Toning Down the Excess"

1959 was a year of refinement for the Corvette and toning down from the excesses of '58. By the end of the 1950s the country was experiencing a minor recession and car sales weren't very good. However, Corvette sales actually increased in '59 to 9,670 units (from 9,168 in '58). While that's not much of an increase, considering the market of the day, no one inside Chevrolet was complaining too much. It was this downturn of the economy that killed the entire Q-Chevrolet concept for

transaxle-equipped cars across the Chevrolet line of cars, the only exception being the Corvair project. Changes to the marginally profitable '59 Corvette were very minimal, requiring a keen eye.

The obvious external changes on the '59 Corvette were the elimination of the louvered hood and the chrome trim on the trunk lid. This was the beginning of a new trend in Detroit for cars with less trim and simpler styles that would take several years to implement. Most subtle was the addition of 10 slots on the hub cap for a little extra brake cooling. Those were the only external points of difference on the '59. The cleaner look was well received.

The interior received a storage bin under the passenger side grab bar and the door knob was moved forward for better ergonomics. A common complaint of the '58 was the almost total lack of side support from the seats.

Those early bucket seats were really just narrow bench seats. So the '59 had reshaped seats to help keep the driver's seat relatively planted behind the wheel. Door panel arm rests were relocated for improved arm room. The calibration of the dash instruments was improved, and the gauge lenses were now concave to eliminate glare and improve readability. All '59 Corvette tachometers now read up to 7,000-rpm. For safety reasons, a T-handle reverse-lockout was added to the 4-speed shifter. Twin sun visors were also a new option.

Under the body, radius rods were added to the rear axle to partially fix the Corvette's wheel hop problem. Shock mount points were improved as well as upgraded nitrogen-filled shocks, and front and rear springs were stiffened to offset additional weight. New performance options included 6.70 x 15 nylon blackwall tires and a simplified off-road braking package. There also was an oversized 24-gallon fuel tank for long trips, or trips specifically lasting 12 or 24 hours. Fewer than 200 oversized tanks ("tanker" Corvettes) were sold between 1959 and 1962. The addition of this option required the auxiliary hardtop without the folding convertible, as there was no storage room behind the seats when equipped with the larger tank. Under the hood, the full line of 283-cubic-inch carbureted and fuel injected engines were available, as they were in 1958.

Thanks to the RPO 684 racer kit option, Corvettes were becoming a force to be reckoned with. In those days, the aftermarket industry was just beginning and there wasn't the vast selection of racing parts, aside from what the factory produced. RPO 684 and its other required racing options provided customers with a foundation to race with the best, and many did just that.

Out on the race track, Bill Mitchell began racing the rebodied SS Corvette mule chassis wearing Bill's new Sting Ray body design. Although the car looked great, it still suffered from inadequate brakes and a new problem - front end lift. This was an areodynamic design issue that plagued the future Grand Sports and production Corvette racers. Corvettes were precluded from the Le Mans race, because rules limited engine size to 3 liters - 183 ci.

New ground may not have been broken this year, but the '59 Corvette was still a very desirable sports car. *Motor Trend* magazine tested a '59 Corvette against a 356 Porsche and concluded that if a buyer liked the idea of having one of the world's quickest sports cars, then pick the Corvette. What more can you say?

1960 Corvette
"Year of the Bait'n Switch!"

The public was ready for something really exciting. Actually what happened was the first of many Corvette "bait-and-switch" setups. The press was also well aware of Bill Mitchell's beautiful Sting Ray racer that was making a name for itself in SCCA racing. *Road & Track* said in January 1959, "We predict that this will be the year of big changes for the Corvette." Rumors had it that Chevrolet was going to release a completely new Corvette for 1960.

Rumors were fueled by speculation concerning the radical Q-Corvette. Unfortunately, this highly advanced 1957 design never made it past the clay model stage, not even a running prototype was built. However, the Q-Corvette's styling would eventually become the 1963 Sting Ray Coupe. The Q-Corvette turned out to be an engineering wish-list of advanced mechanical goodies. What really fanned the flames was the XP-700 show car. This was your basic, overdone show car that was used to test the public's reaction to some new styling ideas. Since Bill Mitchell often drove the car to and from work, some saw it as just an executive perk. That may have been partially true, as it was good to be the Sr. VP of Styling at GM. But XP-700 clearly showed us the upcoming "boat tail" design for 1961 and beyond.

So after all of the press-fed anticipation, the '60 Corvette was somewhat of a disappointment because it looked exactly like a '59 Vette, except for the eight colors to choose from, instead of seven. Aside from Roman Red and Tuxedo Black, the other colors were slightly different with new names. Anticipating this letdown, Zora Arkus-Duntov had planned some good stuff under the hood.

Advertisements announced, "major breakthrough in design and metallurgy." Aluminum heads would be standard on both versions of the optional fuelie engine. This improvement was to save 53 lbs. and bumped the power rating from 250 to 275 hp for the hydraulic lifter version and 290 hp to 315 hp for the solid lifter Fuelie. Extra power came from an enlarged injection plenum, improved combustion chamber design, larger valves and higher compression. Unfortunately, casting irregularities killed the exotic new heads. Aluminum heads wouldn't show up again until the arrival of the '67 L88 option and wouldn't make it into production as part of the standard Corvette engine until '96.

Disappointments and setbacks aside, the 1960 Corvette was still an improved car. A rear stabilizer bar was now standard, along with a thicker front sway bar, eliminating the need for stiffer springs. The $333.60 RPO 684 heavy Duty Brakes and Special Steering optional racing package included stiffer shocks, quicker steering, finned brake drums with metallic brake facings, and cooling scoops. Required with this option was either the 270-hp 283 engine with two 4-bbl carburetors or the 290-hp Fuelie engine, along with the manual 4-speed transmission and Positraction rear. And for racers there was the optional 24-gallon fuel tank, for $161.40. Aluminum was used to save 18 lbs. on the bellhousing and the fuel injection cars now used an aluminum core radiator. Perhaps the most unusual detail of the '60 Corvette was that at $3,872 list price, the car cost $3 LESS than the '59 model. All '60 Corvette ordered for racing totaled just over $5,000.

On the race track, the big news for 1960 was Briggs Cunningham Le Mans assault. Briggs took a team of three specially prepared Corvettes with backdoor help from Duntov and finished in 8th place overall. The Cunningham Corvettes qualified using stock Corvette cylinder heads, but on race day, they used cast-iron versions of the big-valve aluminum heads that were supposed to be optional for the '60 Corvettes. This was a huge feather in Chevrolet's cap, having much more status than a class win at Sebring. It clearly let the Europeans know that the Corvette was here to stay.

CHAPTER 1: PRODUCTION CORVETTES

1961 Corvette
"Ushering In the Future"

Zora Arkus-Duntov was a very adaptive engineer. He had built several racing Corvettes that GM's upper management promptly stopped dead in their tracks. Instead, the ever-creative engineer worked to give buyers the best all-around performance car on the market. Duntov's original plan was to sell two different Corvettes, one "street" Corvette and another "racing" Corvette. When the SS Project was killed in '57, Duntov decided to create a tough-guy street performer that could become a competitive

racer with the right parts from Chevrolet. This tactic made for great marketing and advertising.

Corvettes took a lot of heat from the sports car crowd for being a drag racer rather than a road racer. Cars from Detroit were not known to be able to gracefully traverse high speed corners. But by the late '50s and early '60s, Corvettes began to dominate SCCA class racing. It took Carroll Shelby's 2,000- lb. Cobras to break the Corvette dominance.

The '61 Corvette with the fuel injection option would run 0-60 in 5.5 seconds and 14.2 seconds in the quarter-mile. Top speed was 130-mph. *Sports Car Illustrated* magazine referred to the '61 Corvette this way, "One of the most remarkable marriages of touring comfort and violent performance we have ever enjoyed, especially at the price." What Corvettes had that the

high-winding, exotic European sports cars did not have was copious amounts of TORQUE - that other horsepower.

1961 was the first of several big changes for the Corvette's styling, leading up to the stunning 1963 Sting Ray. Except for minor trim, styling was static for '58 to '60. If often took a keen eye and the right angle of view to differentiate the models. Corvette styling chief Bill Mitchell was busy testing the public's opinion with his XP-700 show car. The front end was overdone, but the "boat tail" back end looked great on the '61 model. This included what is a Corvette styling tradition that continues on today - the four round taillights, in two groups of two.

For the production Corvette, the vertical bumpers from the show car were replaced with horizontal bumpers that matched the bumpers on the front of the '58 to '60 design. A Corvette styling queue passed on, as the exhaust tips exited under the body, instead of through the body, as it had done since '53.

Other styling changes were more subtle. The heavy, nine- tooth shark-like front grille was replaced with an argent silver-finished, mesh-style grille, and the chrome headlight trim was now body-colored. This was part of the toning down of the excess binge of chrome bling that had its high-point in '58. Crossed flags replaced the round Corvette badge on the nose and "C O R V E T T E" spelled out under the badge like the SS Racer. The interior had a narrower transmission cover for more leg room, updated seat upholstery and door panel trim. Former options were now standard, and included; the courtesy light, windshield washers, parking brake alarm, and sun visors. The heater was still optional and air conditioning wouldn't arrive until '63. There were no power changes under the hood, however the cross-flow aluminum radiator and thermostatically-controlled fan were new. Also, the 4-speed transmission case was now aluminum. Duntov was gradually seeding aluminum parts into the car.

Corvettes got a big PR boost with the start of the CBS TV program, "Route 66." From the Fall of 1960 through '64, characters Tod Styles and Buz Murdock traveled the nation, seeking adventure, always in a new Corvette. Sales figures for 1961 were 10,939 units, up from 1960 sales of 10,261. The Corvette was now a respectable sports car with real racing potential. 1962 would bring more changes aimed toward the '63 Sting Ray. The days of the solid-axle Corvette were almost over.

1962 Corvette
"Last of the Live-Axle Corvettes"

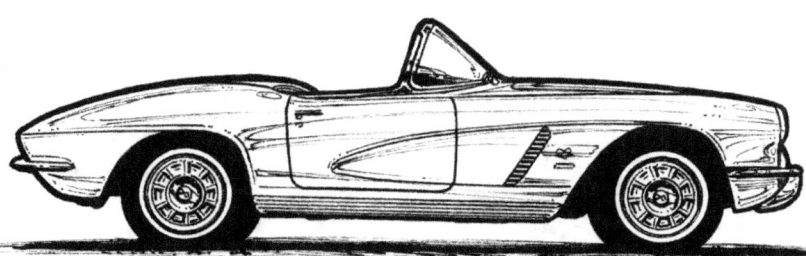

1962 was the end of the line for the first generation Corvette - the last of the C1 Corvettes, you could say. Despite the highest price ever for a Corvette, $4,038, production was at an all-time high of 14,531 units. Only seven years before, Chevrolet only made 700 '55 Corvettes. The turnaround was astonishing, as many inside GM though the car didn't have a snowball's chance.

While the basic layout hadn't changed, thanks to the Corvette's chief engineer, Zora Arkus-Duntov, the humble little parts bin car was taken about as far as possible for that time. By the end of '62, the Corvette was not only a tough street machine, it was a formable road racer that had picked up numerous SCCA championships.

By late in '59 the decision had been made that the Sting Ray racer design would be the basis of the '63 Corvette. Internal GM photo documents clearly show that by April '60, the overall shape had been flushed out - split-window coupe, and all. It wasn't a secret that Chevy was working on a new Corvette. Bill Mitchell's Sting Ray racer not only won races, it was a rolling test vehicle for the next Corvette's esthetics. Fans loved the new look, so it wasn't a stretch to get the new design approved.

To get existing customers warm to the idea of a radical new shape, the back end of the '61 production Corvette was a sneak-peak into the future Vette. Chrome trim rocker panels were becoming a styling fad, so the '62 Corvette took the new look closer to the upcoming Sting Ray. There was a slow move away from the excesses of chrome trim from the late '50s. The chrome trim that had surrounded the side coves since '56 were gone and the three horizontal cove spears were history too. Since Corvettes had made quite a name for themselves on the race track, the front grille and flanking openings were blacked out for more of a racer look. The chrome strip on top of the front fenders could have been removed, but some styling trends die hard.

Obviously, the interior wasn't going to change very much. Surprisingly, the upholstery design and the door panels were new. And here's a shocker - heaters were now standard equipment. In '61 the heater cost $102.25 and $91.40 in '53. If a customer was planning to race his Corvette, the heater could be deleted.

Good things were happening under the hood. The 283 small-block was bored and stroked to a magical 327 cubic-inches. The 250 hp and 300 hp engines used a single four-barrel Carter carburetor and hydraulic lifters. The 340 hp engine used big-valve heads, solid lifters, and single Carter carb. As before, the big gun was the Fuelie, but for '62, it packed 360 hp, 45 hp more than the previous year. Except for a racing version in '57, the price of the Fuel Injection option never increase from '57 to '62. At $484.20, the Fuelie was the most expensive option for the '62 Vette. However, more Fuelies were sold in '62 than in any other year since its introduction in '57.

Buyers could now order the $188.40, T-10 four-speed transmission in either close or wide-ratio versions. Manual transmission Corvettes accounted for 78 percent of all sales in '62. And for weekend warriors and hard-core racers, all of the previous racer kit parts were still available. Hot parts included; straight-through exhaust pipes, a 24-gallon fuel tank, heavy duty brakes, and suspension parts. A '62 Fuelie order for racing totaled out around $5,200.

Just ten model years before, the Corvette began as Harley Earl's dream machine - a sweet-looking sports car for the average American. The start was pretty rough and many thought the fiberglass Chevy wouldn't make it. But without hard work, guts, glamour, and a wild and crazy Russian pushing the limits, the Corvette never would have become America's sports car.

CHAPTER 1: PRODUCTION CORVETTES

1963 Corvette
"First of the Sting Ray Corvettes"

The '63 Corvette stunned everyone, and not just with its one-of-a-kind, futuristic good looks. Everything worked like a carefully planned symphony. If you spend time looking at a '63 to '67 Sting Ray, it looks perfect from every angle. And unlike the car from 10 years before, the Sting Ray wasn't just a beauty queen.

The engine and transmission had received a healthy boost in '62, aside from that, everything else was completely new. To fully appreciate the '63 Corvette. You have to look at regular cars from '63. There was nothing else in the American market that had the mechanical or styling edge that the new Corvette did.

Styling direction had been defined with the ill-fated '57 Q-Corvette project. Chief of Styling Bill Mitchell loved to say, "I'm the only one around here that designs Corvettes!" Bill took the Q-Corvette styling direction and used it for his privately financed Stingray racer. Aside from being a successful race car in '59 and '60, the public loved its good looks. So in the fall of '59, with the help of young designer, Larry Shinoda, the XP-720 clay prototype was started in Studio X, with the help of young designer, Larry Shinoda. From there, it was a solid, GO, for the new 1963 Corvette Sting Ray.

Enthusiasts got everything they wanted, and then some. But unlike the '53 Corvette, this machine had the right hardware to backup its aggressive looks. The new ladder-style frame was lighter and more rigid than the '50s sedan-based frame. The coupe version actually had a steel cage roll-bar built into the chassis. The perimeter frame allowed the drivetrain and interior to sit lower, helping to drop the car's center of gravity. The fully independent suspension reduced unsprung weight and gave the car superior handling over the older solid-axle cars. Finned brake drums with metallic linings offered outstanding, fade-free braking for a street machine. Unlike the old interior that took some time to get used to, the new Sting Ray was an instant hit to everyone. The steering wheel, shifter, and gauge positions were spot on.

With a coupe or a roadster to choose from, the car looks fantastic in both configurations. One of the first questions asked by many was, "Where are the headlights?" Since headlights were prohibited from being covered, even with clear plastic, the Sting Ray had flip-around headlight pods to keep the front-end clean and sharp-looking.

Although fastback roofs had been featured on high-end cars in the '50s, none of them had the sharp Sting Ray-stinger look. The split-window coupe caused quite a stir and only lasted one year. The strong horizontal crease and distinctive fender humps were totally new and unique design that looks good nearly 50 years later! Aside from the split-window issue, the only other critique was that the decoration was just a little overdone. But, that's just the way upscale cars were designed in those days. Every surface had to have elements of discovery.

Mitchell, Shinoda, and the rest of the styling team were masters of shape and proportion. The new Corvette was smaller in every direction than its predecessor. The car measures 2.1 inches shorter, .8 inches narrower, and 1.7 inches lower. The front track is .75 inches wider, the fuel tank is 3.6-gallons larger, and the total weight is 50 lbs less.

The Corvette had nothing to apologize for. It had become a world-class sports car. *Car Life* magazine awarded the car the Award For Engineering Excellence. The automotive world had never seen anything like it before from a mass-produced automobile. Zora Arkus-Duntov expressed it best when he said, "For the first time, I now can have a Corvette I can be proud to drive in Europe."

1964 Corvette
"Acceptance & Refinement"

Bean counters love round numbers. It wasn't until the '60 Corvette arrived in showrooms that the little sports car sold over 10,000 units. Just 3 years later, thanks to the astonishingly futuristic Sting Ray, sales more than doubled to 21,513 units. The work that goes into a new car design is tremendous. Two things usually happen after a new design is released. One, it often takes a year for the public to warm up to the new design (this happened in '68 and '97). And second, the following year usually only offers minimal changes. By '62, sales jumped to 14,531, and by the end of the first year of the new Sting Ray design, 21,513 units were sold. The demand for new Corvettes was so high that Chevrolet had to start a second production shift. Finally, there was a waiting list for Corvettes.

What little criticism the '63 Corvette got, Chevrolet heard loud and clear. The biggest complaint was Bill Mitchell's pet design element - the split-rear window on the coupe. One magazine said that it was just wide enough to conceal a motorcycle cop! So the split-window was soon gone, making the '63 "Split-Window Coupe" one of the most valuable cars in Corvette history. Bill was from the old design school that made sure there were little design elements to be discovered from every angle of view. While an interesting idea, it can easily lead to an overdone, fussy look.

The '64 Corvette saw much of Mitchell's excess toned way down. Gone were the fake chrome hood grilles, and the chrome trim from the A-pillars. The vents at the B-pillar were made functional, however, the vents on the front fenders were still just decorative. The interior was toned down by eliminating the bright-center dials on all of the instruments.

Amazingly, there was no price increase for '64. The coupe listed for $4,252 and the roadster for $4,037. Although offered in '63, the cast aluminum knock-off wheels were finally available for $322. Only 806 Corvettes were ordered with the knock-offs. The suspension was improved by adding new variable-rate springs that gave the car a reasonably soft ride under normal driving, but stiffened up when pushed in heavy cornering. Body and interior noise was reduced with improved insulator mounts, foil-backed firewall insulation and thicker fiberglass in the body's rear section.

There was also exciting new hardware offered under the hood. Buyers had their choice of four small-block engines. The base 327-ci engine and the optional 300 hp L75 were unchanged from '63. but the solid-lifter, big carb L76 option was up 25 hp to 365 hp, and the L84 Fuelie got a 15-hp bump to 375 hp. The price of the top-shelf L84 Fuelie was up from $108 to $538.

For those with racing on their minds, the '63 Z06 package was off the order sheet. Much of what had been in the $1,818.45 Z06 was now part of the $695.50 Special Sintered Metallic Brake Package. You could still get all of the Z06 hardware, you just had to know which parts to order from your friendly Chevrolet Parts Manager.

Because of the slight bump in power for the two performance engine options, '64 Corvettes were better than ever. Ordered with one of the optional performance engines, the $188.30 four-speed, and the $43.05 Posi rear, the '64 Corvette could be a potent customer. One automotive publication tested a fuel-injected '64 Corvette with 4.11:1 gears and clicked off 0-60-mph in only 5.6 seconds, and ran the quarter-mile in 14.2 seconds @ 100 mph! With more power than ever, and a fully independent suspension, the Corvette Sting Ray was coming into its own in '64. Actually, things were just warming up.

CHAPTER 1: PRODUCTION CORVETTES

1965 Corvette
"Balance vs Raw Power"

Not only was the 1965 Sting Ray the middle of the second generation Corvette, but it was the end of an era and the beginning of another. The days of the Rochester Fuel Injection option were over after '65 and a 10-year run of the Mark IV big-block began. Raw power would never be this inexpensive.

Duntov's mission for the Corvette customers was to give them the option of a mild-mannered street car or a rip-snortin, semi-racing machine.

Since 1957, the Fuel Injection option was the hot setup for maximum performance and racing. By combining the right parts with the small-block engine, the Corvette could be a formidable sports car and race car. However, for street use, living with the Fuelie wasn't always easy. Many owners actually replaced the Rochester setup in favor of a four-barrel carburetor after too many trips to the service department. The '65 Vette was unique because both the L84 Fuel Injection setup and the L78 396 big-block were available.

Unfortunately for the Fuelie, cubic inches were cheaper than an elaborate fuel delivery system. The Fuel Injection option cost $538, while the 396 big-block cost only $292. Plus, according to the brochures, the 396 cranked 425 hp to 50 hp more than the Fuelie! And what wasn't revealed until many years later (although it was suspected from the beginning) was that the L78's horsepower rating was supposed to be 450-hp, but management decided to tone it down some, at least on paper. The question for performance hounds

additional engine clearance. Although the big-block might not have been as nimble as the small-block, this was one tough customer.

The other big performance leap was standard four-wheel disc brakes. The '65 Corvette was the first American car to offer four-wheel disc brakes as standard equipment. The Corvette's drum brakes had been a sore spot for years, especially with racers. In the '50s and '60s, only exotic European sports cars had disc brakes. The big, 11.75-inch rotors and four-piston calipers provided unprecedented stopping power to match the new power under the hood. And if the Corvette's extreme good-looks didn't draw enough attention, there was the very noisy, Side-Mounted Exhaust System, for $134. The system used a long, chambered straight pipe, mounted under a beautifully-styled, ribbed aluminum cover. They looked great and got louder as they aged.

The body received minor changes. Vertical vents on the front fenders were functional and the fake hood vents were removed. The horizontal grille bars were now black. The interior had new seats, door panels, and black, flat-face gauges. Base price of the 1965 Corvette was $4,321, and total production was 23,562 units.

The 1965 was the middle-year for the C2 Corvettes. Buyers had more options than ever and

was would you like your Vette light weight and nimble, or a stump-pulling brute?

Not that the big-block tripped over it's feet. The 396 engine option wasn't just an engine swap. Everything from the flywheel to the rear-axle half-shafts were beefed up to handle the monstrous torque of the new engine. The suspension was also beefed up to handle the extra weight, and a cool-looking new domed hood was designed for

Chevrolet was selling every Corvette they could make. Sales totaled 23,564 units, of which 53.2 percent were roadsters. While the '66 and '67 models had a few additional options and details were revised, the '65 model was almost complete. With the release of the Mark IV 396, Corvettes were just entering into a new level of performance.

1966 427 Corvette
"The Mark IV Grows Up"

Chevrolet had all the bases covered for 1966. The bar had been significantly raised at both ends of the performance spectrum. The base Corvette engine was now a 300 hp small-block - a 50-hp increase over the '65 offering! The 375-hp Fuelie was gone, but the 396 big-block was now a 427 monster. Performance had taken a quantum leap.

The '65 big-block 396 was bored out to 427 cubic inches for '66, taking the street-driven Corvette to undreamed of high performance. The factory power rating for the new L72 427 was 425-hp at 5,600 rpm - same as the L78 396. However, the real redline was more like 6,500 rpm, with well over 450 horsepower! This was 75 hp more than the 1965 fuel-injection setup. Duntov joked that engine size increase was to save weight. After all, 31 cubic inches of cast iron is a significant weight savings. If a 427 solid-lifter beast was too much, the L36 hydraulic-lifter version was good for 390-hp. Corvettes were now at the top of the performance feeding chain.

Subtle changes for the 1966 Corvette made it stand out from previous cars. The egg-crate grille and hub caps were obvious on coupes and convertibles. "Corvette" script on the hood was new and the b-pillar roof vents on the coupe were gone and the three vertical fender vents were carry-overs from '65. Spotting a '66 coupe was easy, however, convertibles with aftermarket wheels were much harder to spot. Big-block '66 Vettes used the same hood from '65. If you could tolerate the exhaust noise, side pipes were a bargain at $131.65. While it was never published that there was any power increase from the side-pipes option, they sure looked cool! The interior trim was changed, in addition to new optional head rests and hazard lights.

Duntov was working on a new racer kit for big-block Corvette racers that wouldn't arrive until '67. Racers and wanna be's had plenty of hardware to choose from that was available from their local Chevrolet Parts Department. The L72 427/425 engine cost $312.85. The M-22 "Rock Crusher" four-speed was $237, and the special heavy-duty brakes cost $342.30. The F41 special front and rear suspension was a super deal at $36.90. While customers were buying individual racing parts for their Corvettes, Roger Penske was doing some field-testing in an L88 prototype. Zora knew how to take good care of his Corvette racing family.

Although the base Corvette cost $4,295, down $26 from 1965, total production for 1966 was 22,940, down from 65's total of 27,720 cars. Car magazines were all over the new Mako Shark-II show car and it was obvious that a new Shark-inspired Corvette was in the works. That may have had something to do with the drop in sales.

But GM didn't mind too much, since the press was gushing all over the new 427 Corvette. Tests from 0-to-60 mph ranged from 4.8 to 5.7 seconds with quarter mile times of 12.8 to 14 seconds. Some saw top speeds of between 130 and 152-mph, depending on gearing and the driver's nerve. For its day, performance like that was the stuff a bench racing banter.

1966 was supposed to be the last year for the Sting Ray design, but making the Mako Shark styling streetable for '67 was a big challenge. As hot as the '66 Corvette was, the '67 was about to get even hotter.

1967 Corvette
"The Finished Sting Ray"

Sometimes unexpected efforts turn out the best. Such is the case with the '67 Sting Ray. It is common for designers to be working on the next generation as soon as a new model comes out. As soon as the '63 Sting Ray hit the showrooms, Bill Mitchell and his team of top designers were working on the car's replacement. When the non-running Mako Shark II was shown to GM brass in March '65, it was obvious - the new Shark HAD to be the next Corvette.

The excitement was so intense, marketing wanted the new design to be the '67 model! That left just 18-months to make the show car into a '67 production car. While Chevrolet was GM's sales flagship, there were troubles with the line. The Corvair was becoming a nightmare and the Mustang caught Chevrolet with their pants down. The Nova-based Camaro was rushed into production and the Mako Shark-II was just too sweet to let go. While the Shark looked slick, the new shape actually had more front-end lift that the Sting Ray - which already had considerable front-end lift. Also, there was the issue of the Shark's mountainous front fenders. The trick was toning them down, yet maintaining the proportions for the rest of the car. Getting the Shark design into production was a major project.

Meanwhile, Corvette product planners and engineers had a production Vette to keep fresh and exciting. Of course, Duntov seemed to always have a few more go-fast goodies in his back pocket to keep things lively. When it was obvious that the Shark wasn't going to happen for '67, stylists had to spruce up the '66 model to keep interesting. The end result was a totally unique version that is unmistakable from the previous Sting Rays. Many consider the '67 to be the "finished" Sting Ray.

Not that there was anything wrong with the '66 model, but the '67 got a few styling touches that really pulled it all together. The most obvious change was the new front fender vents. The five, forward leaning vents looked tough. Badges on the front fenders were removed and the backup light was placed over top of the rear license plate. Traditional hub caps were replaced with 5-slot steel wheels with a chrome beauty ring and a small center cap. This wheel style would continue on until 1982. Real knock-off wheels were gone, but knock-off-style wheels were still available for $263. Big-block cars got the new "stinger" hood with "427" badges that went on to be a styling classic.

Performance hounds went wild over the new L71 427/435. The new 3-2 bbl carb setup was designed with a progressive, vacuum operated linkage that only used the center two-barrel carburetor for normal driving. If you put your boot into it, the remaining two carburetors cranked out amazing power. With the right gears and a four-speed, quarter-mile times in the 13s were standard, with a top speed of 140+ mph! Every possible performance option was available.

For the racing crowd, Duntov had a new racer kit called the L88. This was the most aggressive racer option Zora had ever created and was NOT intended for street use. Duntov purposely set the power figure at 430 hp to discourage buyers from just checking off the engine option with the largest number. The true power rating was closer to 500 hp!

For a model that was technically a carry over, Chevy did all right, selling 22,940 cars, costing over $5,000 each. Although sales were down 4,780 units from '66, the 1967 427/435 model went on to become one of the most desired and valued cars in Corvette history.

1968 Corvette
"From Show Car To Road Machine"

In retrospect, it's astonishing that the shark-design made it into production by September '67. After all, the non-running prototype was shown to GM's brass in March '65, just 1-1/2 years before the production cars were available. And here's the kicker - the new Shark was supposed to be the '67 model! It's easy to see how that happened. After all, the Shark design sits on the Sting Ray's chassis design and drive train. How hard could a new body and interior be? There were two Mako Shark-II cars built. The non-running model was shown at the '65 New York International Car Show and the New York World's Fair. By September, the running version was shown to the press at GM's Tech Center. The new design was a smash hit and production was a "GO!"

But show cars are one thing and real cars are another. Photos of the Mako Shark II next to a production '68 Corvette show how small and compact the show car really was. Real cars need space for production and maintenance. Then there was the issue of those famous front fender humps. On the show car, they look fantastic, but from behind the wheel, they severely restricted forward vision. It took quite a lot of finessing to make the design useable. Consequently, along the way to production, a lot changed.

looked like a 200-mph sex-goddess in your driveway. Even though the new Corvette picked up almost all of its running gear from the '63 to '67 Corvettes, much had to be modified and much was new. New external features included vacuum-operated pop-up headlights and a vacuum-operated closet to conceal the windshield wipers. The coupe version had lift-out roof panels for a semi-roadster look and the near vertical rear window was removable for free-flowing air. The 427-optioned Corvettes had a hood bulge with "427" badges on both sides. While the new car looked bigger, it was only marginally so. The pointed nose made the car 7.4 inches longer, it was .6 inches narrower, 2 inches lower, and the front and rear tracks were 1.5 inches and 1.4 inches wider respectively. And the total weight was only 55 pounds more.

The interior was totally new, with its dash raking back with two main gauges behind the steering wheel. Other gauges were located on the console, and Aero bucket seats had built-in head rests. The new three-speed Turbo-Hydramatic was optional along with dozens of other goodies.

All the glamour and guts was fantastic, but when customers finally took delivery, things weren't good. Overall fit, finish, and quality was dismal

Behind the scenes, not everyone was on the same page. Battles raged between engineering, styling and marketing. Some wanted the new Corvette to be based on the Corvair, while others were concerned that the Z-28 Camaro would eat into the Corvette's sales volume. Mitchell wanted the Mako Shark to be the next Vette, while Duntov was pushing for a mid-engine Corvette. When the wraps came off in September '66, it wasn't quite the Mako Shark-II, but it was definitely a Corvette.

Corvettes were always unique, but there was nothing like the C3 on either side of the Atlantic. "Looks Italian" was as close as one could get because of all the curves. It and owners were not happy. And while Chevrolet earned kudos for the much improved '69 model, they really should have extended the Sting Ray into the '68 model year to allow time to get the Shark right. What would a '68 "Sting Ray" have looked like? That's an interesting notion. Corvette lovers bought 28,566 Corvettes in '68, a nice improvement from the 22,940 '67 units sold. At least the GM bean-counters were happy. And hey, it was still a Vette, and it ran like nobody's business!

CHAPTER 1: PRODUCTION CORVETTES

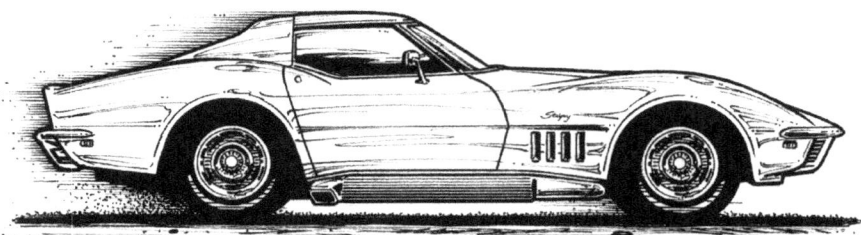

1969 Corvette
"Getting Its Act Together"

After all the brouhaha over the new Corvette's Mako Shark styling, reality set in and the magazine testers and customers figured out that the '68 model wasn't really done. Quality, fit, and finish were a major concerns. There was a lot that wasn't right - so much so that the '68 Corvette never enjoyed the same status as the first 1963 Sting Ray.

Designers knew that the Mako Shark II-inspired '68 Corvette was rushed into production and considered a transition model. Considering the flak they caught, a '69 introduction might have been a better move. But much of what they'd hoped to have on the '68 car made it into the '69 model. The Stingray name was back, however, instead of being a two word name, it was now just, "Stingray."

Visually, the Stingray had minor changes. The most obvious one was the "Stingray" script lettering over the front fender vents. The front grille was now completely blacked out and the taillights had integrated backup lights built into the inboard taillights. The door handles were flush mounted and operated by squeezing down. What had been the door handle button was now the door lock. The Rally Wheels didn't look much different, but now measured 8 inches in width and helped fill the wheel openings for a more aggressive look. Tires remained the same as where used on the '68 car - F70-15 bias-ply Firestone Wide Oval or Goodyear Wide Treads. Perhaps the hottest option was the off-road exhaust pipes. Side-pipes had been a standard feature on racing Corvettes since the late '50s, but it wasn't until '65 that customers could have either their new small-block or big-block outfitted with these booming exhaust pipes. The C2 versions were nothing more than a piece of long, chambered straight pipe. "Chambered" meant that the pipes had crimps that functioned as mild baffles. The baffles tended to burn off after a few years of use, yielding the car with essentially open, unmuffled exhaust - i.e., LOUD! The '69 versions had an oval-shaped mufflers that wereonly slightly quieter. The side-pipe covers were beautifully styled to fit the rocker panel's shape. The $147 option gave the new Stingray a tough look.

Under the hood, the small-block engines grew from 327 cubic inches to 350, but power ratings remained the same. All four 427 engines were unchanged for 1969 except for the $3,000, optional, all-aluminum 427 ZL-1. This was essentially an L88 with an aluminum block and was an extension of the L88 racer kit option, NOT intended for street use. Transmissions and suspension options were carry-overs from '68.

The interior saw new door panels for additional shoulder room and a small-diameter steering wheel, since most Stingrays had power steering. The dash now had map pockets and the seats had built-in headrests. The console area had a few new warning lights and there was a plate indicating which of the five engines was under the hood. An alarm system was a new option for '69.

The changes were mostly well received. Nearly all of the shortcomings of the '68 model were fixed. Flaws aside, the public wanted the new car so much that the then new Chevrolet general manager, 44-year-old John Delorean, extended the '69 production to December '69 to fulfill the demand for '69 Corvettes.

Consequently, the '69 Corvette set a new

production record of 38,762 units. Walking away from what had been the best Vette yet, the '63-'67 line, was a big gamble, but Mitchell, Shinoda, Duntov and the rest of the Corvette team scored big-time!

One magazine described the small-blocks as "marginally fast and very civilized, while the big-blocks were marginally civilized and very fast." The Stingray was still criticized for having a "harsh" suspension. Duntov explained that it was tuned for speeds between 80 and 120 mph. He didn't want to, "penalize the man who's going to drive fast." Wise words from the Godfather.

1970-1/2 Corvette
"Lots of Hot Stuff!"

Corvette lovers had much to catch up with and get very warm about for the '70 Corvette. There were subtle, but significant, body and interior alterations, and big changes under the hood.

By the numbers, sales for the '69 model were the best to date, due to then Chevrolet General Manager John DeLorean's decision to extend the sales year of the Corvette, Camaro, and Firebird to make up time lost to a worker's strike earlier in

the year. Sales for the '69 Corvette were 38,762 units, up from '68 production of 28,566. It seemed like it took a year for the public to warm up to the new Shark body style, allowing customers extra time to get their cars. Plus, the extra time allowed the Corvette team to better refine the new model. So, GM's bean counters were very happy. Production of the '70 Corvettes didn't start until January 1970. Traditionally, GM starts producing new cars in September. And to compound the low production numbers for the '70 Vettes, the St. Louis plant was shut down for the month of April because of a Teamsters strike. Consequently, sales numbers for the '70 model were only 17,316 units.

The body changes weren't a total surprise, as the Aero Coupe show car tipped the hand for the new styling. But it was a fresh change that few complained about. The new front grille was an eggcrate design sporting rectangular turn signals with clear lens and amber lights in the corners of the grille. The front fender vents used a similar eggcrate design.

All four wheel openings were flared at the back to protect the sculpted

sides from road debris. Exhaust outlets were now rectangular shaped. Interior mods included reshaped seats for more headroom and an optional trim package that included cut-pile carpet and imitation wood trim on the console and door panels. Tinted glass, Positraction rear, and the wide-ratio 4-speed transmission were now standard. The Turbo-Hydramatic 3-speed automatic transmission was a no-cost option. John DeLorean decided that Corvettes should move in a more upscale direction. The $158 Custom Interior Trim package included leather seats, wood-grain and carpet trim on the door panels, wood grain trim on the console, and cut-pile carpeting. Customers seemed to like the enhancements, as 3,191 cars were so equipped.

The really hot news was under the hood. The muscle car wars were still raging in Detroit and fans had gotten used to new hardware every year. The trusty, eight-year-old 327 was stroked to 350 cubic-inches and the beastly 427 was stroked to 454 cubic-inches. The 454 LS5 engine had 390 hp and 500 ft-lb of torque. Duntov scored a victory with his LT1 option. Zora wanted to do whatever he could to keep the weight down and the power up. On the street, the LT1 was only a tick slower than the big-block. However, it handled more like the sports car Duntov wanted the Corvette to be.

For the first time, Corvette's base price was over five thousand dollars. $5,192 was the new entry price for a Corvette. The most expensive street option was the $447.60 for the LT1. The LS5 454 engine option was only $289.65. A loaded LT1 could cost over $7-grand!

Duntov never wanted his legions of Corvette racers to be without the latest racing parts. The ZR1 option cost $968.95 and included the LT1 engine, transistor ignition, the M22 four-speed, power brakes, an aluminum radiator, and beefed-up suspension. With this package, you couldn't get power windows, power steering, air conditioning, or a radio. Only 25 ZR1 cars were ordered. Planned, but not sold, was a ZR2 option that included all of the ZR1 parts, but with a 465-horsepower 454! The ZR1 was essentially an LT1-powered L88. And like the L88, it was a "for off-road use" vehicle.

This was the big-block's best year. Engines had not yet been detuned to run lead-free gas, and emission controls were minimal. With insurance and emissions concerns, the rip-snort'n 454 was history by '75. The LT1 only lasted until the end of '72, not to return for 20 years.

1970-1/2 454 Corvette
"Gobs of Power & Confusion"

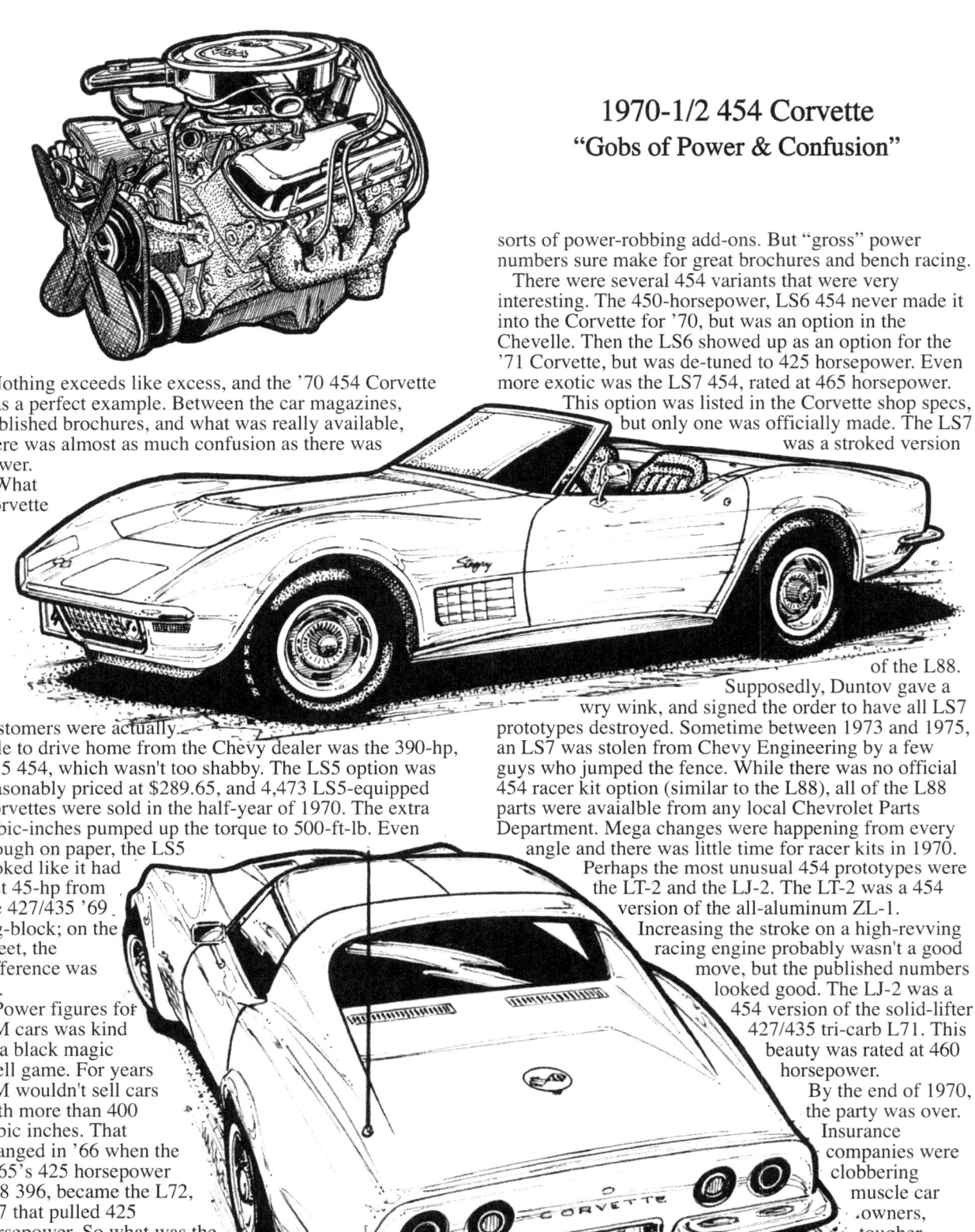

Nothing exceeds like excess, and the '70 454 Corvette was a perfect example. Between the car magazines, published brochures, and what was really available, there was almost as much confusion as there was power.

What Corvette customers were actually able to drive home from the Chevy dealer was the 390-hp, LS5 454, which wasn't too shabby. The LS5 option was reasonably priced at $289.65, and 4,473 LS5-equipped Corvettes were sold in the half-year of 1970. The extra cubic-inches pumped up the torque to 500-ft-lb. Even though on paper, the LS5 looked like it had lost 45-hp from the 427/435 '69 big-block; on the street, the difference was nil.

Power figures for GM cars was kind of a black magic shell game. For years GM wouldn't sell cars with more than 400 cubic inches. That changed in '66 when the 1965's 425 horsepower L78 396, became the L72, 427 that pulled 425 horsepower. So what was the real power of the 427? The L72 almost got a decal reading "450 horsepower," but corporate politics downplayed the figure. The '67, '68, and '69 L71, 427/435 tri-carb engine was rated at 435 horsepower, but was closer to 450 to 475 horsepower. All of the Detroit power numbers were somewhat misleading because published figures were "gross" power ratings. Engines were power-tested without mufflers, accessories, or even a fan. Real cars have all sorts of power-robbing add-ons. But "gross" power numbers sure make for great brochures and bench racing.

There were several 454 variants that were very interesting. The 450-horsepower, LS6 454 never made it into the Corvette for '70, but was an option in the Chevelle. Then the LS6 showed up as an option for the '71 Corvette, but was de-tuned to 425 horsepower. Even more exotic was the LS7 454, rated at 465 horsepower. This option was listed in the Corvette shop specs, but only one was officially made. The LS7 was a stroked version of the L88. Supposedly, Duntov gave a wry wink, and signed the order to have all LS7 prototypes destroyed. Sometime between 1973 and 1975, an LS7 was stolen from Chevy Engineering by a few guys who jumped the fence. While there was no official 454 racer kit option (similar to the L88), all of the L88 parts were avaialble from any local Chevrolet Parts Department. Mega changes were happening from every angle and there was little time for racer kits in 1970.

Perhaps the most unusual 454 prototypes were the LT-2 and the LJ-2. The LT-2 was a 454 version of the all-aluminum ZL-1. Increasing the stroke on a high-revving racing engine probably wasn't a good move, but the published numbers looked good. The LJ-2 was a 454 version of the solid-lifter 427/435 tri-carb L71. This beauty was rated at 460 horsepower.

By the end of 1970, the party was over. Insurance companies were clobbering muscle car owners, tougher emissions regulations were mandated by federal law, and no-lead gas put a lid on high compression ratios on engines. In retrospect, big-block engines took the Corvette away from "sports car" to "street bruiser." Duntov liked the easy-to-make power, but didn't miss the weight of the big-block. But oh, the wonderful sound of a big-block Corvette with side pipes!

THE ILLUSTRATED CORVETTE SERIES

1971 Corvette
"High-Performance Takes A Long Nap"

By 1971, the performance party wasn't over, but it was getting quieter, and the hangover hadn't kicked in yet. Once again, the Corvette's survival was called into question. Bean counters and marketing people, being what they are, can only see "what is and what was." In 1969, customers bought a, then record-setting, 38,762 Corvettes. But three months into the '70 model production, the St. Louis assembly plant had to shut

down, due to a lack of parts, due to a Teamsters strike. Although the strike only lasted one month, the disruption caused the production total to tank 44-percent to 17,316 for '70 - thus opening the question, "Is the Corvette finished?" Were it not for the Corvette's high prestige level, the GM bean counters probably would have killed the performance flagship. What was hurting the Corvette was the perception of reduced performance and a Cadillac-priced car with very poor quality.

John DeLorean was just 44-years old when Ed Cole promoted him to general manager of the Chevrolet division to rein in the division's overhead and to do damage control over the failed Corvair. John's involvement and leadership was something of a mixed blessing for the Corvette. After *Car & Driver* named the '70 Corvette "Car Of The Year," DeLorean pushed for higher production, hurting overall quality. The car magazines had been bashing the Corvette since '68 over the quality issue, so DeLorean initiated a quality improvement program that was at best marginally effective. He also initiated the luxury Corvette by adding interior trim upgrades and he bumped the price of the '71 model to $5,496, up $304 from the '70 model. DeLorean reasoned that if there was a demand, the buyers would pay the extra cost. While that may well have been true, John also proposed making the Corvette on the lesser expensive Camaro/Nova chassis as a way to increase the Corvette's profit margin. Fortunately, that idea died.

Production figures for 1971 were 26,844 units, up 4,258 from 1970, but down by 11,918 from 1969. When you factor in price increases, high insurance rates, and the performance car's fall from grace, it's amazing that this low volume car ever survived.

There were no changes to the body of the '71 Corvette. Under the hood, Corvette's bargain priced ($158) L46 350-hp 350 was dropped in order to save the LT1. Compression ratios of all GM cars were reduced so that cars could start running on lead-free gas. Also, power figures were listed at "net" ratings, creating, on paper, what looked like a huge power drop. However, on the street, the '71 Corvette could still rip up the pavement. The $483, LT1 Corvette ran 0-to-60 in 6.0 seconds, while the $1,221, LS6 454 optioned Corvette could run 0-to-60 in just 5.3 seconds, while the $1,221, LS6 454 ran 0 to 60 in just 5.3 seconds. Not bad for a big-block car weighing almost 3,700 lbs!

While street Corvettes had their challenges, Duntov made sure that the racers could still order hot Corvettes. On the $1,010 ZR1 option, nearly everything was heavy duty and no luxury options were available. Only eight ZR1s were made. The ZR2 option cost a whopping $1,747 and was the same as the ZR1, except for the LS6 454 engine. Only 12 ZR2s were made.

What saved the Corvette in the '70s wasn't horsepower, but loyalty and style. Considering the challenges of the '70s, the Corvette's survival was truly an automotive miracle.

CHAPTER 1: PRODUCTION CORVETTES

1972 Corvette
"Staying the Course"

Despite the storm clouds that loomed over Detroit's performance cars, the 1972 Corvette was thriving, at least in sales. The base price of the '72 Corvette was $5,553, up only $37 from the '71 model. But sales went from 21,801 in '71, to 27,004 in '72 an increase of 5,203 units. Not bad for a limited use sports car with a high ticket price and sky-high insurance premiums. Chevrolet must have been doing something right.

However, on paper, things looked bleak. There were now only three engine options; the base 350 small-block ZQ-3, with 200 hp, the 350 small-block LT1, with 255 hp, and the 454 big-block LS5, with 270 hp. By the numbers, these power figures look bad, but keep in mind, these are "net" not "gross" power ratings. Due to cars now using lead-free gas, compression and power rates were down, but not as much as it might have seemed.

Magazine tests still raved about the '72 Corvette, especially the LT1. One writer referred to the LT1 as a "real tiger." With 3.70 gears, the LT1 was a solid low 14-second car. With 4.11 gears, high 13s were possible. The only complaint was a lack of torque under 3,500 rpm but from there up to the 7,000 rpm, the LT1 was a delight to experience.

Like the '71 Vettes, there were no notable external visual changes. However, '72 was the last year for several items that included; the front and rear chrome bumpers, the egg-crate front grille and side-vents, the rectangular exhaust tips, the removable rear window, the windshield wiper closet, and bias-ply tires.

The LS5 454 was not emissions certified in California, and an alarm system replaced the fiber-optic lighting monitoring system. Also, this was the last year for the nearly unstreetable, $1,010.05 ZR1 option, which provided a base car for racers. Only 20 ZR1 equipped Corvettes were built in '72. This was the last of the "For Off-Road Use" C3 racer kits.

The C3 Corvettes had three distinct phases: the '68 to '73 chrome bumper cars, the '73 to '79 soft bumper cars, and the '80 to '82 integrated spoiler cars. This was the end of the first phase of C3 Corvettes. But in spite of all the changes and reductions, the '72 Corvette did surprisingly well. But challenges were on the horizon that no one anticipated. Ultimately, the Corvette had developed into a much better performance car, even if it took almost 12 years to make it so. Meanwhile, out on the race track, John Greenwood

The performance dilemma was this: for $483.45, the LT1 was a fast, balanced car. The LS5 made 15 more horses for only $294.90, but the car seemed heavy and sluggish. Chevrolet was doing its best to make the Corvette a true GT car. There was a custom interior trim option, and air conditioning was now available with the LT1, but with a lower redline of only 5,600 rpm, in order to keep the A/C belts from flying off. Also, the close-ratio four-speed and three-speed automatic were standard.

was making quite a name for himself. In '72 Greenwood's BF Goodrich 427 ZL1 Corvette broke the speed record at Le Mans on the Mulsanne Straight with a 211-mph blast on the 3.7-mile long straight. John was leading the GT class until the ZL1 threw a piston and had to drop out. John's cars were notorious for qualifying first, setting records, and breaking small parts. Such is the life of an independent road racer – even with a bad-ass big-block Corvette.

1973 Corvette
"First of the Soft-Bumper Vettes"

It was a strange time to be a Corvette. Chief engineer Duntov clearly saw that speed, power, and performance were obviously "out." So Duntov set out to make his Corvette the best he could. In 1972, while showing one of his mid-engine prototypes, a GM board member commented, "What do you want a new car for? You're selling all you can right now!"

That's like saying, "If it ain't broke, don't fix it!" But you can make it better.

Duntov wanted to use his final years at General Motors to make the Corvette a quality automobile. The demand for the new C3 Corvette was so high that extra production shifts were added and quality seriously suffered. By '72 "quality" was the least-liked feature of the Corvette. Customers didn't like the Cadillac price with a Vega finish. Thus, Duntov began polishing the '73 Corvette to meet new performance standards.

Corvette sales had been rising since 1972, and continued through the decade Although serious cars guys bemoaned the lackluster power and soft touches, Corvettes were more popular than ever. The accounting-types with the purse strings were very happy.

The most obvious change for '73 was the new front bumper and hood. All cars now had to have 5 mph crash-bumpers. The bumpers added 2 inches to the car's length and 35 lbs of weight to the front end that did not help the front-to-back weight ratio. When it was announced that beginning in '73, all car had to have crash bumpers, many wondered what the Corvette design team would come up with. Their solution was just brilliant. The new hood featured a cowl-induction system, and eliminated the troublesome "wiper closet" from earlier C3s. The doors now had steel guard-beams for added safety. Extra sound-deadening material was sprayed onto the inside of various body panels as well as rubber body mounts to make the car quieter inside. GR70x15 steel-belted radial tires also helped ride quality. Corvette coupes from '68 to '72 had a removable rear window. Unfortunately, when removed, there was considerable interior air buffeting. So, for '73 coupes, the rear window was fixed in place.

In 1973, only three engines were available: the base 190 horsepower 350, the $299 L82 350 with 250 hp, and the $250 LS4 454 with 275 hp. Solid-lifter engines were no longer available. And lastly, very nice-looking, polished, 8-slot aluminum wheels were a $175 option, but had to be recalled due to structural problems. It took until '76 for supplier Kelsey Hayes to work out a porosity problem that kept the tires from holding proper inflation.

Despite the added weight and the soft touches, buyers didn't care. In 1973 30,464 Corvettes were sold. Duntov spent '68 to '72 making the C3 a rip-snort'n pavement burner. His final efforts actually saved the car in the '70s. Thanks Zora!

CHAPTER 1: PRODUCTION CORVETTES

1974 Corvette
"Happy Bean Counters"

While the automotive world was in the doldrums over the death of performance cars, Chevrolet couldn't make enough Corvettes to satisfy customers! Duntov's objective was to make the Corvette a quality performance car. Obviously, his efforts paid off. And despite major social changes, Chevrolet sold 37,502 Corvettes in '74, that's up 7,038 from '73 sales of 30,464. This made the GM bean counters very happy!

The name of the game in business is sales. If nobody is buying, it won't be sold for long. Remember the Fiero? The marketplace was changing and Duntov made enough changes in creature comfort and quality to strike a chord with the buyers. Demand was so high for new Corvettes that the production was bumped from 8 to 9 hours. And even then, there were 8,200 orders returned to dealers "unfilled." Buyers wanted Cadillac quality for their $6,000. A major car magazine awarded the Corvette Best All-Around Car in '73 and '74. Considering the performance drop, this was amazing!

The obvious visual difference on the '74 Corvette was the new rear bumper. While other cars had huge chrome railroad ties for bumpers, the Corvette's new look was smooth and clean. The Corvettes and the Firebirds had the best-looking crash-bumper covers. The Camaros got the big, chrome bumpers that were common to most cars of the time. The '74 rear bumper cover was made of two pieces, later year cars used a one-peice cover. The crash-bumper was an aluminum impact bar mounted on two telescopic brackets.

In an effort to improve life inside the Corvette, two small resonators (mini mufflers) were added to the exhaust system to tone things down. 1974 was also the last year for non-catalytic exhaust, as well as the last year for real dual-exhausts. There were no exhaust tips for the Corvette, the tailpipe exited below the rear bumper cover, like a regular car. The big-block 454 would be gone in '75 and this was the last year for leaded gas.

Under the hood there were three engines available. The base 195 hp 350, the optional $299 L82 350 with 250 hp, or the $250 LS4 454 with 270-hp. Transmission choice was a no-charge option of either the close-ratio four-speed or 3-speed Turbo Hydramatic. The option buy of the year was the $7 "Gymkhana" suspension that got you a thicker front anti-roll bar and high-rate springs. This was available on all Corvettes, but only 1,905 were ordered. If the $7, EF7 Gymkhana option wasn't quite taut enough for you, there was the $400 Z07 Off-Road Suspension and Brake Package. This bundle of goodies got you stiffer front and rear springs and heavy-duty front and rear power brakes. Only 47 '74 Corvettes were ordered with this option - a real indicator of the changing Corvette market. The only changes to the interior was a new 10-inch wide rear-view mirror and modified seatbelts.

All of the extras added cost and weight to the Corvette. The base price for the '74 Corvette was now 6,001.50, But again, it didn't seem to matter to buyers. The Corvette was over 20 years-old and now had a solid performance image even though the mean machine days were over. The three most popular options were now power steering, power brakes, and telescopic steering column. Buyers taste had changed and Duntov was right on target.

December 31, 1974 wasn't just the end of a year, it was the end of an era. Zora Arkus-Duntov retired after a 21-1/2 years of service to GM. During his last year, Zora built two racer mule Corvettes on a '74 Corvette prototype. Both cars were built as racers and looked the part. One car had L88 wheel flares, header side-pipes, and racing wheels and tires. The other, also based on a '74 Corvette, was called the "Silhouette Racer" and was used to develop the IMSA body kit popularized by John Greenwood and others through the mid-to-late '70s. For a senior citizen, the man just wouldn't stop. There would never be another like him.

1975 Corvette
"Pavement Burner to GT Car"

Considering the sad state of the economy in '75, the Corvette was doing rather well. The new direction for the Corvette was style and comfort, and despite rising costs, buyers didn't mind at all.

From a performance point of view, things were dismal. Zora Arkus-Duntov was headed for pasture, car shows, consulting, and other business opportunities Fortunately for the Corvette team, there were only two other American performance cars for buyers to choose from; the Trans-Am Firebird and the Z-28 Camaro. They cost a little less than the Corvette, but lacked the strong image, born of the Corvette's racing heritage.

1975 was a mixed bag of firsts and lasts for the Corvette. Due to sagging sales and pending roll-over safety regulations, '75 would be the last year customers would be able to buy a convertible, until '86. This was also the last time a convertible cost less than a coupe. Future Corvette roadsters would all be premium versions. The big-block 454 option was gone, and there was only one engine option, the toned down $336, 205-hp L82. The new catalytic converter system was a pseudo dual exhaust, using a Y-pipe off the engine into a single converter, then branching off into two pipes and two mufflers. It was also the first year for the HEI (High Energy Ignition) pointless distributor. Other firsts included a bladder-type fuel cell and kilometers-per-hour markings on the speedometer.

For the go-fast crowd, the Z07 suspension was still available, but only with the no-charge M21 close-ratio 4-speed transmission, and the optional $336 L82 engine. For $400 you got special front and rear suspension parts, heavy-duty brakes, and the gymkhana over-sized antiroll bars. Only 144 Corvettes were sold with the Z07 option and the combined engine-transmission package, totalling $736. This was as stout as a '75 Vette could be.

The exterior changes were minimal. The rear bumper cover was now one piece - the previous version was a two-piece design. Both the front and rear bumper covers had simulated black bumper-pads. The side view mirror was wider, and the car sat just over a quarter-inch higher. The custom interior option still cost just $154 and included; leather seats, special cut-pile carpeting, carpet trim on the lower part of the door panels, and wood-grain accents on the console. On the down side, the car packed on 141 pounds, weighing 3,529 pounds. That's an extra 319 pounds since '68! The base cost was up as well by $809 from '74, to $6,810 for the coupe.

For a lot of reasons, the lack of grunt, extra weight and cost didn't matter to buyers. Sales were up 963 units from '74, to 38,465 for '75. Sales were in a near vertical climb through the entire '70s decade. Corvettes weren't just winning sales due to attrition of the dead muscle car market. It seemed that America finally "got" the Corvette. And they lined up in droves, just to have a Vette.

Meanwhile, out on the race track, where legends are made, John Greenwood kept Corvette's racing status alive by winning the SCCA Trans-Am Championship. There was still something to cheer about. And in the hallowed halls of Chevrolet, the Corvette got a new field commander. Dave McLellan was the new Corvette Chief of Engineering, and did he have some big shoes to fill. Plus, he had a new Corvette to design in a few years.

CHAPTER 1: PRODUCTION CORVETTES

1976 Corvette
"Entering the Golden Sales Years"

Depending on what department you worked in at General Motors, it was the best of times or it was the worst of times. Despite our passions for performance, business is business, and not turning a profit can turn automotive gold into lead. Fortunately for the Corvette team, the '76 Corvette was golden in an age of non-performance.

Those pesky bean counters couldn't have been much happier with the '76 Corvette. Sales of the Corvette hit a best-to-date, all-time high of 46,558 units. That was up 8,093 units from '75. And considering

the hefty price hike in '76, those sales figures were astounding. The base price of the '76 Corvette was $7,606, up $794 from '75. Part of the increase came from inflation and the rest was the fact that the Corvette came with more standard equipment than ever before.

Although not official, many in the Corvette design and engineering groups knew the possibility of a new mid-engine performance Corvette was close to zero, so they set out to make a better car. Power steering and brakes were now standard equipment. From there, all other improvements were incremental. The base engine was up 15 hp to 180 hp, and the optional "performance" L82 was up 5 hp to 210 hp. The power boost came from allowing the engines to run hotter. To offset the extra heat in the interior, the '76 Corvette had a partial steel underbelly. And to quiet things inside, the air intake was forward of the radiator, eliminating the intake howl from cowl-induction hood.

Over 30-years later, Corvettes are still getting dinged for a "less than acceptable for a premium car" steering wheel.

Like the mid-year C2 Corvettes, exterior changes were slight and one had to have a sharp eye. The hood was unique to '76, as it was missing the cowl induction features. The rear bumper cover sported a new Corvette script badge that replaced the individual die-cast Corvette letters. There were actually two badge versions, one with smaller recessed lettering, and the other with larger lettering that wasn't recessed. Also, the air vents on the top of the rear deck were gone because Astro Ventilation was cut in '76. The RPO YJ8 aluminum Kelsey-Hayes wheels first shown in '73 were finally available as a $299 option. The RPO FE7 Gymkhana Suspension option that included a larger front stabilizer bar and stiffer springs was up from $7 in '75 to $35 in '76. But for all the add-ons and new parts, the '76 Corvette actually lost weight. Curb weight was down 52 pounds to 3,608. Not a lot, but better than a weight gain.

Older guys and performance addicts called the '76 Corvette "soft," while defenders said it was merely evolving into a true GT - Grand Touring road machine. However, performance was way off. 0-60 time was 7.1 seconds, the 1/4-mile time was 15.3, and top speed was only 124 mph - way off from a few years before. Considering the times, that was as good as it got.

In the interior, the unit was now a new AC Delco maintenance-free battery. The $164 custom interior option was very popular with the Corvette's new buyers. Catalytic converters needed for emission controls can get very hot. To keep the interior cooler and added structural rigidity, a steel underbelly in the forward section was added. Over the years, Corvettes were often criticized for being parts bin cars. Chevrolet didn't help matters by using the small-diameter steering wheel from the Vega! At least the steering wheel had a Corvette horn button.

However, there was a guy named Greenwood with a wild-looking, 221-mph IMSA racer (some called it "The Batmobile") that had everyone's attention. Actually, you couldn't miss it! The over the top body kit was developed by Duntov, Gib Hufstader, and John Greenwood. This was to be Zora's last racer kit effort. For several years, Greenwood's cars were always contenders and almost always broke something small that put him out of the race. Too bad he couldn't have gotten a little more help from the ol' gray fox - Duntov.

1977 Corvette
"The Refinement Process Continues"

General Motors' management was happy. The '77 Corvette was the most successful Corvette to date, selling 49,213 units – up 2,655 from '76. What makes that figure even more amazing was the fact that the base '77 Corvette cost more than ever – $8,647, up $1,043 from the year before. But it flat-out didn't matter, America clearly loved the new, kinder, gentler Corvette.

The design department knew what was in the works for the 25th Anniversary '78 Corvette, so the '77 model was loaded with under-the-skin refinements that all added up to a better, easier-to-live-with Corvette.

The only exterior changes to the '77 Corvette were the removal of the "Stingray" script on the front fenders, a new cross-flag badge on the nose, and black A-pillars. These slight changes make the '77 model completely unique and easy to spot. Everything else was identical to the '76 model, including engine power ratings and transmission options.

Incremental changes were made throughout the car. Power steering and power brakes were now standard. Power for the base model came from a 180 hp 350-CID engine. The optional 210 hp L82 engine now cost $495 – that's $12 more than the last LT-1 option in '72. In California, only the base, 180 hp engine with an automatic transmission was available. And transmission choice was a no-cost option. But you could have all the other luxury options you could afford. And for something completely insignificant, the early Corvette engines were painted traditional Chevy orange, while the later engines were painted blue.

To improve interior ergonomics, the new four-spoke steering wheel was 2-inches closer to the dash for a more "arms-out" driving position, as well as improving ingress and egress. Leather seats and a leather-trimmed steering wheel were now standard, as well as a new headlight and windshield washer control stalk off the steering column. The modified console now housed heater and air conditioning controls – allowing the use of a standard AC Delco stereo radio. The AM/FM stereo 8-track sound system was a $414 option, and was ordered on nearly half of all '77 Corvettes.

Customers had to have something to play those disco 8-track tapes with.

Other improvements included stainless steel shields on the mufflers, steel reinforcements in the hood, and a redesigned rack to hold the T-tops and free up limited interior space. Special NA6 emissions equipment for $22 was required for Corvettes sold in altitude areas over 4,000 feet. The optional FE7 Gymkhana Suspension with a larger front sway bar and stiffer springs was bargan-priced at only $38.

While '77 Corvettes cost more than ever and weren't laying down rubber with thunder, they were still in the game, and more popular than ever. In March of '77 the St. Louis assembly plant built its 500,00th Corvette that was equipped with almost every option - topping out at $15,000. Corvettes from this era tend to get beat up because of their extra weight and reduced power. However, *Road & Track* magazine tested an L82 Corvette that set a new slalom speed record, beating out a 911 Turbo Carrera! Late-'70s Vettes could still kick some butt!

What's particularly odd is that late-'70s Corvettes are currently (2011) the least expensive to buy. Many are shockingly inexpensive - some for under $5,000. If you don't mind a mechanical, pre-electronic era Corvette, these cars are an easy place to enter the Corvette hobby.

CHAPTER 1: PRODUCTION CORVETTES

1978 Corvette
"Finally, A New Look"

As the Corvette's silver anniversary was approaching, there was quite a lot of excitement in the automotive press over the possibility of an all-new, mid-engine '78 Corvette. This was not pure speculation though. Since '68, Chevrolet had teased Corvette fans with seven mid-engine prototypes!

But, it was not to be. Why? Corvettes were just too successful.

The 500,000th Corvette rolled off the St. Louis assembly line on March 15, 1977. This was due in large part to the huge surge in sales beginning in '72. From GM's management perspective, "Is something wrong with the Corvette?" Then in June of '78 Chevrolet decided to end all further development of mid-engine Corvettes. So, where to from here? By '77, the overall styling was 10-years old and getting a little stale. The front and rear bumpers, hood, and fenders had been updated, so the only thing left to change was the roof. The new glass fastback roof was a refreshing improvement that made the car much more useful by opening up the rear storage area. Too bad they didn't make it a hatchback from the beginning.

The '78 Corvette had three variations: the stock Corvette with the new roof and all the new options, the Silver Anniversary paint option, and the Pace Car Replica option. (To be covered next.)

The improved package was a winner with buyers, selling 46,776 units, down from '77, but higher than '76. Overall, it was a solid hit. The base price of the '78 Corvette was up $704 from '77, to $9,351. Well-optioned cars cost over $11,000. Besides the new fastback roof, there were many other improvements. The base engine got another 5 hp, and the optional $525 L82 was up 10 hp, to 220 hp. A wide-ratio four-speed gear box, T-top, and leather interior was standard. The Corvette finally had optional 60-series tires for $216, and the gas tank how held 24 gallons. The interior had new features as well. The dash had a square housing around the speedometer and tachometer, new wiper controls, a real glove box, new door panels, and a roller-type screen for the fastback area.

Finally, the $349 glass T-top panels were available. Special 25th Anniversary badges were on the nose and the gas filler cap, and there was a $399, two-tone, light and dark silver paint option.

The '78 Corvette was a much-improved car. But, at 3,595 pounds, the extra 20 hp in the L82 had little affect on performance. Chief of Corvette Engineering Dave McLellan's mission was to satisfy the current Corvette customers who wanted style and comfort, not neck-snapping performance. Dwindling power and performance didn't matter to buyers. It's hard to tell if Duntov could have made a difference. After all, this is General Motors, and "sales" is the bottom line.

1979 Corvette
"The Best Sales Year Ever!"

Despite the huge price increases, weight increases, and lack-luster power, the '79 Corvette set an all-time sales record of 53,807 units, General Motors accountants were never happier with the Corvette. This was a very strange time. The only GM survivors from the muscle car era were the Camaro, Firebird, and Corvette - all of whom were shadows of their former performance past. Ford had a new Mustang, but it looked nothing like a real Mustang. But it didn't matter, buyers just wanted a sporty car, and after all, the Corvette was still a "Vette."

From a performance perspective, the '79 Corvette was quite unremarkable. The biggest news for the '79 Corvette was price. Inflation was driving everyone nuts in the late 1970s and it was showing up big-time on the Corvette spec sheet. In the beginning of the year, the base price was $10,220, up $869 from '78. By the end of '79, the base price was $12,313, up $2,962 from 1978! Although inflation was part of the increase, the growing list of luxury options that were now "standard," also helped drive up the base price. Statistics showed that buyers wanted cushy Corvettes, and Chevrolet was happy to oblige them. Air conditioning was ordered on 87 percent of '79 Corvettes, and 77-percent were ordered with automatic transmissions. The $439 AM/FM/CB radio was the third most expensive option.

Once again, improvements were incremental. Between the new "open flow" mufflers and the dual-snorkel air cleaner, the L48 engine was up 10-hp to 195-hp and the L82 was up 5 hp to 225 hp. Automatic transmission equipped Corvettes now had 3.55:1 rear gears for improved "off-the-line" performance. Only 7-percent of '79 Corvettes had the close-ratio four-speed. The low-profile, 60-series tire option was only $226.

Appearance and comfort defined the '79 Corvette. The '78 Pace Car front and rear spoilers were a $265 option and improved mileage by 1/2 mpg. Lightweight leather seats from the '78 Pace Car saved 24 lbs, but curb weight was 3,665 lbs, up 60 lbs from '78. Tungsten-halogen headlights and 85 mph speedometers were phased in during the year.

Prices jumped over 100 percent from 1968 to '78! A loaded '79 Corvette cost between $14,000 and $16,000 depending on when the car was ordered. Obviously, performance hounds weren't happy with the '79 model. Perhaps the best thing one could say about the new Vette was that it was a very nice car. With reduced speed limits and increased fuel prices, buyers seemed more interested in their Corvette being more of a GT car than a stump-pulling screamer. The record sales also provided the justification for a new Corvette design. In June '78 Dave McLellan started development of a new front-engine Corvette. Then in January '79, he received approval for a complete redesign for the next Corvette. The C4 was underway.

CHAPTER 1: PRODUCTION CORVETTES

1980 Corvette
"The Shark's Final Makeover"

Chevrolet could have left the Corvette's styling alone for 1980. But the soft-nose look was seven years old and needed a makeover. Sales success of the previous year simply caught everyone by surprise. 1980 was the beginning of the last few rounds of incremental changes as the Shark years were coming to a close.

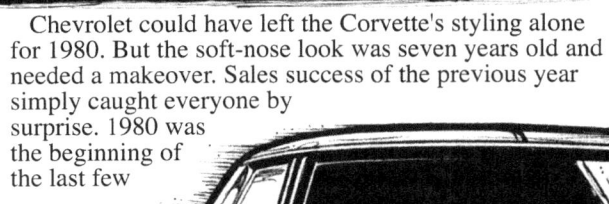

The '80 Corvette was a mixed bag of good and bad. On the good side, the new hood and front and rear bumper covers not only created a new look, but also reduced drag coefficient from .503 for the '79 car to .443 for the '80 model. Engineers also put the '80 Corvette on a diet, taking 160 pounds out of the car by using thinner hood and door parts, as well as an aluminum differential, crossmembers, and various attaching parts. The diet was part of Chevrolet's effort to meet new, tougher CAFE standards.

On the not-so-good side was the price. GM's marketing people knew that Corvette buyers were more interested in comfort and luxury than performance, so previous optional items, such as power windows, air conditioning, and tilt-telescope steering, were now standard. The base price started out at $13,145 and went up to $14,345 by the end of the model year. Inflation was raising the price of everything it takes to make a car. Other tweaks included a federally mandated 85-mph speedometer, a relocated power lock button, and a new storage compartment.

1980 Corvette engines were an odd mix. California buyers could only order the 180-hp LG4. This was a mildly enhanced passenger car engine that used stainless steel headers and a computer module to control timing and carburetor settings. The LG4 was only available with the automatic transmission featuring the new lock-up torque converter. The good news was that the L82 power rating was bumped up 5 hp to 230 hp, the best since '74. However, the 4-speed transmission was not available with the L82, except for a few early production builds. The only other performance option was the $55 gymkhana suspension that was ordered on just 9,907 '80 Corvettes.

Many wondered where the Corvette was going. Rumors were circulating about a "new" Corvette, but that wasn't anything new, as the automotive press was always talking about a new Vette. However, design work on the C4 was indeed underway.

Sales for the 1980 were down to 40,614, from 53,807 in '79, but prices were up enough to make General Motors very happy. A loaded '80 Corvette could cost over $17,000. An L82, four-speed model could do 0-60 in 7.1-seconds and the quarter-mile in 16-seconds. Not great, but still hanging in there.

1981 Corvette
"Price Way Up... Sales Flat-Lined"

Detroit was experiencing real pain in 1981. Sales hit a 20-year low with only 6.2 million cars built. Despite a 23 percent price hike, General Motors was very happy with their flagship Corvette. Even though '81 sales were almost the same as the '80 sales figure, and was down considerably from the all-time high of 53,807 units in '79, 40,606 units for '81 wasn't too shabby.

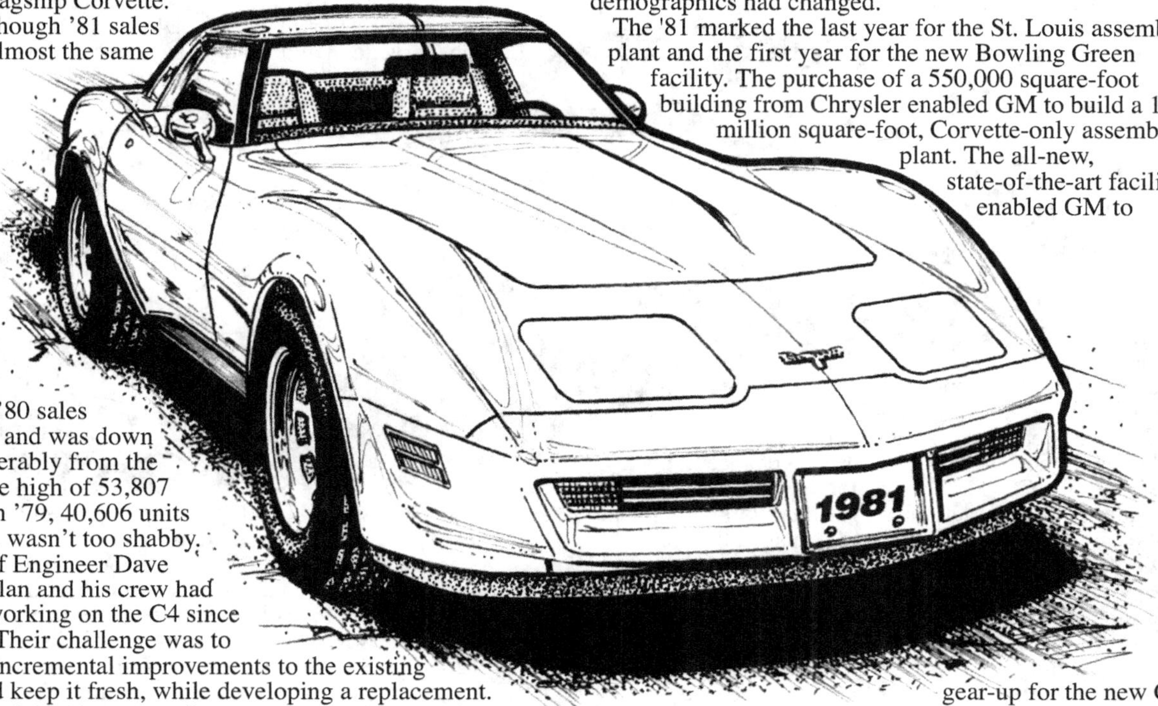

Chief Engineer Dave McLellan and his crew had been working on the C4 since 1979. Their challenge was to make incremental improvements to the existing car and keep it fresh, while developing a replacement.

One of the biggest challenges was weight control versus horsepower. In 1981, the Corvette lost 150-pounds of weight with the use of a new fiberglass mono-leaf rear spring, magnesium valve covers, steel tube headers, and thinner door glass. The Corvette went from 3,495 pounds in 1980, to 3,345 pounds in '81.

Unfortunately, the optional 230 hp L82 engine was no longer available. Only the base 190 hp 350 engine was available. This was the first time since '55 that there was no optional performance engine for Corvette customers. However, buyers did have a no-cost choice between a four-speed and an automatic transmission with the new lock-up torque converter for second and third gears. Only 5,757 (14 percent) were 4-speed cars. Unfortunately, the loss of the optional L82 (and its extra 40 hp) canceled out any performance advantage from the weight reduction. Yes, Corvette demographics had changed.

The '81 marked the last year for the St. Louis assembly plant and the first year for the new Bowling Green facility. The purchase of a 550,000 square-foot building from Chrysler enabled GM to build a 1 million square-foot, Corvette-only assembly plant. The all-new, state-of-the-art facility enabled GM to gear-up for the new C4 Corvettes as well as the use of the new clear-coat painting process. The first Bowling Green Corvette rolled out on June 1, 1981, while the last St. Louis Corvette was built on August 1, 1981. Only 8,995 of the 40,606 '81 Corvettes were built in the new Bowling Green plant.

The '81 Corvette saw a huge price hike of $3,118 over the '80 model. "Soft" options such as aluminum wheels, two-tone paint, glass roof panels, 60-series tires, and am-fm cassette/CB radio, could jack the price as high as $19,750!

While it is true that C3 Corvettes were now marketed to a different buyer base, the car was still alive and well. Sales numbers proved that people still wanted Corvettes, even though they weren't the loud, tire-burning beasts of the '60s. Besides, McLellan and his crew were working on great things for 1984.

1982 Corvette
"The Last of the C3 Sharks"

Speculation by the automotive press about what Chevrolet was up to with the Corvette has been sport since the mid '50s. By 1982, word was out that there would finally be a new Corvette, soon.

Thanks to the sales success of the Corvette in the late '70s, the General Motors bean counters commanded, "Sales are great – keep making them!" Although enthusiasts were dying for a new Corvette, the delaying of the C4 gave engineering a chance to make the last of the C3 Corvettes as good as they could, considering the restrictions they had to work with. While Dave McLellan and his team had managed to trim 230 lbs out of the car since '78, with only 200 hp under the hood, it was better to talk about what a nice car the Corvette was and don't mention the "p" word - performance.

The only thing faster than a Corvette in early '80s America was inflation. The last C3 was also the most expensive of the Shark Corvettes. The new base price was $18,290 – up $2,032 from '81! And to send the C3 into the history books with a splash, Chevrolet offered the "Collector Edition Corvette" for a whopping $22,537 – making it the first Corvette to bust the $20K barrier. But because the press was all a buzz over the pending C4, buyers opted to wait-and-see. Consequently, the '82 C3 Corvette only sold 25,407 units – down 15,199 from '81. That was the lowest sales year since 1971.

Chief engineer, Dave McLellan decided that the Collector Edition would offer, "...A unique combination of color, equipment, and innovation – resulting in one of the most comprehensive packages ever offered to the Corvette buyer." For an extra $4,247 the Collector's Edition Corvette included hood and sidebody decals, pinstriping, a frameless lift-back rear window hatch, knock-off-style aluminum wheels, silver and beige paint, matching leather interior, special carpeting, and special emblems. To prevent imitation versions, the car had special i.d. plates.

By the end of the year, 6,759 Collector Editions were sold – slightly less then the '78 Corvette Pace Car. Many felt that the Collector Edition splash was to distract the fact that there was only one engine available, the 200 hp L83 and a manual transmission was not available. The new "Cross-Fire Injection" engine wasn't real fuel-injection, instead, the system used two injectors with a computer control module to better regulate fuel metering. While it was the first Corvette engine to not have a carburetor since '65, it hardly got any notice.

The best thing one can say about the '82 Corvette is that it was a nice car. Considering that it was the end of the line for the shark body style and a chassis that had been production since '63, the Collector Edition was an acceptable send-off to what has to be considered a very successful production run.

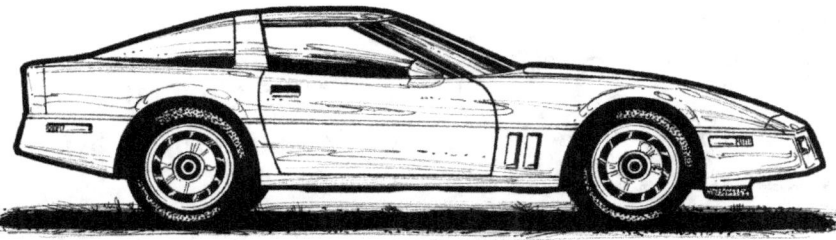

1984 Corvette
"Finally... A New Corvette!"

Anticipation couldn't have been higher. The C3 Corvette had lasted an amazing 15 model years andtook the Corvette through extreme highs and lows. Designing a new Corvette is said to be one of the most challenging tasks in the car business. It has to look new, but still look like a Corvette. On top of that, everyone has their own idea of what the car should be and look like. And to stoke expectation even higher, because completion was late, there was no '83 model. Fuzzy spy photos captured prototypes and mule cars that kept everyone guessing.

When the new Corvette was officially shown to the public, many were let down saying that because of the sloped nose, it looked tame and too much like the '82 Camaro and Firebird designs. However, once the magazine testers drove the car, minds were blown, socks went up and down, and all the carping about Camaros and Firebirds went away!

Everyone got warm because the new Corvette handled like no street production car ever dreamed of. On the General Motors test track, a new Corvette with the optional Z51 suspension maxed out on the skidpad with a 0.95g! That's race car territory. Corvettes have always had a weight issue. The '78 model topped out at 3,572 lbs to 380 lbs more than the new C4. Between the weight reduction, a slight increase in power and the new suspension, this was the Vette that performance enthusiasts had been waiting for. The new Corvette had FINALLY arrived.

The new design mandate was that the car have increased ground clearance, a larger interior, and less height. The only carry over from the '82 model was the Cross Fire injection 350 engine with a new air cleaner bonnet. The cast-iron motor was mounted closer to the middle of the car and the exhausts were run through a larger transmission tunnel. This layout helped create a quasi front-mid-engine design that no doubt helped the car dominate the SCCA Showroom Stock racing Series. The design trade-off was slightly less space in the interior footwells. Transmission choices were a four-speed automatic or the new Doug Nash 4+3 manual with overdrive in the top three gears. The all-new suspension included a five-link rear suspension, a rear stabilizer bar, monoleaf fiberglass front and rear springs, and forged aluminum suspension components. It all looked very race car-like. The Girlock four-wheel disc brakes had aluminum calipers and semi-metallic brake linings. New turbine-styled 16-inch wheels helped pull air through the wheels to cool the brakes. Small turbine vanes has been part of the old racer kit options from the early '60s.

The new body was designed so that there were no seams on any of the exposed panels. Seams were at the black rub strip that surrounds the car. A new clam shell hood design tipped forward to allow maximum accessibility to the engine, plus, it looked really cool. The windshield was raked back a whopping 64 degrees and the lift-out roof panels were now one piece. The rear hatch was finally standard. This was something that should have been done back in '78. The new interior had cloth, aircraft-style seats and broad, flat dash with full digital gauges.

Good thing the new car was a runner, as the new base price was $21,800 – up $3,510 from '82. But it didn't matter to buyers. The C4 was released in March of '83 as an '84 model, consequently, the '84 model had an extended production run. Just as well, because the demand for the new C4 was very high. The '84 Corvette scored the second best sales year with 51,547 units sold. The new C4 was a fantastic beginning for the next generation of Corvette.

CHAPTER 1: PRODUCTION CORVETTES

1985 Corvette
"The Refining Process Begins"

The new C4 Corvette was on the cover of just about every car magazine in the automotive business. Although the '84 Corvette posted amazing skid-pad figures, using the car on real roads was no fun. The two main improvements of the '85 model were a softer suspension and more power.

When the automotive press got to drive the new C4 Corvette on GM's test facility during the '84 preview, they were blown away by the car's handling. But in the real world, on real roads, they were less enthusiastic. Some were in pain, the ride was so harsh. Chevrolet improved the situation by decreasing the spring rates by 26 percent in the front and 25-percent in the rear. The springs in the optional Z51 package were reduced by 16-percent in the front and 25 percent in the rear. Despite the changes, some still complained about the ride.

The most exciting new feature for the '85 Corvette was under the hood. The Cross-Fire Injection 350 was replaced with the new Tuned Port Injection L98, fuel-injected engine. There hadn't been a real fuelie Corvette since '65, and after years of wheezy performance, this was a welcome change. The new L98 engine was rated at 230-hp – up 25-hp and had 330 ft-lb of torque up 40 ft-lb from the '84 engine, and fuel economy increased by 11 percent.

The additional horsepower and torque really improved the Corvette's performance. *Car & Driver* magazine awarded the '85 Corvette as the "Fastest Car in America," beating out Porsche with a top speed of 150-mph. On the skid pad, the new Corvette tied with the Porsche with a .84 g-force rating. The 0-to-60 times were between 6.0 and 5.7 seconds! While these figures don't seem all that stupendous, in '85, this was hot stuff!

The only exterior change on the '85 Corvette was the "Tuned Port Injection" inscription on the horizontal body molding behind the front wheelwell. Paint options were the same as the '84 model – 10 solid colors and three two-tone potions. And the optional $595 Removable Transparent Roof Panels had stronger sun screening.

The interior received subtle improvements. Dash instruments graphics were simplified with larger, easier to read digital numbers on the center cluster displays and a map strap was added to the driver's sun visor. The optional sport seats were now available in leather for only $1,025!

The Z51 suspension was priced at only $470. Included were FG3 Delco-Bilstein shocks, heavy-duty cooling, an extra radiator fan, heavy-duty front and rear springs, stabilizer bars, bushings, fast-ratio steering, and 16x9.5-inch aluminum wheels. The Z51 lowered the car by 3/4-inch. The heavy-duty Delco-Bilstein shocks and the Heavy Duty Cooling were available separately. If you were into gymkhana racing or just liked a tough handling Vette, and didn't mind the bone-jarring ride, the Z51 was a hot ticket.

Base price of the '85 Corvette was now $24,403 – up $2,603 from the previous model. A loaded '85 Corvette cost close to $28,500! Sales were good, but off from '84 with 39,729 units sold.

Showroom Stock racing brought the new fuelie Corvette some much-needed racing interest. The Vettes ran so fast that Porsche bought two Corvettes and took them apart to see why they were so quick! Considering where the Corvette was in the late '70s, this was sweet revenge for Chevrolet.

THE ILLUSTRATED CORVETTE SERIES

1986 Corvette
"The Return of the Roadster"

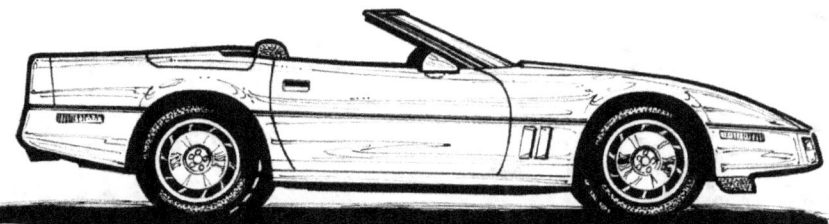

Outside the Corvette community, Harley Earl is mostly known for his Buick and Cadillac cars. Earl also created the GM Motorama to showcase advanced designs for possible future GM cars. For car people in the '50s and '60s, this was pure automotive magic. The Corvette was Harley's dream of an American sports car to compete with Europe's best - at least in the styling department. Right from the beginning, the seriously underpowered Corvette was a roadster. Thirty years later, when Dave McLellan and his design staff were working on the new C4 Corvette, they had in mind that the C4 Corvette might soon become a roadster again.

Since the basic C4 frame was designed with a possible future convertible in mind, major changes to the structure were not required. All that was needed was an x-brace on the frame, larger k-braces, thicker sections on several connecting bars, and a few other minor additions. The x-brace under the bottom of the main frame required that the ride height be increased by 10mm. The American Sunroof Company was contracted to work out the details of the top mechanism and everything else was developed by the Corvette engineering team. Extra space was needed for the convertible top, so the gas tank size was reduced from 20 gallons to 18 gallons.

There was a much-anticipated major change under the hood as well for '86 – aluminum heads. What was once exotic in the '60s with the L88 and L89 427 big-blocks was now stock. The new cylinder heads shaved 40 pounds off the front end. It would be another 11 years before an all-aluminum engine would become standard. Other engine changes included triple catalytic converters and an increase in compression from 9:1 to 9.5: 1. The net result was a 5 hp increase to 235 hp.

The only visual change for '86, besides the roadster version, was the mandated third brake light. Most cars had tacked-on third brake lights, but the roadster had a very nicely integrated light at the top edge of the rear bumper cover. The suspension setup on the roadster was stiffer than a stock Corvette, but not as stiff as a Z51 optioned car, and all roadsters got the wider Z51 wheels.

ABS braking was standard on all Corvettes for '86. Journalists loved the handling of the new roadster, but everyone had to get used to the "thumper" ABS brake system. The only changes in the interior were slightly angled instruments for better day-time readability and an all-new electronic air- conditioning system. A new cloth material was used for the stock seats.

The new roadster picked up some extra kudos by pacing the Indy 500 for the second time. The last time a Corvette paced the 500 was in '78, and boy, did Chevrolet create a ruckus. Only 300 '78 Pace Car Replicas were planned, but after dealers howled, Chevrolet decided to build one for every dealer - with 6,502 built for the year. Speculators went wild and some dealers wanted double the list price for their Pace Car. So, when it came time for another Pace Car replica, Chevrolet decided that ALL '86 Corvette roadsters would be "pace car replicas" with a set of dealer or customer applied decals to prove it.

Aside from the obvious visual difference of the convertible top, the only other exterior change was several new colors and slightly revised wheels. The new wheels now had a brushed finish on the center section.

All of the wonderful changes came at a very hefty price. The stock Corvette was up $2,624 from the '85 price to $27,027. The roadster was a $5,005 option that hiked the price to $32,032! Sales dropped from 39,729 the year before, to 35,109 in '86, with 7,315 "Pace Car replica" convertibles built. But it didn't matter, the rave reviews and the sheer open-air, driving fun of the new roadster was well worth the wait.

CHAPTER 1: PRODUCTION CORVETTES

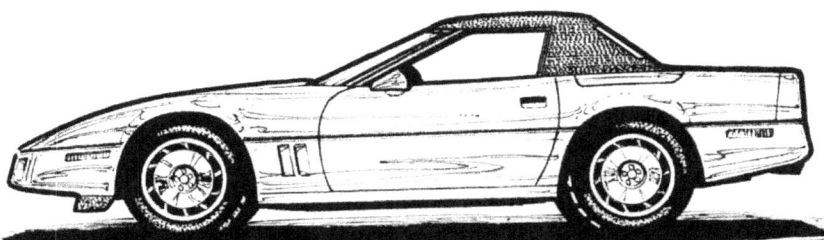

1987 Corvette
"Return to Greatness"

After having been kicked around for over 15 years as an overweight, under-powered has-been, the '87 Corvette reestablished itself as America's performance car.

You have to go back to the '70-1/2 LT1 and LS6 454 big-block to see performance figures like those of the '87 Corvette. Although there was only a 5-hp increase in power, testers reported that it felt more like 25 hp. With 0-60 mph times of 6.3 seconds and a top speed of 152 mph, critics, the competition, and racers were beginning to notice. It is possible that the tuned port-injection L98 engine was deliberately underrated. This would not have been the first time a Corvette engine had "low" power figures. Remember the 430-hp L88? This might be why the Corvettes dominated the Showroom Stock Series.

The fuel-injected 350 engine only received two improvements. The old-style hydraulic lifters were replaced with racer-like, roller valve lifters, and the spark plugs were relocated to the center of the combustion chambers.

The overall performance of the '87 Corvette was vastly improved with the new Z52 "sport package." For $470, the '87 Corvette was treated to most of the parts used on the Z51 package, but with the softer, stock suspension. Z52 extras included a radiator boost fan, Bilstein shocks, an engine oil-cooler, a heavy-duty radiator, 16 x 9.5-inch wheels, faster 13:1 steering, and a larger front stabilizer bar. The Z52 option was available with the coupe and convertible, manual or automatic transmission.

And in keeping with the Duntov "racer kit" tradition, the Z51 option included all of the before mentioned, plus the stiffer suspension, as well as the extra structural stiffening from the convertible. This was not an option designed for street use. The possible underrated L98, plus the $795 Z51 option, formed the basis of the SCCA Showroom Stock competition Corvettes that went undefeated for four years straight!

Visual changes on the '87 Corvette are hard to spot. One has to look closely at the wheels to notice the paint change to argent gray on the center-section and radial slots. Interior changes included relocating the "overdrive engage" light to the tachometer display area, a lighted vanity mirror, heated side-view mirrors, rear window defogger, six-way power seats, and standard electronic air-conditioning. Two antitheft devices were now used: major parts received I.D. tags and if not properly started, the fuel pump was disengaged. Base price of a coupe was $27,999 and the roadster's price was $33,172. And if you happened to have an extra $20k, there was the 345-hp, 177-mph Callaway Twin-Turbo option. This was the first time a non-GM installed option was on the Corvette order sheet.

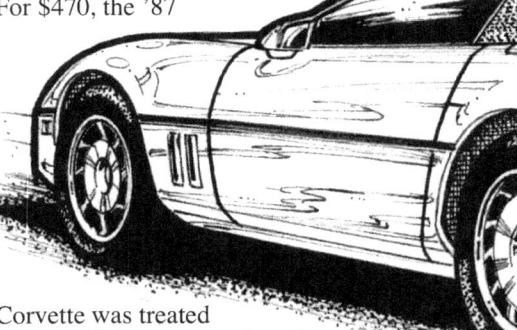

Callaway converted 188 '87 Corvettes to supercar status. This option would be available for the next five years. Eventually the price topped out at $33,000, but the package also included extensive body changes and was very exclusive.

Successful racing is what has always made the Corvette a performance icon. The SCCA Showroom Stock Corvettes were so fast that Porsche bought two '87 Corvettes to dissect to try to learn why their 944 racers couldn't keep up with them. Revenge can be sweet!

THE ILLUSTRATED CORVETTE SERIES

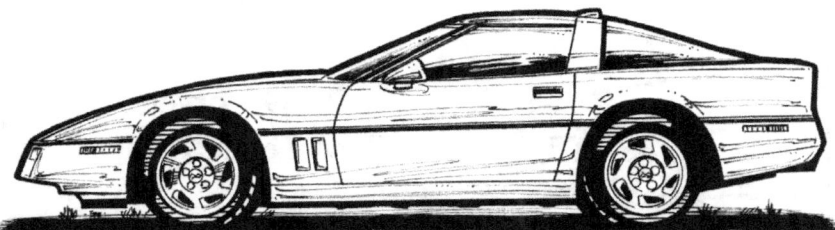

1988 Corvette
"Fantastic Options!"

The '88 Corvette looked nearly identical to the previous years C4 Corvettes, but under the surface there were three very exciting new options to choose from. Not since the late '60s had there been so many choices for Corvette buyers.

The only visual difference on the '88 Corvette was the restyled wheels, which were only offered in '88. The standard six-slot wheels were actually quite rare because of the 22,789 '88 Corvettes built, all but 5,463 cars did not have the optional Z51 or Z52 suspension options that included the 12-slot design wheels. The order sheet showed three distinctive options: An improved Z51 Performance Handling Package, the 35th Anniversary Edition, and the amazing Callaway Twin Turbo.

The base price of the '88 Vette was up $1,490 from the previous year, to $29,489. The car had minor but significant improvements in its engine, suspension, brakes, and interior. Items such as power door locks, cruise control, and stereo cassette were now standard.

For performance buffs, the $1,295 Z51 option was the hot setup and only 1,309 were ordered. The "new" Z51 package included huge P275/40ZR-15 Z-rated tires on restyled 17-inch wheels, a heavy-duty suspension, fast-ratio steering, larger front rotors and calipers, a radiator boost fan, a finned power-steering cooler, Delco-Bilstein shocks, an engine oil cooler, and higher rate springs.

The 35th Anniversary Package was a $4,795 option and featured a special all-white body with badges on the front fenders, black B-pillars and roof bar, tinted roof panels, and white 17-inch wheels from the Z51 package. The running gear was stock, but the interior came with embroidered leather seats and trim, a special anniversary plaque, and every creature-comfort option available. Only 2,050 were built.

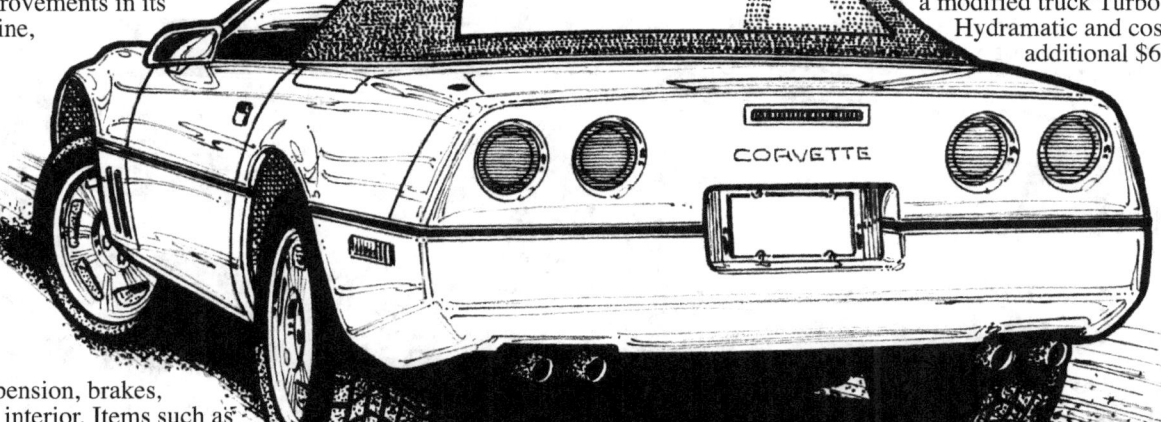

The big gun for '88 was the optional $25,895 Callaway Twin-Turbo. This was the most aggressive out-sourced specialty Corvette ever made. The Twin Turbo L98 350 engine packed 382 net horsepower with 562 ft-lb of torque. Even more impressive was the fact that the engine met EPA emissions standards while providing owners with a car that had a top speed of over 190 mph! An automatic version was available that used a modified truck Turbo-Hydramatic and cost an additional $6,000!

And to keep the racing crowd stoked, Chevrolet built 56 street-legal Corvettes for the SCCA Corvette Challenge Series. These cars had matched power output engines and full rollcages.

It was almost like the old days, plus a lot more cash, and minus the booming sidepipes.

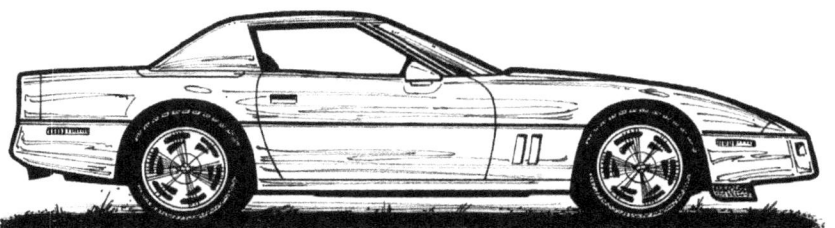

1989 Corvette
"Return of the Hardtop"

Rumors and spy photos were flying around the automotive press over the details of the new super-Corvette that Dave McLellan and his team were working on. The few dozen '89 ZR-1s were built as press review cars raised expectations to a fever pitch. But development delays with the Mercury Marine-built LT5 engine caused the ZR-1 to be postponed until 1990. However, that didn't mean that the production Corvette was being ignored. Far from it. The '89 Corvette saw a host of interesting upgrades and new features that made it a solid performer.

Spotting the new '89 Vette wasn't easy. While the base Corvette technically had new standard wheels, they were the same units that were part of the '88 Z51 Performance and Handling option and the Z52 Sport Handling option. Of the 22,789 '88 Corvettes, 17,326 of them had the Z51 and Z52 option that included the 12-slot wheel design. So, from the outside, the '89 looked just like 75-percent of the '88 cars. This had been a common practice with Corvettes, in that, what was once an option, became standard. The '89 Corvette was the last of the digital-dash Corvettes and considered by some to be the best of these digital Corvettes. Except for two new options, all improvements were under the skin. Sales were up 3,623 units to 26,412 for 1989, and the base price took a $2,056 jump to $31,545. The roadster had a $5,240 premium listing for $36,785. A loaded roadster cost over $43,000.

New option number one was for roadster buyers who lived in colder areas A hardtop hadn't been seen on a Corvette since 1975. Of the 9,749 convertibles ordered in 1989, 1,573 had the ASC-produced $1,995 option. Weighing only 64 pounds, the urethane and fiberglass top included heated rear glass and a finished roof liner. The new top could be used on '86 to '88 roadsters. Under the hood, the fuel injection system had improved injector calibration for better fuel atomization. Horsepower stayed at 245.

The Doug Nash 4+3 transmission was replaced with the all-new ZF six-speed gearbox. The new unit was fully synchronized and used an internal rail shift mechanism. Engineers called it the "tiger-pussycat" because it was docile at low speeds, yet tough at highway speed. The second big option was the $1,695 FX3, Selective Ride and Handling Package that gave drivers three distinctive suspension settings for cushy cruising, or Corvette Challenge racer-like setting. This was the first mass-produced car to ever offer this kind of technology and was a direct outgrowth of GM's ownership of Lotus.

A much improved anti-theft system initiated a four-minute shutdown of the fuel pump and started if the standard starting procedure wasn't used. It was so effective that insurance companies actually lowered Corvette rates. And lastly, the new $325 Low Tire Pressure Warning option informed the driver of tire underinflation. Expensive low-profile tires can look properly inflated, yet be up to 40 percent low.

The '89 Corvette didn't set any new records, but small improvements made the car an even better performance value. Car magazines gushed all over the car, calling it the "Best Vette Yet!" Ah, but they didn't really know what was ahead for 1990!

THE ILLUSTRATED CORVETTE SERIES

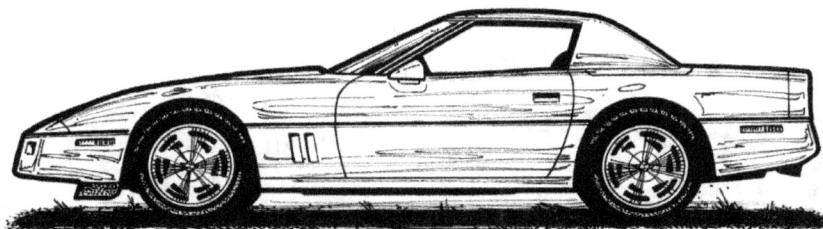

1990 Corvette
"In the Shadow of the ZR-1"

The introduction of the C4 '84 Corvette in the autumn of 1983 saved the car's reputation as a true sports car. Every succeeding year, things got just a little bit better, and the 1990 Corvette was no exception. Unfortunately, the base model Corvette stood in the shadow of the ZR-1.

Chevrolet had been stoking the Corvette fans since 1988 with the news of the soon-to-arrive "Super Vette," the ZR-1. What seemed like embarrassing delays only served to create a mountain of expectation for the car. Consequently, the "regular" Corvette got as much attention as Frank Sinatra, Jr.

The ZR-1 aside, Chevrolet had a great selection for Corvette buyers for 1990. To start off with, the car did not have another big price jump. The new list price for the '90 Corvette was $31,979 up only $434 from '89. The Z51 handling package was reduced by $115 to $434. On the other end of the options scale, the ZR-1 cost an extra $27,016 and the exotic Callaway Twin-Turbo option cost $26,895!

Even though the ante for a super Corvette was as much as an 84 percent premium over the stock version, Chevrolet public relations spin masters were quick to point out that even a nearly $60,000 Corvette was a bargain compared to a Porsche or a Ferrari. Actually, this has been the Corvette's market position for decades

Like previous C4 Corvettes, the 1990 model was peppered with small improvements. Under the hood, the fuel-injected L98 engine got another five horsepower as a result of adjustments in the air-intake speed-density control system, increased compression, a modified camshaft, and less restrictive exhausts. The new sloped-back radiator design eliminated the need for a heavy-duty radiator. Also, the radiator boost-fan was now standard. The 17-inch wheels were lighter than the previous year, but the wheel's design and size remained the sale as the '89 wheels. For more spirited driving, the $460 Z51 Performance Handling Package was still available on coupes only. Or, for maximum versatility, there was the $1,696 RPO FX3 Selective Ride and Handling option that included three suspension settings controlled by a console switch.

There were no exterior changes for the 1990 Corvette, so to spot a 1990 model, you'll have to look into the interior. The new wraparound dash had analog gauges in front of the driver and digital gauges in the center console. The new steering wheel had the first generation airbag and the car now had a real glovebox. It was also the first year for the new Bosch-Delco 200-watt CD player and the oil gauge now measured useful oil life.

ZR-1 aside, '90 was a pretty typical year for the Corvette, with lots of incremental changes that made for an improved car. The 1990 Corvette with the six-speed transmission and optional handling package would have been the Corvette flagship were it not for the ZR-1. This was a solid 150-mph sports car with the bargain price in the low-$30,000 range. Behind closed doors in the upper echelons of GM, the decision was made to cancel plans to reskin the Corvette for '95. Instead, a $250 million dollar budget was approved for an all-new Corvette, the C5.

CHAPTER 1: PRODUCTION CORVETTES

1991 Corvette
60's Performance...'90's Style"

Here's a shocker for you. While the ZR-1 was getting all of the attention, Dave McClellan and his team of engineers were quietly raising the performance bar. The stock '91 Corvette could rip off a 0-to-60 time of just 5.3-seconds. That's quicker that a '69 427/435 big-block Corvette, without the thunderous side pipes!

The country was in the doldrums in '91. Recession, inflation, and federal deficits had a damper on the economy. SUVs hadn't arrived yet and very few people were interested in performance cars. Despite the bad mood of the economy, the Corvette was running better than ever. *Car & Driver* magazine featured a face-off between a ZR-1 Corvette and a 911 Porsche Turbo. The Porsche lost.

Corvettes usually only make incremental improvements and '91 was no exception. There were no serious changes under the hood, as this would be the last year for the tried and true L98 that had served the C4 so well since '85. Although the power rating hadn't changed, new low-pressure mufflers improved performance and made the car slightly quieter. There was a new finned power steering cooler and a "low oil" sensor pickup was added to the oil pan. The most obvious change for '91 was the first face-lift since the C4 Corvette arrived in '84. The front bumper cover now had the side-marker lights incorporated into the design and the rear bumper cover now had squared-off tail lights, similar to those on the ZR-1. The front fender vents now had four horizontal slots - this design would be used through to the '94 model. The wheels were restyled with a new turbine look with the familiar center button section.

Wheel size was the same as the '90 model. The formerly black horizontal body molding was now body color, for a cleaner, monochromatic look. Other minor details included the placement of the third brake light at the top of the rear bumper cover. The list price for the '91 coupe was $32,455, up only $476 from the '90 model. The roadster started at $38,770. Total production was only 20,639, down 3,007 units from the '90 model - a reflection of the crummy economy of the day.

The famous Z51 performance suspension option was replaced with the new Z07 option. The new option offered all of the Z51 suspension parts, plus the old FX3 adjustable suspension option. However, the suspension settings were "firm-to-very firm," and it wasn't cheap. The Z07 cost $2,155. Only 773 cars were ordered with this option.

1991 was also the last year for the official Callaway conversion Corvettes. Callaway also built the 500th Callaway Corvette on September 26, 1991. The ZR-1 market was cooling off as well. Only 2,044 of the $67,000 beasts were built in '91. That down from the 3,049 made in 1990.

The '91 Corvette had come a long way in the ten years since the dog-days of '81. Corvettes were winning races, there were two exotic Corvettes offered, and performance was better than ever. And just over the horizon, a famous old gun from the early '70s was about to return: the LT1.

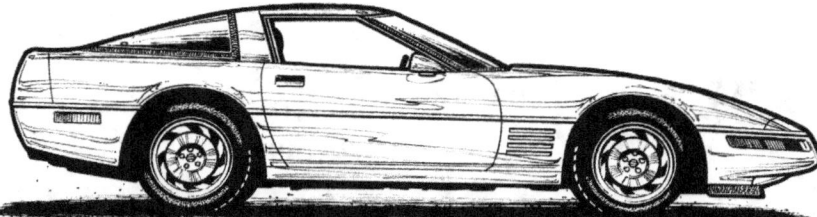

1992 Corvette
"The Return of the LT1"

Back in the late '70s, the dog days of performance, who would have thought that the famous LT1 would make a return? But this wasn't just an expensive, resurrected old performance badge as an option. The new LT1 packed 300 hp and was standard on every '92 Corvette!

Except for the rectangular exhaust tips and a few new interior and exterior colors, the '92 Corvette looks the same as the '91 Corvette. But under the pretty fiberglass there was plenty of new gear that made the '92 model the best standard Corvette to date. Some said that it was what the '84 model should have been.

Since the first V-8 Corvette in '55, Corvettes have always been about what's under the hood. The 1970-1/2 LT1 Corvette had been one of Zora Arkus-Duntov's favorite Corvettes. The high-revving, solid-lifter LT1 350 engine gave the driver an excellent mix of power, torque, and handling balance.

McLellan and his team broght back the LT1 magic. Everything from intake to exhaust was overhauled. A new Rochester multi-port injection system was built with the latest computer-controlled ignition system. The ports in the cylinder heads were opened up to better use the new 10.5:1 compression ratio and cast-iron exhaust manifolds connected with a new, dual catalytic converter exhaust system. A new cooling system flowed coolant to the heads first and the use of synthetic oil eliminated the need for an oil cooler. The net result was an increase of 50-hp!

The new standard ASR (Acceleration Slip Regulation) feature controlled both traction control and ABS breaking systems. For enthusiasts, this feature had an "off" switch on the dash. The new Goodyear GS-C tires were directional

The original LT-1 was rated at 370 "gross" hp. The new LT1, with its 300 net hp, was probably stronger than the original LT1. As good as the '91 model was, the '92 was better.

The new LT1 Corvette could do 0-60 mph in just five seconds, the quarter-mile in 13.6 seconds at 104-mph and had a top speed of 161-mph! Building a production performance car is a challenge, but thanks to some new electronics, there were a few basic hot rod tricks, for each side of the car with an asymmetric tread pattern that replaced the "Gatorback" design.

The only complaints came from ZR-1 owners because the new stock Corvette was only a few ticks slower than the ZR-1. For all of the extra hardware, the '92 model was up only $1,180 from the '91 car, making it a genuine performance bargain.

1993 40th Anniversary Corvette
"Ruby Red"

When the anemic '78 Corvette anniversary model came out, no one could have imagined how good things would be for the Corvette's 40th anniversary. When you consider the Corvette's low volume sales figures compared to other Chevys, it's amazing that GM kept the car in the Chevrolet lineup. But the improvements to the C4 during the '80s and early '90s were so impressive, Chevrolet dished out a delicious, special edition for the 40th anniversary of America's only true sports car.

To avoid the feeding frenzy of the '78 25th Anniversary Indy 500 Pace Car, Corvette planners decided to make the 40th Anniversary edition an option available on all three Corvette models - the coupe, convertible, and ZR-1. Although a few collectors complained, it was a good move for customers. A total of 6,749 40th Anniversary models were built for 1993. Compare those figures to the '88 35th Anniversary figures of 2,050, and to the 6,502 for the '78 25th Anniversary Indy Pace Car replica. Many people bought the '78 Pace Cars and paid nearly double the price, thinking their "collectible Corvette" would skyrocket in value. Perhaps by '93, the public's attitude to collectible cars had become more realistic.

The first thing you notice about the 40th Anniversary Corvette is its stunning, metallic Ruby Red paint. This paint was only available with the 40th Anniversary option. The rest of the details just sweetened the package. Included were Ruby Red leather sport seats, a power driver's seat, and the special wheel center trim caps, embroidered headrests and wheel center trim using the 40th Anniversary logo. Convertible editions got a Ruby Red-colored soft top.

There were several mechanical improvements for the '93 model. The engine was quieter due to new heat shields, new polyester valve covers, and a modified exhaust cam lobe. The front wheels were reduced in size to 8.5x17 with P255/45ZR-17 tires while the rear tires were increased to P285/40ZR-17.

The red-meat-performance news was with the nose-bleed-expensive ZR-1 option. With a few old fashioned hot rod tricks, the ZR-1's power was bumped from 375 to 405 hp. The heads were ported and polished with a new 4-degree valve overlap, for slightly less exhaust back pressure. The block now had 4-bolt main bearing caps and a modified oil pan with race car baffles, capable of controlling oil in 1.5g turns. The piston assembly was lightened and the injectors were opened up. The ZR-1 now used platinum-tipped spark plugs and Mobil 1 synthetic oil. It was a lot of little "hot rodder" details that added up to an extra 30 hp, allowing the ZR-1 to do 0-60 in 4.49-seconds, the quarter-mile in 13.03 @ 112.2 mph, 0.95 on the skidpad, and a top speed of 179 mph!

All that for an extra $31,683 on top of the base price of $34,595. This made the ZR-1 option '93 Corvette the most expensive Vette yet, at a whopping $66,278. In '93, 448 ZR-1s were sold, of which 245 units were equipped with RPO Z25, the 40th Anniversary option. With the adjustable suspension option, cruise control, and the Bose stereo CD sound system, the ZR-1 could be a race track screamer or a GT cruiser. A fully loaded ZR-1 could cost over $72,000!

The '93 Corvette was the first car to use the new GM passive keyless entry system. The system had many interesting functions, but was tricky to operate, and replacement keys were very expensive. For club racers, the $2,045 Z07 suspension option now included 9.5x17 wheels with P275/40ZR17 tires on the front and rear. All this made the standard Corvette look like a bargain. The base price was up $90 to $34,595 for the coupe and up $1,050 to $41,195 for the convertible. Sales were up slightly in '93 by 1,111 units, for a total of 21,590. But, the accolades coming in more than made up for the okay sales. Besides, the C5 model had just been approved for development.

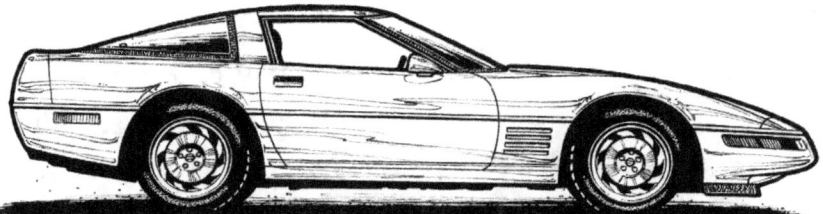

1994 Corvette
"No Revolution, Just Solid Evolution"

On June 14, 1993 when Corvette Chief Engineer Dave Hill and program manager Russ McLean got approval from GM president, John Smith for the '97 C5 Corvette, it put Hill and the C4 in a tough spot. Of course, it wasn't long before word got out that the next generation Corvette would soon be a reality. Hill and his team not only had to complete the design and implementation of a totally new car, they had to keep the remaining years of the C4 interesting and exciting.

With the C4 Corvette's scheduled demise, there

obviously weren't going to be any more big improvements made to the Corvette. After all, at this point, the design of the car was over 12 years old and had already racked up a long list of very impressive accomplishments. And considering the state of the last C3 model, the Corvette's performance resurrection was an automotive miracle. The goal for the remaining years of the C4 was to refine the car to the limits of its basic design, keep costs in check, and maintain customer interest in the light of the upcoming all-new '97 Corvette.

Let's face it, as a car owner, you spend most of your time looking at your car through the steering wheel in your interior. The '94 Corvette received a complete revamping of its cockpit. Most obvious was the new 2-spoke steering wheel and the new standard leather seats. Someone decided that a $30,000 car should not have cloth seats. And down at your feet there was new carpeting. The new floor covering was premium material, thicker, and more durable. The door panels were revised to coordinate with the two-tone dash.

Passengers received added protection with their own air bag. The new air bag took up the space where the glove box used to be, so a new storage compartment was designed into the center armrest. The plastic Roadster rear glass was replaced with real glass. Instruments were revised for better visibility and the car was subjected to a "squeak and rattle track" to isolate and eliminate rattles. An excellent thing for a premium automobile.

The 1994 Corvette didn't just get new interior digs. While engine power levels of the LT1 and the ZR-1 remained the same, numerous mechanical improvements were made. Both engines received the latest Sequential Fuel Injection units for better throttle response, idle, and lower emissions. The LT1 engine received an improved oil pan with a new oil sensor, a new coolant pump, and composite rocker arms. The 4-speed automatic was redesigned with new electronic controls for improved shift quality and rpm shift-point consistency.

For sport enthusiasts, the $1,695 FX3 Selective Ride and handling option received slightly softer springs for improved ride quality. But the big suspension news was the new Goodyear run-flat tires and low-pressure warning indicator. The new tires could be driven at 55-mph for 200 miles with zero tire pressure! That's why the pressure indicator was necessary.

Price increase for the '94 model wasn't too bad. The new list price for the coupe was $36,185 (up $1,590 from '93) and $42,443 for the roadster (up $1,765 from '93). The ZR-1 option was down $425 to $31,258! That's part why only 448 ZR-1s were ordered in '94. The ZR-1 models could be easily spotted by their new unidirectional 5-spoke aluminum alloy wheels with "ZR-1" enscribed on one of the spokes.

Of course, no one ever buys a basic stripo Corvette. A "loaded" coupe cost almost $43,000, while a roadster was over $50,000. A similarly equipped ZR-1 cost almost $70,000! It all added up to an evolutionary sales improvement, with total sales at 23,330 units, up 1,740 from '93. Not too shabby for the 11th season of a car with only three years before retirement. The final three years of the C4 Corvette would prove to be some of the generation's best.

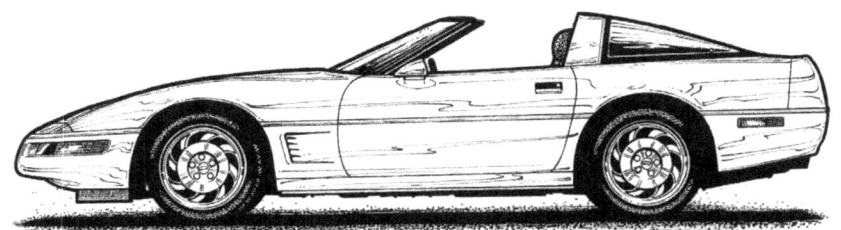

1995 Corvette
"Small Improvements Equal A Better Corvette"

It's funny how the mind remembers things. When you mention muscle cars, we usually think of Hemi 'Cudas, GTOs, 396 Camaros, or Boss 429 Mustangs. A '95 Corvette certainly doesn't come to mind. But the fact is Dave Hill and his team slowly and carefully honed the Corvette into what would have been hailed as one of the baddest of pavement burners of the muscle car era.

When you consider the dark days of '81 when Chevrolet actually dropped a 305 passenger car engine into the Corvette, the base model '95 Corvette is

nothing less than amazing. In the good old days, '67 to '70 big-block 427 and 454 Corvettes were at the top of the feeding chain. Quarter-mile times in the low 14s and high 13s made enthusiasts' head spin. The '95 base model Corvette ran 0-to-60 in just 5.1 seconds and the quarter-mile in 13.7 seconds at 103 mph! Remember, that's with a 350-ci small-block engine. And lets not forget the 161-mph top speed! Of course the icing on the Corvette cake was the EPA gas mileage of 17 mpg in the city, and 27 mpg on the highway.

The C4 Corvette was a example of how factory participation in racing can dramatically improve a performance car. Through the '80s we saw spectacular factory-supported cars such as the Showroom Stock Series Corvettes, the Corvette Challenge racers, the Chevrolet-powered GTP Lola chassis racers, and the jewel-like, world class ZR-1. Lessons learned from those

efforts were gradually integrated into base-model Vettes.

1995 was a significant year for two other reasons. It was the last year for the ZR-1 and it was the third time the Corvette was chosen to pace the Indy 500. Although the ZR-1 was not a sales success, it was a record setting, high-speed performance machine. The Indy 500 Pace Car Replica was the rarest of the three Corvette pace cars offered to that date, with only 527 units built and sold.

Although the '95 Corvette was essentially a carry over car, there were several improvements made on the car. The only visual change for the '95 model was the redesign of the front fender vents and new windshield wipers that eliminated chatter and floating at high speeds. Dark purple metallic paint was the only new color for the '95 model.

The power rating of the LT1 engine was unchanged, however new powdered-metal connecting rods were used for increased strength and uniformity of weight. At the top end of the LT1, the fuel injectors were improved to better cope with alcohol-blended fuels and to eliminate fuel dripping after the engine was shut off. A quieter fan was installed for overall noise improvement.

A new shifter for the 6-speed manual transmission replaced the reverse-lock with a high detent design for easier operation. Automatic transmission equipped cars had improved clutch controls and a lighter torque converter.

Suspension improvements included softer springs for better ride quality and cars with the optional adjustable suspension were equipped with the 13-inch brakes from the ZR-1.

Small interior improvements included a transmission temperature readout on the dash, Velcro straps to reduce rattling, improved stitching on the optional sport seats, and improved weather stripping to reduce water intrusion.

Overall, the '95 Corvette was a stunning car, making the number one spot in many car magazine reader's polls. The end of the C4 lineage was fast approaching and the "Grand Sport" was about to make another appearance.

1996 Collector Edition Corvette
"Going Out In Style!"

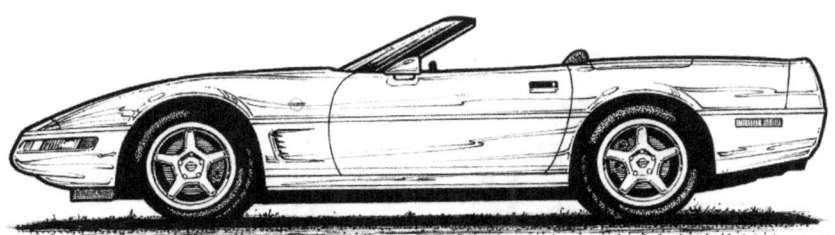

By '96, car magazines were teasing readers with "spy photos" of the upcoming '97 Corvette. Meanwhile at Chevrolet dealer showrooms, there were two delicious optional special edition Corvettes. The Grand Sport was a salute to the '63 Grand Sport racers. The Collector's Edition was just plain gorgeous.

The '84 model was a huge leap in technology for the Corvette. After all, the '82 Corvette was riding around on a chassis and suspension that was designed in early '60 and introduced in '63! While the '84 Corvette only had a 30-hp power increase over the '82 model, it was only packing 230 hp under the hood. Fast forward to '96 and the optional LT4 engine produced 330 hp! And remember, that was "net" horsepower. In the golden days of "gross" power ratings, the new LT4 engine would have been in the low 400-hp range. That means that a '96 LT4 Corvette was in the performance range of the old 427/435 L71 big-block Corvette.

Actual performance figures prove this out with 0-to-60 times in the low 5-second range and quarter-miles numbers in the mid-13s! High performance was back folks, and the car handled better and got improved gas mileage - it just wasn't as loud and rough. And another thing is that the '96 Corvette didn't just get better mileage, it got double the fuel economy of a '67 big-block Vette!

A '96 Corvette Collector's Edition could be ordered with the optional LT4 engine and other performance options that made this one of the sweetest package Corvettes made to that point. Performance was just a tick off the stump puller ZR-1 and 2/3s the price. The Sebring Silver paint and the ZR-1-styled allow wheels gave the car beauty to go along with its new LT4 brawn.

The RPO Z15 Collector's Edition package was very reasonably priced at $1,250. Included was the special Sebring Silver paint, painted ZR-1, 5-spoke alloy wheels, black brake calipers with polished raised "Corvette" lettering, and embroidered seats. Available interior colors were black, red, or gray. Convertible optioned cars all had black tops. Since there were no production limits for the Collector's Edition, a total of 5,412 units were sold, accounting for 25 percent of the total '96 Corvette production run.

The C4's life cycle saw one revolutionary leap (the ZR-1) and evolutionary growth every year - and 1996 was no exception. The optional 330-horsepower LT4 engine was an intermediary step towards what would be the standard LS1 engine in the '97 C5 model. The F45 Selective Real Time Dampening system was a $1,695 option that provided Corvettes with a mechanical-electronic active suspension. The Bosch ABS/ASR, anti-locking and acceleration slip system was standard, as were Goodyear run-flat tires, and a low tire pressure sensor. The passive-keyless entry Pass-Key II was also standard. And remember, these upgrades were on top of 12 previous years of improvements.

Through the '80s and '90s car magazines kept announcing, "The Best Vette Yet!" And each year it was true. A loaded '96 Collectors Edition coupe cost slightly over $43,000 and a roadster close to $51,000. Still twice as much as a regular Chevy, but 2/3s the cost of some of the sacred cows from Europe. Plus, the Corvette did nearly everything better and had a solid 43-year heritage!

CHAPTER 1: PRODUCTION CORVETTES

1997 Corvette
"The C5 Arrives"

The C5 was supposed to be released in '93, but GM was having serious financial problems in the early '90s. When the C5 project was finally approved, it was given a $250-million dollar development budget - not much to develop a completely new car. Dave Hill and his team got to work and the results were better than anyone expected.

The C5 was the first Corvette to be completely redesigned using virtually no carryover parts. Designers were very aware of the Corvette's short comings and set out to fix everything that wasn't right. The only carryover part was the 4L60-E automatic transmission and a few fasteners.

The basic layout and materials selection was first pitched in the '57 "Q-Corvette" concept study. Duntov had proposed a new Corvette featuring a fuel-injected, all-aluminum engine, a transaxle, 4-wheel independent suspension, and more. It took 40-years, but the essence of the Q-Corvette lives on in the new C5 Corvette.

The new C5 was bigger in every dimension, yet it weighed 80 pounds less than the '96 Corvette. The length went from 178.5 inches to 179.7 inches, the width went from 70.7 inches to 73.6-inches, the height went from 46.3 inches to 47.8 inches, the front track was increased 4.4 inches in the front and 2.9 inches in the rear. Even thought the car was larger in every direction, the new styling was lean and slick.

The new LS1 engine was like the ghost of the famous ZL1, 28 years before. The LS1 was an all-aluminum engine with cross-bolted 4-bolt main bearing caps, cast-in cylinder liners, a shallow aluminum oil pan with side reservoirs, a composite intake manifold, and aluminum valve covers. Also included was a hollow camshaft, separate ignition coils for each spark plug with crankshaft and camshaft sensors, and double-lined exhaust manifolds. The complete engine weighed 44 pounds less than the '96 LT4. Horsepower was 345, up from the LT4 rating of 330.

Using a transaxle in the back end helped create a near 50/50 front-to-rear weight ratio. Buyers had a no-extra cost choice of either an electronically-controlled 4-speed automatic or the new Borg-Warner 6-speed manual with a limited-slip Getrag rear axle.

The all-new interior featured Lear leather seats, complete analog gauges, a centrally-located parking brake handle, and a glove box located under the passenger-side air bag. The suspension used front and rear double wish bones, transverse composite mono-leaf springs, and thicker brake rotors with no-pulse anti-lock calipers. The new perimeter frame was made of stainless hydro-formed tube steel, with aluminum and magnesium bracing.

Car magazine writers were impressed with the fact that the new C5 did everything better that the '96 Corvette. A long-standing complaint about Corvettes has been body rattles and noise. Engineers were able to get the body vibrational frequency up from 15 hertz to 23 hertz. The Mercedes SL Convertible had a frequency of 19 hertz. But the real kicker was the price increase - up only $270 from the '96 model! Yet performance was better that the exotic ZR-1, with 0-60-mph times of just 4.7 seconds, quarter-mile times of 13.3-seconds at 109 mph, and a top-speed of 172 mph. Corvette team created a winner with the new C5 Corvette, but it took the public a year to catch on the new design. Sales for the '97 Corvette were less than half of the '96 figures, only selling 9,752 units. However, the following year sales more than tripled to 31,084 units. The '97 C5 was just the beginning of an amazing generation of Corvettes. C5s would pace the Indy 500 in '98, '03, and '04, and win the ultimate world-class sports car event, Le Mans, in the GT class in '01, '02, and '04. In '04, the C5-R team won every race of the season!

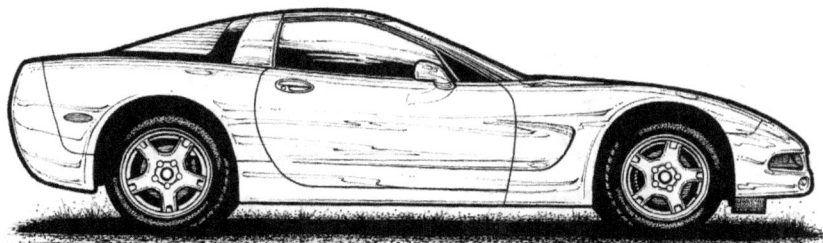

1998 Corvette
"Praise Comes Pouring In"

Perhaps it just took a year for Corvette fans to get used to the new C5. Sales more than tripled over the '97 model, making the '98 edition the best-selling Corvette since '86. With total sales of 31,084 units, the C5 was finally beginning to show returns on GM's $250 million investment in development costs. The buyers were back, and they were loving what they saw.

Chevrolet rolled out one major variation and several very juicy options for the Corvette in '98. The biggest news was the return of the roadster. Although the roadster was a $6,930 option, it was a stunning package and was considered by many to be the best topless Corvette ever made. Next, there was the Indy Pace Car Replica, which added another $5,804 on top of the roadster's steep premium. Only 1,163 units were built, making it the second-most collectible of the four Corvette Pace Car replicas to that date.

Although the Selective Ride and Handling option had been available since '89, '98 brought a new suspension option, the $500 Active Handling System. This advanced system used traction control and anti-lock braking to maintain vehicle stability.

For the first time ever, Corvette buyers could order real magnesium wheels. These beautifully styled 5-spoke rims were similar to the 5-spoke aluminum alloys used on the ZR-1 in '94 and '95, as well as on the '96 Grand Sport and Collector's Edition. The new "mag" wheels were a $3,000 option!

Engineers are constantly making mechanical improvements to the Corvette. By deleting a brace on the rear of the alternator and revising the accessory-drive tensioner, they were able to eliminate a high-speed whine. A quieter electric fuel pump was installed, and clips were added to better hold the glass to the seals during high-speed driving, reducing interior noise. To improve tracking, the steering caster angle of the front suspension was slightly increased. Finally, the automatic transmission had a new second-gear-start mode to reduce wheelspin on slippery roads.

The more people got behind the wheel of the new Corvette, the more they loved it. *Motor Trend* gave the '98 Corvette its Car of the Year Award, a telling accomplishment for a car whose predecessor had long since fallen out of contention for such accolades. Former Corvette owners raved over the new car. "Makes me feel like a kid again!" was a typical comment.

And why wouldn't they rave? The new Corvette accelerated quicker, went faster, stopped shorter, and handled better than even the stoutest 427 Corvettes. One magazine ran a '98 Corvette to a top speed of 173.9 mph, with a 0-60 time of 4.8-seconds and a quarter-mile time of 13.2 seconds @109.3 mph. Further sweetening the deal, there was no price increase over the '97 model.

The base '98 Corvette went for $37,495, while the roadster commanded $44,425. While that's still not cheap, the new Corvette had tradition, unique styling, and did everything as well or better than sports cars costing much more. And remember, the C5 was just getting warmed up... many more amazing things were in the works.

1998 Corvette Convertible
"The Roadster Returns"

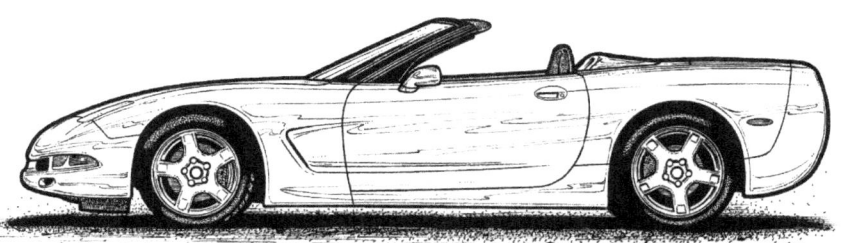

In the early '80s when the C4 Corvette was being designed, a convertible version was not part of the plan. Convertibles had fallen out of favor in the '70s. When the decision was made to make a roadster C4 Corvette, an add-on X-brace was needed for structural rigidity. The fix worked and it was great to have the Roadster back. But unlike the C4, the C5 was designed to be a roadster right from the beginning.

During the eleven-year run from '86 to '96, Chevrolet sold 74,651 Corvette Roadsters. This accounted for approximately 25-percent of the Corvette's annual sales. Chief Engineer Dave Hill wasn't about to let the new C5 Roadster be a second-thought version.

Magazine writers who road tested the '98 Roadster were astonished at how the car was just as rigid as the coupe version. The usual convertible "wiggle" was hardly noticeable. The new C5 Roadster weighed 114 pounds less than the '96 C4 version and the chassis was four times stiffer than the C4. One magazine tested the car and found that the slalom times were on par with the Ferrari 550 Maranello and the Jaguar XK8 Coupe. The cynics were almost speechless.

The aesthetics of the new Roadster were picture perfect. Unlike most convertibles, a hard tonneau cover was already part of the body design. Lowering the top required releasing two latches at the top of the windshield, pushing a button to release the tonneau cover, then manually lowering the top into the trunk. It only took 6-to-10-seconds to get the top down. An electric system would have been nice, but the manual system kept the weight to just one-pound more than the coupe.

Except for a few noise reduction adjustments, the '98 Corvette was the same as the '97 model. However, the Roadster had several very nice features. The convertible top was fully insulated and the rear glass was heated. A separate "trunk" with outside access hadn't been available since '62. The storage space was slightly more than half of the Coupe at 13.9 cubic feet, versus 24.8 cubic feet. And with the top down, there was 11.1 cubic feet of space. The stereo system was speed sensitive and would increase in volume at higher speeds with the top down.

For a roadster, the aerodynamics were excellent. The coefficient of drag was .33 for the '98 Roadster and .29 for the '98 Coupe. Considering that the coefficient of drag for the '84 Corvette Coupe was .34, this was amazing.

Since '86, Corvette Roadsters have carried a premium, and the new C5 Roadster was no exception. The $6,930 option priced the car at $44,425 before any other options. However, this was $635 less than a '96 Roadster! A fully loaded '98 Roadster cost over $52,000 - not including the $5,039 Indy 500 Pace Car Replica package.

The '98 Corvette Roadster was bloody fast as well. One road test reported an automatic version with 0-60 times of 4.9 seconds, quarter-mile times of 13.4 seconds at 105.5 mph, and a top speed of 167 mph with the top down. The Roadster was back and it was better than ever!

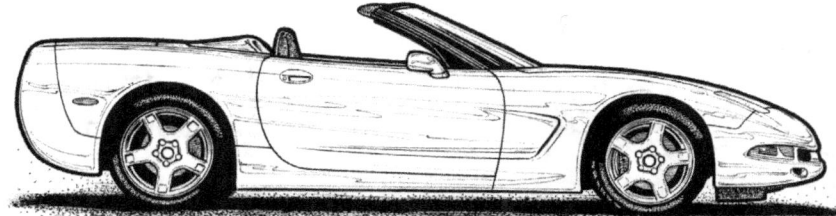

1999 Production Corvette
"Another GREAT Year"

What we didn't know in '97 was that there was to be a three-stage rollout for the new Corvette. First, there was the big-splash debut of the C5 in '97 - the first new edition in 13 years. The following year, the '98 convertible stunned the motoring press. And finally, in '99 we saw the arrival of the new Corvette hardtop. This was the first fixed-roof Vette since 1967.

Automotive journalists were simply enraptured by the '99 model. Car and Driver magazine voted the car to its "10 Best Cars of 1999" list, while the readers of AutoWeek magazine voted it "Best Car of the Year." You can't buy advertising like that! When testers can only complain about flimsy seatback latches or having to get out of the car to put the top down, it's clear that all the fundamental elements of a design are in place.

All of this netted GM increased sales for '99. Even though the base price was increased $1,667, to $39,171, buyers drove home 33,270 Corvettes, up 2,186 from 1998. The GM bean counters were very happy.

The other big news for 1999 was the Corvette's return to factory-supported racing. Chevrolet contracted race-car builders Pratt & Miller to build two C5-R Corvettes to compete against the Vipers, Porsches, Ferraris, and others in production-based racing classes. The C5-R had 600 horsepower and weighed 2,510 pounds, paving the way for the 2006 C6.R Corvette racer. The spirit of the '63 Grand Sport lives on.

Chevrolet has a reputation for regular evolutionary improvements and an occasional revolutionary leap. While the hardtop was a revolutionary development, it did set the stage for what would become a legendary Corvette, the '01 to '04 Z06. Although only 92-lbs lighter than the coupe, it was the lightest Corvette since the 3,015-lb '63 Sting Ray coupe. Aside from the introduction of the hardtop version of the car, the '99 Corvette had three new options and a host of minor improvements. The "Telescoping Steering Column" option allowed a 20-mm forward-to-aft adjustment for only $350. For $375, buyers could order the "Head Up Instrument Display," which projected all or partial instrument information onto the base of the windshield. Back in hte '60s, this used to be the stuff of Bill Mitchell's exotic show cars. And for only $60, customers could get the "Twilight Sentinel," which used a low-light sensor to automatically open the headlight covers and turn on the lights. Minor improvements included a new doorsill plate and improved, "next-generation" airbags. Aside from a revised cylinder-head design, the 345 hp LS1 engine was unchanged.

Since the '99 Corvette didn't gain or lose any weight, and the engine was the same, performance was as spectacular as on the '98 model: 0-to-60 in just 4.8 seconds, 13.2 in the quarter-mile, and a top speed of 175 mph. The automotive press finally caught on to the C5. *Car & Driver* awarded the '99 Corvette one of the top-best cars. *AutoWeek* readers voted the '99 Vette as America's best! You could say that the Corvette definitely had its "mojo" back!

CHAPTER 1: PRODUCTION CORVETTES

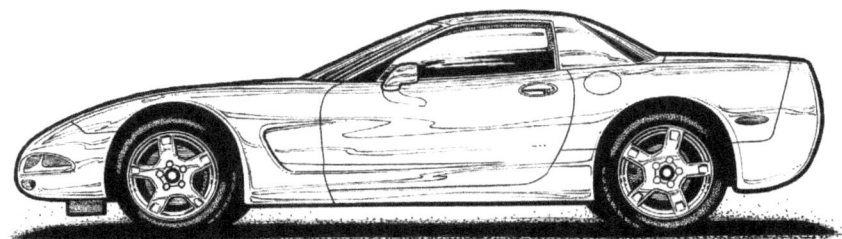

1999 Hardtop Corvette
"Return of the Hardtop"

In the car industry, if you don't sell enough of a particular model, it won't be around for long. In the years leading up to the debut of the C5, Corvette sales were dismal. The sales record holder was the '79 Corvette, at 53,807 units, with the '84 model coming in second at 51,547. Despite improvements to the C4, as the years rolled on, sales were in a steady decline.

When the new C5 was being developed, management issued a mandate: Sell 25,000 units per year, or else.

Fortunately, Dave Hill and his team had a three-year plan to ensure the Corvette hit its sales numbers. Thanks in part to a truncated model year, 1997 sales came in at only 9,752. But with the introduction of the new convertible in '98, sales for that year rocketed to 31,084.

Almost from the beginning, some within GM marketing have wanted to make the Vette something other than a thoroughbred sports car. (Remember the proposed four-seat '63 Stingray and the XP-819 rear-engine Corvette?) The C5 was no exception. In an attempt to boost sales, a "cheap" Corvette with a non-removable roof panel was seriously considered for '99. The base model was to have a smaller 4.8- or 5.3-liter engine, cloth seats, roll-up windows, and smaller wheels and tires. Sounds exciting, doesn't it?

A few prototypes were built, and marketing tests were ordered. Fortunately, the budget Vette didn't light anyone's fire. Those surveyed felt that a $32,000 Corvette would cheapen the entire line. So, the decision was to make the hardtop a performance model, available only with a manual transmission and the Z51 suspension. This hardtop would be only slightly cheaper, with limited options, a little less weight, and slightly better acceleration.

But Hill's engineering department had a surprise the product planners hadn't anticipated. Starting with the convertible body and chassis, a hardtop was permanently bolted and bonded in place. The net result was a 12-percent increase in chassis stiffness, making the new hardtop the stiffest production Corvette ever. Automotive writers had been complaining since the '50s about the Corvette's squeaks, rattles, and lack of structural rigidity. No longer. With its rigid platform and 345 hp engine, this was a setup the magazine guys loved. Buyers scooped up 4,031 hardtops in '99, accounting for 12 percent of total Corvette sales that year.

The GM bean-counters must have hated this project. In order to keep the price below that of the standard Vette ($39,171), they had to limit the availability of many options. The $38,777 hardtop option included the LS1 engine, 6-speed manual transmission, Z51 Performance Handling Package, black interior with black leather seats, and six exterior colors. Items not available with the hardtop included the automatic transmission, magnesium wheels, power sport seats, and Selective Real Time Damping. However, the Active Handling Suspension option was available on the hardtop.

Even though the plan of a cheap Corvette didn't quite work out as envisioned, the hardtop proved the perfect choice for buyers who wanted that slight extra edge in performance. Meanwhile, the sales figures for the coupe and convertible alone were well above management's 25,000-units-per-year mandate.

The basic Corvette comes with more horsepower than most people will ever experience. The addition of a fixed roof allowed the car's suspension to handle all that power with race-car-like responsiveness. The hardtop's roof line wasn't as slippery as the coupe's, limiting the car to a top speed of "only" 170 mph. (The coupe topped out at 175.) Zero-to-60 and quarter-mile times were 4.4 and 13.3 @ 108-mph, respectively. Behine the scenes, Dave Hill and his team were hard at work on developing the next legendary, ground-pounding hot-rod Corvette - the 2001 Z06.

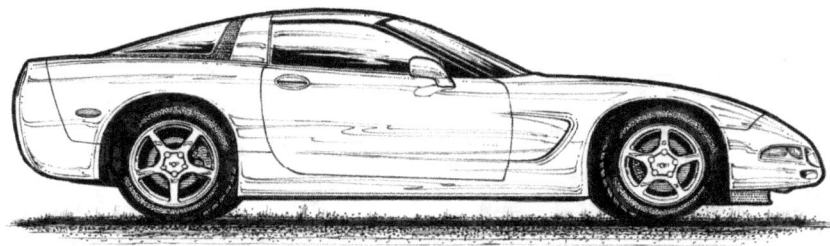

2000 Corvette
"Taking A Breather!"

The first three years of the C5 were unlike any previously seen in the Corvette's long history. The overall design of the car was so good that all there was left to do was make minor improvements. With 345 net horsepower and 350 ft-lbs of torque delivering 0-to-60 mph in less than 5 seconds and drag strip times in the low 13s, what was there to complain about?

Not only was the car bloody fast, it was an unrivaled performance bargain. Excluding true supercars that are handmade by the dozens, the only cars capable of matching or exceeding the Corvette's performance were the Dodge Viper and the Porsche 911. Both cost just over $25,000 more than the Chevy. The base price of the '00 Corvette Coupe was $39,475, the convertible cost $45,900, and the "entry-level" hardtop model was only $38,900.

The pricing of the new C5 Corvettes was just right. Even better, the base price had only gone up $1,980 since the car's '97 launch. Although only 9,752 Corvettes were sold during the abbreviated '97 model year, sales in '98 rocketed to 31,084. In 2000, there were 33,682 Corvettes sold. Clearly, the word was out that the new Corvette was better than ever, without all of the previous car's squeeks and rattles.

Spotting a new '00 Corvette was easy. Most noticeable were new 5-spoke mag-style forged aluminum wheels, which were standard on all Vettes. The only other external change was the elimination of the passenger-side door lock. When the new Passive Keyless Entry system replaced the previous Active Keyless Entry system, the second lock was deemed unnecessary.

There was a bit of confusion about the "standard" wheels. Initially, they were made from forged aluminum and had a flow-formed rim. A polished version of the wheel was also offered as an $895 option. Then, in January 2000, Chevrolet announced that the new standard wheel would be painted silver. This would allow the supplier to increase production of the polished version.

Also announced was a price reduction for the optional magnesium wheels—from $3,000 to $2,000.

Other minor improvements included a revised shifter for better gear location and selection, improved hatch seals to eliminate water leakage, revised dual-zone air conditioning calibrations, and more-durable seat material. Two new colors were also added to the palette - Millennium Yellow and Dark Bowling Green Metallic. The new hues were a $500 option, the extra cost being attributable to a special process of applying tinted clearcoat.

Proving it was possible to have high performance while still being friendly to the environment, the '00 Vette met the EPA's Low Emissions Vehicle (LEV) standard. And for customers who wanted that extra edge on the track, the $350 Z51 Performance Handling Package got slightly larger stabilizer bars and recalibrated shock valving. The changes didn't produce a stiffer ride, but they did improve handling by increasing roll stiffness.

What an extraordinary time for Corvettes. The cars were faster, quicker, more economical, and handled better than ever—traits that made the cars popular with enthusiasts and and journalists alike. The car's success even convinced Chevrolet to launch a factory-backed Corvette racing team, with Le Mans in its sights. Could it get much better?

Even though it looked like Chevrolet had taken a breather, behind the scenes engineers were sorting out the next Corvette legend - the Z06.

CHAPTER 1: PRODUCTION CORVETTES

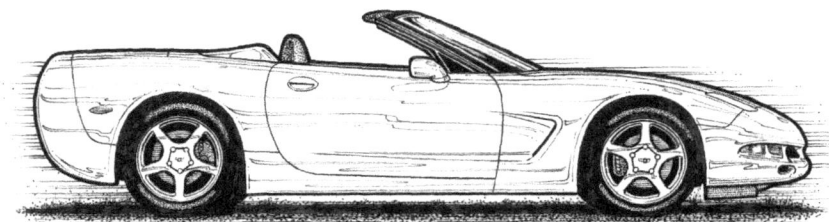

2001 Corvette
"In The Shadow of the Z06"

A funny thing happened to the '01 Corvette on the way to the showroom. It got lost in the shadow of its own offspring - the new Z06. The base '01 Vette could smoke almost any machine from the glory days of the '60s and early '70s and still get 30 mpg on the highway. But because the Z06 took Corvette performance to the level of quasi-racer, with street manners intact, car magazines hardly noticed the standard model.

Corvette product planners have an interesting way of rolling out new options and features. The first three years of the C5 saw a splashy introduction in '97, followed by the convertible in '98 and the hardtop in '99. To kick off the new millennium, all Corvettes got revised five-spoke alloy wheels and a host of small improvements. They were just catching their breath in '00.

The Z06 debut in '01 was so big that hardly anyone noticed the next round of incremental improvements. Earlier generations drew fire from reviewers over the fact that the car cost as much as a Cadillac but had the fit and finish of a Chevette. By '01, those days were over. Chevy officials had long since realized that while the Corvette could get by on the strength of its performance, there was no reason it couldn't exhibit excellent quality as well.

Aside from a few color changes and the addition of chrome exhaust tips, the '01 Corvette was identical to the '00 model. Under the hood, engineers were able to squeeze an extra 5 horsepower and 25 lb-ft of torque from the LS1 by revising the intake manifold with a larger plenum and smoothing out the intake runners. The base engine now packed 350 hp and 375 ft-lb when paired with a manual transmission.

To handle the extra power, a stronger clutch was installed, yet the pedal effort was reduced. Unlike the clutch on the old L71 of the '60s, one could actually live with this new system. Another subtle improvement was the use of a lightweight, absorbent glass-mat battery. This new battery was more heat resistant and could be recharged more often, important features in a car with luxury-car-type electrical amenities.

All Corvettes now had the active suspension as standard equipment, and small improvements were made to both the manual and automatic transmissions. Automatic cars had smoother shifting, thanks to a new alternator clutch pulley, while manual cars had their synchronizers upgraded. Reflecting advancements in both engine build quality and synthetic-oil technology, Chevrolet now recommended oil changes every 15,000 miles, up from the previous 10,000-mile recommendation.

The convertible tops were improved with new weather stripping to reduce interior noise and improved insulation for a smoother exterior look. Auto writers were impressed with the car's seat comfort, instrument layout, and cabin-noise level and gave the car's interior rave reviews.

Sales saw an increase of 1,945 units, for a total of 35,627 for the year. That's the highest number since '85! Of those, 5,773 units were hardtop Z06s. Ironically, the hardtop Corvette had gone from being the least expensive to the most expensive model, now listing for $47,000. The base price for the Vette was up $1,000 for the coupe (to $40,475) and $1,200 for the convertible ($47,000). '01 sales included 14,173 convertibles and 15,681 coupes, the most even distribution between the two configurations in the car's history. A fully loaded '01 Corvette convertible with the optional paint went for close to $57,000.

Performance figures for the '01 Corvette would have been the stuff of wild daydreams of the past. The car ran 0-to-60 mph in just 4.5 seconds in manual form and 5.0-seconds for an automatic. Quarter-mile times were in the low 13s.

In the early days the base Corvette was pretty tame. No one would have imagined a day when all Corvettes would be thoroughbred runners.

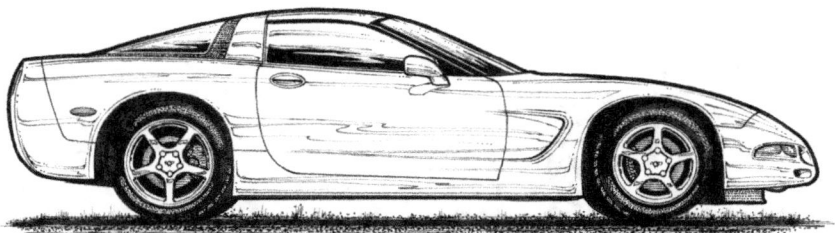

2002 Corvette
"Record Sales & More Z06 Juice"

The C5 Corvette was just getting better every year, and the '02 model year was no exception. The '02 edition hit a sales high for the fifth-generation cars, and the Z06's output climbed to an even more impressive 405 horsepower.

Dave Hill and his gang did such a superb job with the basic layout of the car that the only thing left to do was make incremental enhancements. Even better, the car's base price had only increased $3,955 over the six years since its 1997 introduction. Keeping the price in check, while making gradual performance improvements, played a major role in the C5's surging sales. The icing on the Corvette cake was the C5-R's second consecutive 1-2 class finish at the 24 Hours of Le Mans. The overwhelming success of the C5 virtually guaranteed corporate approval of the upcoming C6 program.

The base price of the '02 Coupe was $41,450, up $975 from the previous year. The Convertible's base price was $47,975, up $500 from '01. And, lastly, the Z06's price was $50,150, up $2,650. But despite this comparatively steep price hike, a total of 8,297 Z06s were sold – more than triple the '01 sales total. At the end of the year, total

production for all models stood at 35,767 units - up 140 from '01

The coupe and convertible saw only minor changes in '02. The front stabilizer bar was now the same size as the Z51 unit and was made of aluminum. Convertibles with heads-up display had thinner, lighter windshields, the same as the Z06. Two exterior colors were dropped, and one new color added.

For performance fans, the real action centered around the Z06 package. The LS6's output increased from 385 to 405 hp, and torque went from 385 to 400 lb-ft. To celebrate this new high-water mark in Chevy small-block engines, the Z06 received a front-fender badge that read "Z06 405 HORSEPOWER."

The extra 20-hp was squeezed out with slight improvements in the intake, exhaust system, and valvetrain. Airflow through the induction system increased 5 percent, and a new camshaft - with the highest lift in Chevy-small-block history - netted another 5-percent flow increase. Lighter intake and exhaust valves were used, and new valve springs increased seat load by 14 percent. At the back end, exhaust pressure was reduced by 14 percent by removing two small catalytic converters and adjusting the material used in the remaining pair. Other Z06 improvements included revised rear shocks, an improved clutch, a thicker front sway bar, a new front brake-pad composition, and a modified steering system that took two feet off the car's turning radius.

Road testers simply adored the latest Vette. They loved how civilized and powerful the coupe was. They were amazed at how the convertible had no cowl shake. And they were just beside themselves over the Z06 and how easy it was to drive so close to the edge. The price was right, and the performance was world class. With just two years left for the C5, Corvette planners had two more special Vettes waiting in the wings.

CHAPTER 1: PRODUCTION CORVETTES

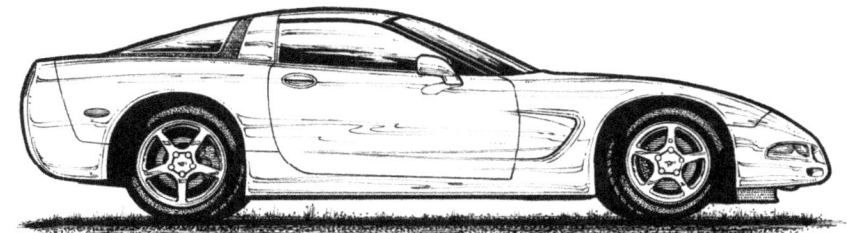

2003 Corvette
"Another Banner Year"

By '03, half a century had passed since Harley Earl's dream sports car began its first year of production. Although Earl, Cole, Mitchell, and Duntov were gone, there were plenty of passionate Corvette team members to carry the flame into the 21st century.

By the time the '03 model year wound down, Chevrolet had sold 35,469 Corvettes. While that wasn't the C5's best sales year, it was only 298 units off the '02 high of 35,767 units.

The base price of the '03 coupe was up $2,445, to $43,895. Sales of the coupe were off by 1,948 units. The $51,155 Z06, meanwhile, logged its best sales year to date, and sold 8,635 units, up 338 from '02. The convertible's price was up $2,395, to $50,370, and sales of this version were up 1,312 units. For the only time in the C5 run, buyers were actually more enthusiastic about the roadster than they were about the coupe.

The big option for '03 was the 50th Anniversary Edition. This $5,000 package was only available on coupe and convertible models. A total of 11,632 units were sold - 4,085 coupes and 7,547 convertibles. This option accounted for nearly a third of all sales in '03.

To top things off, the '03 Indy 500 was paced by a near-stock 50th Anniversary Edition coupe, that only needed a 5-point safety harnesses and a set of strobe lights. Everything else on the car was bone stock. There was no pace-car option like there was in '98, but the pace-car graphics were available for an additional $495.

still packed 350 hp, and the Z06 LS6 had 405 horses under the hood. Many items that previously had been optional were included on the '03 models. Fog lamps, sport seats, a power passenger seat, dual-zone air conditioning, a parcel net, and a luggage shade were now part of the standard-equipment list. These upgrades undoubtedly contributed to the $2,445 increase in base price for '03.

Thanks to tougher occupant-protection standards, the '03 Corvette was a little safer. The A-pillars on all Vettes and the A and B-pillars on the coupe and Z06 were beefed up. Z06 headliners were also thicker. And to show that the new Corvette was sensitive to family needs, child-seat hooks were added to the passenger side.

Visually, the '03 model year saw the arrival of two new paint colors. Medium Spiral Gray replaced Pewter, and 50th Anniversary Red replaced Magnetic Red Metallic. Perhaps the most interesting improvement for '03 was the F55 Magnetic Selective Ride Control option, which replaced the F45 Selective Real Time Damping option. The new system provided faster response time by using shocks filled with a magnetic fluid. Called "magneto-rheological," the fluid held iron particles in suspension. An electronic coil on each shock received input from a sensor, then varied an electrical charge to adjust the fluid's viscosity and flow rate. The system could adjust shock damping an amazing 1,000 times per second, allowing it to react to every inch

Out on the race track, C5-R team did not have its best year, but the cars still took five First-place and five Second-place wins out of 10 races. The C5-Rs became so dominant that race-sanctioning bodies were forced to put restrictions on the Vettes to ensure parity in the field.

From the beginning, Corvette advancement has been mostly evolutionary, with an occasional revolutionary leap. Since the C6 Corvette was already in the works, '03 would be another evolutionary year. The base LS1 engine

of road surface at 60 mph. Best of all, the new system had no extra moving parts as compared with its electro-mechanical predecessor.

With just one year left in the C5 era, the '03 Corvette was the most thoroughly refined fifth-generation model yet. Customers were lining up like they hadn't in 17 years, the 50th Anniversary Edition was truly a collector car, and the C5-R team was still a powerful presence on the race track. Could it get much better?

2004 Production Corvette
"The Last of the C5s"

2004 was the end of the line for the C5 Corvette, and the '04 model was arguably the finest Vette offered to that point. After all, aside from offering an optional supercharger, turbocharger, or all-wheel-drive, there wasn't much else that Corvette designers could do with the C5 platform. The car was as good as it would ever be and that was pretty darned good.

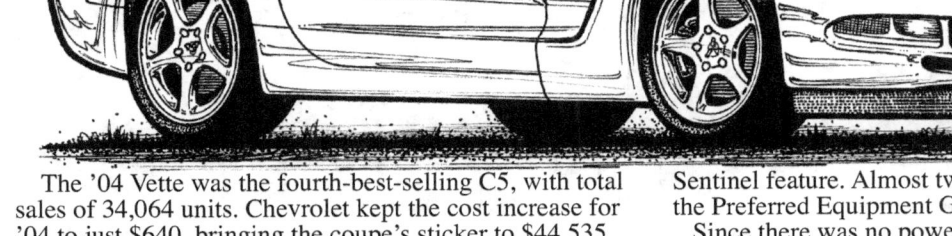

The '04 Vette was the fourth-best-selling C5, with total sales of 34,064 units. Chevrolet kept the cost increase for '04 to just $640, bringing the coupe's sticker to $44,535. The roadster model jumped by $1,165, to $51,535, while the Z06 climbed by $1,230, to $52,385.

The sweetest option for the '04 Vette was the Commemorative Edition, which saluted Corvette Racing's class victories at the 24 Hours of Le Mans in 2001 and 2002. Unlike the '03 50th Anniversary option, this one was available on all Corvettes, including the Z06. This homage to the C5-R was not inexpensive, costing $3,700 on the coupe and roadster and $4,335 on the Z06. Although there were no performance enhancements, the Commemorative Edition cars were stylish and distinctive.

In '04 the Corvette made its sixth appearance pacing the Indy 500, this time with actor Morgan Freeman behind the wheel. A basically stock C5 Vette had also paced the legendary race in 1998 and 2002. Obviously, the Brickyard likes Corvettes.

By '04, equipment that was once optional had become standard. All models included active suspension, traction control, leather seats, a six-way power driver's seat, a Delco stereo CD player, dual-zone electronic air conditioning, tilt steering, cruise control, fog lights, and floor mats. The Preferred Equipment Group was a $1,200 option that included heads-up display, power-telescoping steering wheel, auto-dimming mirrors, a memory package, and the Twilight Sentinel feature. Almost two-thirds of all '04 Vettes had the Preferred Equipment Group option.

Since there was no power increase, the performance of the '04 Corvette was much the same as that of the '01 through '03 models. Top speeds were 175 mph for the coupe and 162 mph for the roadster. Sprints from 0-60 took less than five seconds for the manual-transmission cars and were in the mid-five-second range for the automatics. Quarter-mile times were in the 13.20 range. The Z06 posted 0-60 times in the low-four-second range, with quarter-mile times in the mid-12s. Suspension settings for the Z06 were reworked at the famous Nürburgring race track by refining the shock-absorber valving and using softer rear sway-bar bushings. The modifications enabled the '04 Z06 to break the eight-minute-lap barrier, the unofficial benchmark for supercars. Commemorative Edition Z06s also sported a carbon-fiber hood, which cut just over 10-pounds from the car's curb weight.

The C5 Corvette was so well rounded that the only things road testers had to complain about were the seatback latches and door handles. Lame complaints, but that's how good the car had become. Chevrolet might have been able to continue on with the C5 platform, but the time was right for a new Vette. Thanks to Dave Hill and his team, and the line workers at Bowling Green assembly plant, the C5 Corvette was the best to date. But wait, here comes the C6!

2004 also marked the first time the Corvette's platform was shared with another GM vehicle. The Cadillac XLR began production on the Bowling Green assembly line that year and was soon garnering the same kind of critical acclaim previously heaped on its platform mate. This marriage of convenience gave GM two world-class performance cars based on the same underpinnings.

2005 C6 Corvette
"WOW!!!"

Chief designer Tom Peters began designing the C6's shape in fall of '99. While that might seem a little premature, it's actually quite common for designers to start working on a replacement design not long after a new car comes out. Designers had fixed almost everything they weren't happy with on the C5, to do any more, they would have to create a new car. So in '99, Corvette designers

were hoping for the C6 to be an '03 model to coincide with the Corvette's 50th anniversary - which would have been very cool. But after the economy tanked in '01, the projected release date for the C6 was pushed back to '05. While some were disappointed, it gave them more time to refine the car. Dave Hill said, "We're not inventing, we're perfecting.

The team wanted the C6 to be tight, crisp, and trim, with at least 400 hp to match the C5 Z06, reduced interior noise, and improved ride comfort. Hill summed it up by saying, "You drive a C5 500 miles and you still feel good. You drive a C6 600 miles and feel great."

Peters' source of inspiration was the '63 to '67 Corvettes. This shows up on the C6 when you look at the fender bulges and the rear hatch shape. There's also a slight coke-bottle shape on the side rocker panels, reminiscent of the C3 Vettes. While the overall look is somewhat similar to the C5, especially in the back end, the body creases are more defined with more

surface details and facets.

Dimensional changes helped create the C6's new look that is deceiving small. Look at the C6 next to the new Camaro or Mustang and you'll immediately see how small the car really is. The length was shortened to 5.1 inches, to 174.6-inches, while the wheelbase was lengthened to 105.7-inches. The width was reduced 1.1-inches, to 72.6 inches, and the height was increased to 49.1-inches. It also had sxposed headlight configuration, which has not seen since '62. This design helped reduce weight and keeps the car aerodynamic when the lights were turned on. The roof section had a more pronounced double-bubble shape, and the taillights followed the traditional round designs of the C2, C3, and C4 Vettes.

Wheel diameter was increased by one-inch all around, to 18 x 8.5-inches on the front and 19 x 10 inches on the rear. Tires were the latest run-flat Goodyear Eagle F1 EMTs, measuring 245/40-18 and 285/35-19, respectively. The suspension is similar to the C5.

Under the hood the new LS2 engine packs 400 hp and 400 ft-lb of torque from 364 ci. The power increase came from an improved intake manifold; larger valves; a higher, 10.9:1 compression ratio; improved, thin-wall, cast iron exhaust manifolds; and less-restrictive exhaust. Buyers could order either the 6-speed manual or a 4-speed automatic transmission at no additional charge.

The new interior was an improved version of the C5's, with materials, fit, finish, switches, and controls that don't look like parts from a Monte Carlo. The only things that weren't standard were the Bose stereo, XM Radio, and OnStar.

The performance of the new C6 was astounding: 0-60 mph in just 4.1 seconds, the quarter-mile in 12.5 seconds, and a top speed of 186 mph - the fastest ever for a Corvette.

All that performance cost just $44,245 for the coupe ($290 less than the '04) and $52,245 for the convertible ($140 less than the '04).

The C6 is arguably the finest Corvette platform ever made. Designed to be either a coupe or roadster, the design easily accommodated the Z06, the ZR1, the Grand Sport, and the C6.R. What a bargain! We'll be talking about this car for a long time.

2005 Corvette Convertible
"Top Down WOW!!!"

The Corvette was born as a roadster in '53, and except for a nine-year stretch from '76 through '85, there has always been a topless Vette available. The C2 coupe's styling is timeless, and the removable-roof-panel coupes from '68 on are terrific. But there's nothing like open-air motoring while driving a Corvette. The new C6 took that roadster experience to a new level.

When Dave Hill took over as Chief Engineer for the Corvette in '92, many wondered, "A Cadillac guy doing Corvettes?" What Hill brought to the party was flagship quality. Beating up on Corvette quality had almost become a sport in the automotive press. Thanks to Hill and his team, the C5 all but put an end to that. But while the basic C5 design was incredibly good, engineers quickly identified numerous areas for further improvement. Enter the C6.

Thanks to the extraordinary power potential of the LS-series engine family, hitting the 400 hp mark wasn't much of a stretch. The new LS2 engine delivered a tractable, easy-to-use 400 horses and 400 ft-lb of torque. Suspension and braking were dialed in to a level unimaginable a few decades before. All that was needed was a platform that performed as if cut from a single piece of billet aluminum. The C6 chassis took everything learned from the C5 and the C5-R race car and delivered an out-of-the-box, world-class sports car for $52,245. That's $140 less than an '04 Vette!

Usually, it takes a year for buyers to warm up to a new-generation Vette, but this was not the case for the '05 model. Buyers put their money down on 3,308 more Corvettes in '05 than in '04. An '05 convertible stickered for $52,245 and 10,644 enthusiasts said, "I'll take one!"

The '05 Corvette was not only faster than ever (top speed was an impressive 186 mph), it was safer as well. Constructed mostly from extruded aluminum, the door pillar and windshield frame passed the federal roof-crush standards without the use of a roll bar. Because the driving experience happens behind the wheel, extra attention was paid to the interior. The classic problem with convertibles is "cowl shake." In the C6, hydroformed frame rails with extra bracing at the suspension-mounting points and a hydroformed lower instrument-panel brace completely eliminated this problem. The roadster's interior received an additional 15 pounds of sound insulation, and there's extra padding for the aerodynamically shaped soft top. The net result was that the roadster had less wind noise and weighs only 20 pounds more than the coupe.

The soft top was available in black, gray, or beige and used a single handle-release mechanism. The built-in tonneau cover is hinged from the back, allowing the top to drop back into the trunk. And for the first time ever in a Vette, there was an optional power top ($1,995) that takes just 18 seconds to transform the car into a roadster. The system uses no additional trunk space, weighs only 15 pounds, and was developed by Car Top Systems, the same company that designed the Cadillac XLR top. If all this wasn't enough, the Bose Autopilot sound system uses a sound-equalizing algorithm to reduce interior noise when the top was down.

Some Corvette buyers were hoping for a roadster version of the Z06. While that wasn't in the cards, the $1,495 Z51 Performance Package did deliver much of the Z06's on-track performance. This bargain-priced option included stiffer shocks and springs; larger, cross-drilled front and rear rotors; engine oil, transmission, and power steering coolers; unidirectional tires; and modified transmission gearing. To top it all off, a red '05 roadster paced the Indy 500 for the sixth time, with General Colin Powell behind the wheel. Sweet!

CHAPTER 1: PRODUCTION CORVETTES

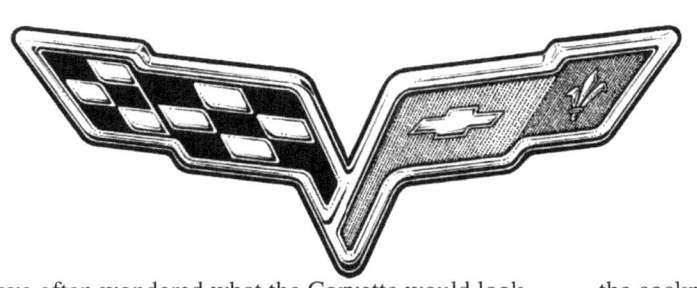

2006 Convertible
"All the Lines Connect"

I have often wondered what the Corvette would look like today had Chevrolet maintained the basic lines of the C2 Sting Ray and allowed them to evolve over the years. That might have happened, had the '65 Mako Shark II show car not come along.

The Mako Shark II's styling was so stunning that Chevy had little choice but to use it as the basis of the next-generation Corvette. The "shark" design has been a part of every Corvette since '68.

At first glance, the C6 looks like an updated C5. But look closer, and you can see there's a lot going on. The C6 is a mix of shark and Sting Ray elements, a fact that may not be apparent until you view the car from above and look closely at its front- and rear-fender details.

Because '63 to '82 Vettes rode on a 98-inch wheelbase, we became used to a certain amount of front and rear overhang. The '84 to '96 Vette had a 96.2-inch wheelbase but maintained roughly the same front and rear proportions. With the introduction of the C5 in '97, the Vette's wheelbase grew to 104.5-inches. To keep the shark-like proportions, the car was stretched 1.2 inches, to 179.7 inches. The C5 was 2.8 inches shorter than the C3, but it looked bigger because of its longer wheelbase.

The C6 Vette took the car's proportions in a completely new direction. The 105.7-inch wheelbase is the longest in Corvette history, while the 174.6-inch overall length makes the car the shortest Vette since '57. The profile still has the distinctive shark fender humps, but when seen from above, the classic Sting Ray fenders are quite obvious. Note how the hood line blends with the edge of the cockpit, then wraps around the rear glass (on the coupe) or the tonneau cover (on the convertible).

The hood bulge is perfectly proportioned to the rest of the hood. The double-bubble roof has two creases close to the center, and the drip molding blends perfectly with the A-pillars. The back end is similar to the C5's but doesn't look nearly as wide. Up front, the most obvious change is the exposed headlights, not seen on a Corvette since '62.

Compared with the C5 Vette, the C6 looks crisp and taught. It is also the slickest Vette ever, with a .29 drag coefficient. All of the body's defining lines flow smoothly, making the car look fast, even when it's just sitting still.

The C6 came out of the gate so fast, there were no significant mechanical changes, save for the arrival of the Z06. The base price for the coupe was up $355, to $44,600, while the convertible's base price was up $90, to $52,335. XM satellite radio became standard with all but the base sound systems, and an optional ($1,250), 6-speed, paddle-shift automatic transmission was introduced. Interior trim was slightly revised, and a new, three-spoke steering wheel replaced the previous design. Aside from the steering wheel and paint choices, the '06 was outwardly identical to the '05 model. Considering the car's price and performance, it's still the bargain of the decade.

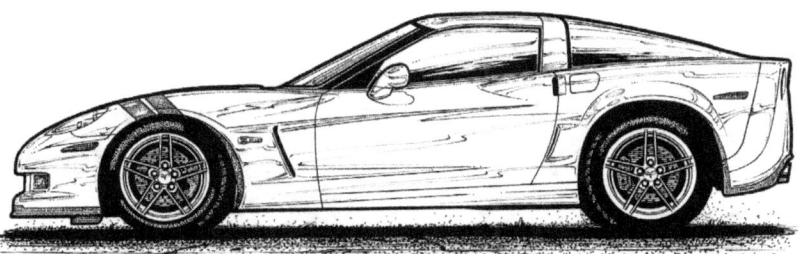

2007 Corvette
"Great Package Deals"

When a sports car is nearly a "Perfect 10," the only place left to go is "special editions." The '07 Corvette had no major mechanical or visual changes, except for color combinations and equipment option groups. Aside for the larger, cross-drilled rotors included with the RPO F55 Magnetic Adjustable Suspension, and the optional Atomic Orange paint, that's all that changed. However, two tantalizing special editions were offered - the Ron Fellows Z06 and the Indy 500 Pace Car.

The Ron Fellows Edition Z06 is noteworthy for three reasons. First, at $77,500, this was the most expensive Corvette to date. Second, it was the first official "signature series" Corvette, with Fellows himself signing and numbering the center-console lid. And third, the car has the longest official name in Corvette history: the '07 Chevrolet Ron Fellows ALMS GT1 Champion Corvette Z06. Had Chevy elected not to abbreviate "American Le Mans Series," the name would have been even longer.

Ron Fellows will likely enter the history books as the most successful Corvette racing driver ever. Ron joined the Corvette Racing Team in '98 and played an important role in the development of the C5-R. To date, Fellows has been part of six consecutive ALMS GT1 Championships for Chevrolet. He was also voted the most popular driver in ALMS in '04 and '05. Born in Ontario, Fellows and his accomplishments are a source of pride not only for Corvette fans, but for Canadian race fans as well.

The Ron Fellows Edition Z06 is a very clean, distinctive car. It's the only C6 Z06 ever offered in Arctic White, and its red fender stripes and polished wheels help accent the Z's aggressive fender bulges and scoops. Also included in the package were a full-width rear spoiler, a windshield banner, and a dark-gray interior with red trim. Only 399 units were built, making it a very rare special edition Vette.

If 77 grand was out of reach for you, there was the '07 Indy 500 Pace Car Corvette. Pacing Indy was becoming a habit for the Corvette. This was the fourth year in a row and the ninth time overall that a Vette got the nod. These days, it's one of the few American cars capable of pacing the race without any performance enhancements. Actor Patrick Dempsey handled the driving duties at Indy in '07.

This was the first pace car special since '98. The '98 version cost just over $50,000, with 1,163 units produced. The '07 edition cost nearly $67,000, with only 500 units built, making this the rarest Corvette Indy 500 Pace Car to date.

All '07 Indy 500 Pace Cars were standard 400 hp convertibles with a delightful assortment of extras. The Atomic Orange paint featured a stream of gold ribbons flowing out of the side vents and along the flanks of the car. In the center of the hood was a Chevy bow tie. Indy 500 graphics adorned the doors, while Indy 500 badges dressed up the front fenders. A Z06 spoiler and new Sebring Silver–painted split-spoke wheels completed the exterior. The interior was Ebony with Atomic Orange accents on the steering wheel, dash, and console trim. The Indy 500 logo was embroidered on the seatbacks. The Z51 suspension package brought heavy-duty shocks, springs, and stabilizers, cross-drilled brake rotors, engine-oil, trans, and steering coolers, and Goodyear F1 Supercar EMT tires. The only options for the Pace Car package were the 6-speed, paddle-shifted automatic transmission, OnStar, and a Bose sound system.

With only 500 units built, the '07 Pace Car Vettes are likely to be among some of the most sought-after special editions in recent history.

CHAPTER 1: PRODUCTION CORVETTES

2008 Production Corvette
"The Mid-Cycle Refresh"

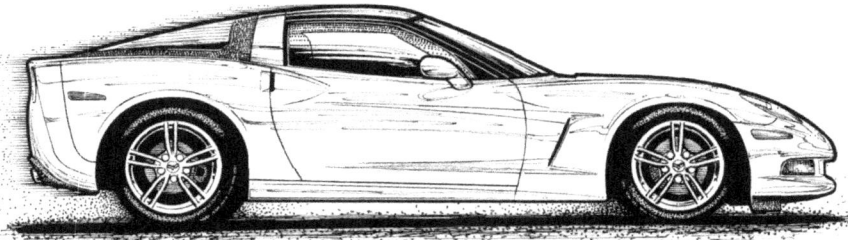

"Mid-cycle refresh" is the term Corvette engineers used when introducing the press to the improved '08 model. "Mid-cycle" suggests to us that the current platform may be halfway through its production run.

If you follow the Internet Corvette rumor mill, it's obvious the gossipers have added a third shift. The internet is practically afire with spy photos and speculation as to what the next Z06 might be like, including the possibility of the car having something "over the top" under the hood and lots of carbon fiber. There's even the rumor that the C7 will be a mid-engine Corvette. Regardless of how the next Vette turns out, one thing is very clear: The days of 10-plus-year production runs are over. Chevy sold 40,561 Vettes in '07. That's 4,794 more units than the best C5 sales year, '02. You'd have to go all the way back to '81 to find better sales figures. This makes GM's accounting department happy enough to leave Corvette engineers alone to improve the car.

Corvette development team members take a systematic, incremental approach to making improvements. They examine everything from the moment air enters the intake manifold to the moment the exhaust leaves the tailpipes. Every facet - from where the rubber touches the road to the feeling of the steering wheel - is carefully tweaked. When Dave Hill was Chief of Corvette Engineering, he brought with him his Cadillac quality background and applied it to the Corvette. Heck, the Cadillac XLR is built at the Bowling Green Corvette plant. When customers talk, Corvette planners and engineers listen.

Spotting an '08 Vette is easy, just look for the new split-spoke wheels. But the big news is under the hood. The new LS3 packs 30 hp more than the LS2, giving it 430 hp and 424 ft-lb of torque. The optional Dual Mode Exhaust, borrowed from the Z06, adds 6 more ponies and a delicious exhaust growl over 3,500 rpm.

Zero-to-60 mph acceleration comes up in 4.1-seconds for the manual car and 4.3-seconds for the automatic. Top speed is 190 mph. This performance bump starts with a new acoustically tuned intake manifold and Z06 injectors. High-flow heads are based on the LS7's and have 9 percent larger intake valves. The camshaft boasts revised timing. The strengthened block received a .06-inch overbore, increasing displacement to 376 ci. The new pistons were designed for high-rpm performance. Pop the hood, and you'll notice the LS3's new engine cover shields the rocker covers and has a noise-reducing insert for a more refined sound.

The drivetrain has an improved manual shifter linkage for quicker shifts and better feel. As for the paddle-shifted automatic, it was also improved for quicker shifts, and there's an optional 2.73 performance axle (included with the Z51 option). Finally, the rack-and-pinion unit was modified for increased road feel at all speeds.

Bowing to customer complaints about the car's interior, designers added brushed-aluminum trim, new doorsill plates, and an optional leather package that adds two-tone hides to the dash, instrument panel, and doors. XM Satellite Radio and OnStar are both standard, plus there's a jack for your iPod.

Don't want to make the stretch to the Z06? The Z51 option has an enhanced suspension, Goodyear Eagle F1 tires, and larger brakes in a package you can live with every day. Could things get any better? They could: Just wait till you see the '09 ZR1!

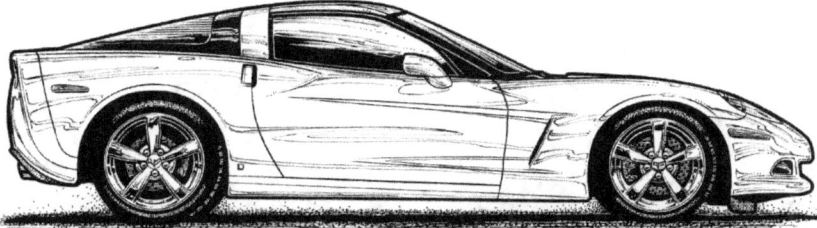

2009 Production Corvette
"Is the C6 Finished?"

Some Corvette historians refer to the '67 model as "the finished Sting Ray." In its day, it looked as if Corvette designers had done everything they wanted with the Sting Ray design before moving on. A somewhat similar situation occurred in '99. Only this time, Corvette engineers really had done all they wanted to do with the C5 platform, so the decision was made to start designing the C6. The new '05 Corvette hit the

ground at nearly top speed and just kept rolling along each year with special-edition models and the Z06.

In 2007, the Corvette rumor mill went into hyper-drive with speculation about a super-Vette. Perhaps the boys at GM saw the financial storm clouds that were over the horizon and decided on an early release for the new model. In December 2007, Chevy officially announced "The Return of the King, the '09 ZR1."

When the '05 Corvette was released, the new LS2 engine produced 400 hp. By '08, the base Corvette's LS3 was packing 430 "net" horsepower. A gross-power figure for the new LS3 would be well into the low-500 range - in the base Corvette! As we rolled into '09, the C6 Corvette was in an interesting position. After the ZR1 debut, the rumor mill picked up on talk of the C7 Corvette. As summer and fall approached and

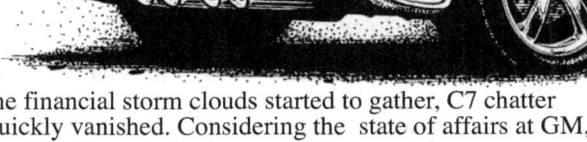

the financial storm clouds started to gather, C7 chatter quickly vanished. Considering the state of affairs at GM, the C6 will probably be around for some time.

For buyers with deep pockets and a lot of nerve, there's the ZR1, GM's first 200 mph, $100k production car A few ticks below the ZR1 is the tried-and-true Z06, and not far behind is the base model Corvette. The performance of the three models is surprisingly close.

The base '09 Corvette has slightly restyled wheels, some very minor changes in interior trim, and no changes to the car's power train. The '09 Z06 distinguishes itself with the same wheels we saw in '08 on the 427 Z06 Special.

Despite a power spread of over 200 hp between the base Corvette and the ZR1, real-world performance is relatively close, making the entry-level '09 with the Z51 and Dual Mode exhaust options the performance bargain of the decade. The base Vette runs 0-60 in just 4.1-seconds, with the Z06 and ZR1 running the same sprint in 3.6 and 3.4 seconds, respectively. Quarter-mile times are close as well: 12.4 @ 117 mph for the base Corvette, 11.7 @ 124 mph for the Z06, and 11.5 @ 128 mph for the ZR1. Top speed is 186-mph for the base car, 198 mph for the Z06, and 205-plus mph for the ZR1. Interestingly, for the price of one ZR1, you could get two base cars with the Z51 and Dual Mode Exhaust options. According to road tests, the driving experiences among the three cars are very different. The ZR1 is civilized up to its limits, the Z06 is a wild, and edgy, and the Z51-optioned base Corvette is fast, crisp, and just a breath behind its bigger brothers.

So, is the C6's evolution finished? With the C7 now on hold, what might Chevrolet do until the C7 arrives? Right now, the grump list is pretty slim, but two consistent complaints center on the steering being somewhat vague and the interior being second rate. Perhaps the steering system from the ZR1 or Z06 and the $8,055 leather interior option will be made standard. Will the C6 will then be finished? One reviewer has already summed up the base Vette this way: "This is as much Corvette as I need."

CHAPTER 1: PRODUCTION CORVETTES

2010 Corvette
"Where To From Here?"

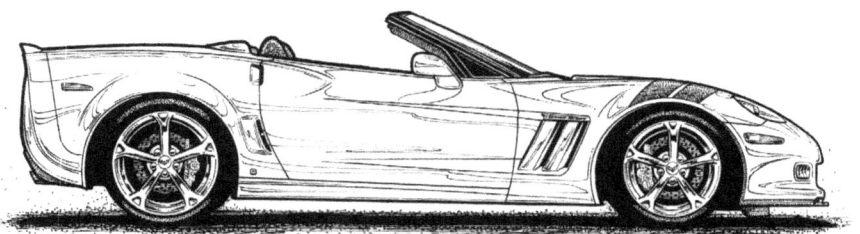

In retrospect, 2009 can be best summed up with a quote from Charles Dickens' classic book, *A Tale of Two Cities*: "It was the best of times, it was the worst of times." 2009 should have been an awesome year for Corvettes, but it turned out to be the worst sales year since '61. Sales went from 35,310 units in '08 to just 13,934—a 60 percent drop! Of course, this led to a lot of Internet speculation that the bottom had dropped out of the market, since nearly all sports-car marques saw sales plummet. So people don't want sports cars anymore? Hardly. It's the economy, stupid.

The '09 Corvette lineup couldn't have been much more enticing. The ZR1 was finally in production, the Z06 was still one tick away from race-car status, and the base Corvette was still packing 430 hp under the hood. Plus, there were two spectacular special-edition Vettes available: the GT1 Championship Edition and the Competition Sport. And if that wasn't enough, starting in April '09, car magazines were all over the upcoming '10 Grand Sport. Chevrolet could not have had better press coverage to whip up interest in Corvettes.

On the other side, there was a nonstop flow of grim news about GM. CEO Rick Wagoner was out, and Fritz Henderson was in. Then Henderson quit and was replaced by Ed Whitacre. Plus, the Camaro SS was finally available, likely draining some sales away from the Corvette. Even the gorgeous special editions didn't generate the projected sales. The GT1 Championship Edition was supposed to have a 600-car run, but only 125 units were built; the Competition Sport package generated just 72 sales.

So, where do we go from here? There have been no special-edition Corvettes announced for '10, but in '11 the Z06 Carbon Edition will be available. In mid-2009 there was a lot of chatter about the C7, but plans for a C6 replacement have been postponed indefinitely. All of this has nothing whatsoever to do with the quality of the car. Like the '09 model, the '10 is awesome, truly the best Vette yet. Even better, some retailers are discounting base and Grand Sport '10 Corvettes by as much as $5,000. And the selection of accessory options is terrific. You can create your own personalized Vette right from your dealer's showroom floor.

What's new for 2010? Not much, but as usual, the car just keeps getting better. New standard items include Launch Control, revised controls for the paddle-shift six-speed automatic, standard side airbags, and interior console trim in either Orbit or Gunmetal patterns. Convertibles now get the taller Z06 rear spoiler. Torch Red paint is back, Z06 cars can opt for the Cashmere interior, and the 3LZ Equipment Group now includes power sport seats and a power passenger seat. Also, Crossed-Flags seat embroidery is a new option. There are no significant changes under the hood, in the driveline, or to the suspension.

Consequently, '10 Corvettes are still the same awesome performers they were in '09.

What an odd situation for GM's flagship performer. In 58 years of production, the car has never been faster, quicker, handled better, or offered more custom accessories. All buffed up and no one to buy, hardly anyone is willing to step up. However, if your personal financial situation has been unaffected by the economic downturn, now is the time to get the Vette of your dreams, just the way you want it!

Chapter 2
Experimental and Prototype Corvettes

Few cars in Detroit generate as much excitement as an experimental or prototype Corvette. While show cars are often "pie in the sky" cars, experimentals and prototypes offer a peek into the thinking of those who endlessly design and develop future Corvettes. These cars often represent ideas that are being seriously considered for production Corvettes.

1957 Q-Corvette
"The Genesis of the C5"

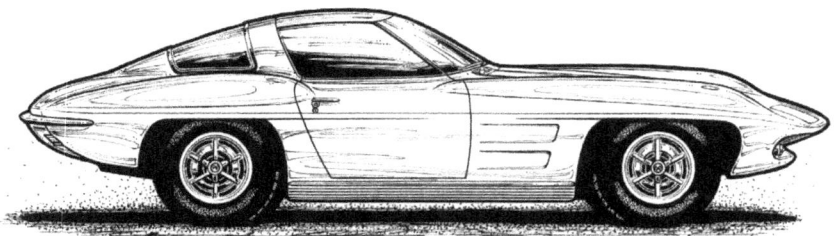

The design and development of the Corvette is one of the most interesting stories in Detroit's history of making cars. Today's Vette is an automotive modern marvel that can outperform anything from the model's glory days.

Once the Corvette finally got some racing exposure, real possibilities began to open up. Thankfully, the car had a powerful friend at the top: Chevrolet general manager Ed Cole. Cole was an engineer and could relate to Duntov's ideas. The gregarious Duntov probably knew more about sports cars than anyone else in Detroit and was the only high-ranking Detroit engineer who had actually raced at Le Mans.

Corvettes aren't just fast cars that handle well. There's also the appearance factor. Since the early days, Vettes have always looked like they were doing 100 mph sitting still. While Harley Earl styled the first Corvette, it was Bill Mitchell and his team of talented designers that gave the later models their aesthetic edge.

In '57, Chevy's engineering group had a revolutionary idea called the "Q-Chevrolets" that would use a rear-mounted transmission and an independent rear suspension. The idea was to improve handling and eliminate the transmission hump from the interior. And yes, part of the lineup included a Q-Corvette.

The list of mechanical goodies planned for the Q-Corvette must have looked like Duntov's Christmas wish list. GM's accounting personnel must have thought he was nuts! No one realized that the basic layout of the Q-Corvette would take 40 years to reach production.

The overall project was guided by designer Bob McLean. Duntov supplied the chassis and running-gear layouts, and Mitchell guiding the styling. This was to be a much smaller Corvette. The wheelbase was 94 inches, the track 53 inches, and the height 46 inches - this compared with the '57 production model's 102-inch wheelbase, 57/59-inch front and rear tracks, and 52-inch height. The target weight was a scant 2,225 pounds. Bucks made for size and space proportions showed a larger interior than that of the production car.

Aluminum was to be used for the transaxle and the fuel-injected 283 engine. A dry-sump oiling setup and a small-diameter flywheel with dual clutch discs allowed the engine to sit as low. To reduce unsprung weight, inboard rear brakes were proposed. The front and rear suspensions used coil springs over shocks, mounted on a steel platform, requiring a steel body. Mitchell proposed a strong horizontal crease with four fender humps, a pointed back roof, pop-up headlights, a windshield with no A-pillar, and roof had lift-out panels. A full-size clay model was presented to the GM brass in December and received glowing reviews.

So what happened? A recession started in 1958, so the entire Q project was canceled. Mitchell did use the Q-Corvette's styling as a starting point for his '59 Sting Ray racer, and the basic look served as the foundation for the C2. Fuel injection has been standard since '85, and disc brakes replaced the inboard drums in '65. Pop-up headlights and lift-out roof panels arrived in 1968. Almost every design parameter of the Q-Corvette was achieved by the time the '97 C5 arrived. Were it not for four pages in Karl Ludvigsen's *"Corvette: America's Star Spangled Sports Car,"* the Q-Corvette likely would have been forgotten as just another design exercise. Fortunately, the basic elements survived and led to the outstanding performance car we enjoy today. Pie-in-the-sky ideas can become reality.

THE ILLUSTRATED CORVETTE SERIES

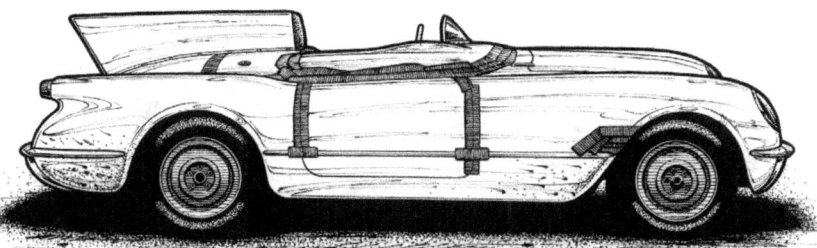

1957 - 1962/1963 Mule Corvettes
"Duntov's Mule Corvettes - Pt. I"

For centuries, farmers have been using mules as beasts of burden for grunt work. They're not pretty or graceful animals, like horses. In the automotive world, engineers often build "mule" cars for R&D work. They're typically slated for test duty only and never experience life on a public road. And like their counterparts in the animal world, they're worked hard, very hard.

While Zora Arkus-Duntov settling into his job, the new Chevy V-8 was still being developed. The '53 show-car Corvette was fitted with a prototype 265-ci engine for testing as an option in the upcoming '55 model. Duntov had used his vacation time to drive a factory-backed Porsche 550 Spyder at Le Mans. After returning to work, it was clear that he was the only man at GM who could make the V-8 Vette into a real race car.

The Corvette was still little more than a '53 Chevy with a lightweight body and a souped-up six-banger engine. The new 195-hp V-8 engine weighed in at 531 lbs, 41 lbs lighter than the 155-hp Blue Flame Six. Duntov took a modified V-8–powered '56 Chevy Pike's Peak, Colorado, and set a new record. While celebrating with Chevrolet Chief Engineer Ed Cole, Zora proposed making 150-mph record run in a special V-8 Corvette! Cole agreed.

Duntov started with a '54 Corvette and installed a short windscreen and a complete belly pan. Calculations showed that 30 more hp were needed to hit 150 mph. As special camshaft that eventually became the "Duntov Cam" allowed the engine to run to 6,500 rpm with no valve float. Zora packed up his mule Corvette and headed for GM's test facility in Phoenix, Arizona. Upon arrival, he added a tonneau cover over the passenger side, blocked-off front grille openings, and added a fin behind the driver's head. With 3.27:1 gearing and stock tires, Duntov was clocked at 163 mph!

The '54 mule Corvette was immediately re-bodied with the new '56 design and prepped as part of a three-car team to compete at the '56 Daytona Beach Record Runs.

But Duntov wanted an all-out Corvette to race at Le Mans. A work order was issued to build one race car that became '57 SS Corvette. Zora ordered extra hardware as "assembly mock-up" parts to get around the one car limit. While Bill Mitchell's styling group worked out a '56-inspired body, Duntov and his crew work on a chassis patterned after the tube-framed Mercedes "birdcage" cars. The body of the racer was to be of lightweight magnesium, but a crude fiberglass version with no doors or rear deck, and a plywood firewall was taped on the functioning mule car for wind-tunnel testing. At the track, Juan Manuel Fangio drove the overweight mule and matched his previous year's practice-lap times set in a Ferrari! The real racer looked great but the magnesium body turned the car into an oven. Between the heat and a failed rear suspension, the car dropped out after its 23rd lap. Thanks to the '57 AMA ban on racing, The SS racer and the mule went into storage. Then in '59, the mule was reborn under Bill Mitchell's beautiful Stingray body.

But Zora was flexible to circumstances. In stead of building race cars, me made parts for customers do the racing. In mid '62 work began on the Z06 racer kit for the new '63 Sting Ray that consisted of suspension and brake upgrades, a 36-gallon fuel tank, the L84 fuel-injected engine, and other racing parts. A mule car using a '63 Z06 frame and running gear, was draped over a body that was part '62 and part '63 Corvette. After tests at Daytona with Duntov driving the mule was never again seen in public.

So what happens to old GM mule cars? They go to GM's glue factory, also known as the crusher. According to Gib Hufstader, mule cars are sometimes stored in various departments inside GM. But ultimately, they end up in the crusher. Such is the life of a Corvette mule.

CHAPTER 2: EXPERIMENTAL AND PROTOTYPE CORVETTES

1969 - 1974 Mule Corvettes
"Duntov's Mule Corvettes - Pt. II"

Zora Arkus-Duntov was the perfect man for his time at GM. Friend and coworker Gib Hufstader explained, "Zora was always anxious for more of everything." Had Duntov come along 20 years later, he wouldn't have gotten away with many of his antics. But while few Corvettes are ever raced, we all get to enjoy the fruits of Duntov's racing passion. Most of his test mules were never seen by the public, but those that were made long lasting impressions.

The introduction of the L88 in '67 floored everyone. This was as close to an all-out, factory-built racing Corvette as the public would ever see. America was in the space age, and race cars were using exotic lightweight materials such as magnesium and aluminum. Duntov had been wanting an all-aluminum engine for the Corvette since 1956. Bolt-on aluminum chassis and engine components were one thing, but complete engine was another. The alloy-headed L88 was a start, but it would take 30 years for the aluminum LS1 to arrive.

At the Milford test facility in the summer of '68 to preview the '69 models, the press wasn't prepared for Duntov's latest toy: the ZL1-powered Corvette. The white ZL1 had killer looks and mega-grunt to match. The formula was simple: take one Corvette roadster, the latest performance parts, and build it like a racer. Everything that didn't belong on a race car was removed. When finished, Duntov and his crew had reduced the weight by about 400 lbs, to 2,965 lbs. The ZL1 engine alone was worth a 175-lb reduction. Missing production items included the radio, heater, insulation, headlights, radiator shroud, upholstery, rear bumpers, and cast-iron exhaust manifolds. Racing equipment included 15 x 9.5-inch magnesium wheels with 10.5-inch front and 12.5-inch rear Goodyear racing tires, a ZL2 cold-air-induction hood with hood pins, and L88 fender flares. Header side pipes really opened up the breathing of the radical ZL1 engine.

Duntov himself gave journalists "believer" rides. On a quarter-mile track, Zora clicked off a 12.1-second e.t. @ 116-mph, despite the car's tallish 3.60 gears. Lower 4.11 or 4.88 gearing would have put the car into the low 11s.

Once, Zora had the hood blow off while making speed test at 180 mph! At GM's Phoenix test track, journalists described white ZL1 as being close to that of a Group 7 race car. Duntov's ZL1 quasi-racer was a shining example of the aluminum racing engine's potential.

Also on hand at the '69 press preview was a mean-looking Monaco Orange ZL1 wearing 9-inch drag slicks. While Corvettes were never designed for drag racing, many racing Corvette as the public would ever see. were quite successful. The pumpkin-colored beast was set up with open headers, a Turbo-400 automatic with a high-stall torque converter, and 4.88:1 gearing. According to Gib Hufstader, who did the transmission work, powertrain engineer Tom Langdon had tuned this particular ZL1 to produce 710 hp!

So how bad was the beast? About 30 guys ran 11-seconds flat, with a best time of 10.89 @ 130 mph. Chevy PR man Bob Clift said, "We all enjoyed driving that car. Zora used to keep us all excited back then."

Before retirement in January '75, Zora was speed testing his wild-looking, "silhouette racer." Working with Gib Hufstader and John Greenwood, Duntov's team developed a body kit to cover the ever-wider racing tires being used in the mid '70s. Chassis and suspension parts for racing had progressed far beyond the racer kits, but racers were still using ZL1 and L88 engines.

The mule car was based on a '74 Corvette and powered by a race-prepared cast-iron ZL1 variant. Included were open-chamber heads, header side pipes, a big Holley double-pumper carb, an L88 cold-air-induction hood, and clear plastic headlight covers over quartz-iodine headlights. Oil coolers were installed behind the mesh-covered front grille openings. The body-kit parts were riveted on and covered over with duct tape. *CARS Magazine* editor Marty Schorr road in the car and reported, "Out on the high-speed test track, Zora was going full tilt, tail slightly out, smoking a cigarette, and explaining big-block engine development. He had great control of this animal car."

Mule Corvettes live hard lives. After tests and evaluations are completed, they always end up in the crusher. You just can't save everything.

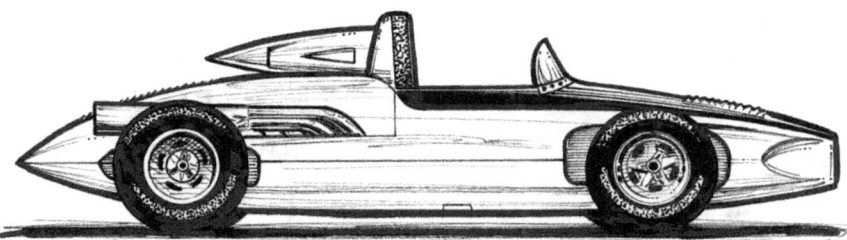

1960 CERV-I
"Duntov's Indy Racer"

At Riverside Raceway in 1960, Zora Arkus-Duntov unveiled one of the most unusual cars of his career. For several years, GM had a hot and cold attitude concerning racing. CERV I's official reason for being was, "A research tool for Chevrolet's continuous investigations into automotive ride and handling phenomena under more realistic conditions." But everyone knew better, or did they?

Duntov first got the idea of building a rear-engine racer in '57 while working out the details on the SS Corvette. A major problem was heat, so why not put the engine behind the driver? R&D work was also going on with the Corvair, so a mid-engine V-8 wasn't outside of legitimate research. Sort of a Super Corvair. This alone may have been what got the project approved.

Duntov built the car to Indy dimensions not to race at Indy, but so the car's performance would have some relevance to all-out race cars. Wheelbase, length, and width were all at Indy specs. The car measures 172 inches in length, 52 inches in width, the wheelbase was the shortest allowable for an Indy car - 96 inches, and the front and rear track was 56-inches.

Obviously, the 283 V-8 wasn't too big for Indy, but it was perfect for the Pikes Peak Hill Climb. So in September 1960, Duntov took the car for extensive testing. But without official timing, he had no idea that the car was performing as well as it was. Instead, they thought they were way off. Actually, his times were below the then record for his class. Before the car was officially named "CERV I," it was known as the "Hill Climber"

The CERV I was loaded with advanced mechanics for 1960. Most interesting was its all-aluminum small-block Corvette engine. Like the '69 ZL-1, the engine used a high-silicon aluminum alloy for the block and forged aluminum Corvette pistons. Attaching components that were cast in aluminum included heads, water pump, clutchplate, and flywheel. The intake manifold and clutch housing were cast in magnesium and the radiator was aluminum. The complete engine weighed 175 lbs less than its cast-iron stock version. Care to imagine an all-aluminum LT1?

Brakes were similar to what was offered in the RPO-684 heavy-duty brake-and-suspension option. The rear brakes were inboard mounted and the fronts were wheel mounted. The rear suspension had upper and lower A-arms with coil springs and shocks. The front suspension also used A-arms with variable-rate springs over shocks. The front also has an 11/16-inch stabilizer bar and re-circulating ball-type with 12:1 steering ratio.

The truss-like frame was made from 7/8-inch and 5/8-inch chrome-moly tubing, and weighed just 125 lbs. Larry Shinoda and Tony Lapine designed the lightweight fiberglass body.

Zora had WAY too much fun with this car. Over the years, various setups were tried; including; twin-turbocharged injected, GMC Root-type supercharged, Hillborn injected, etc. A supercharged, injected version produced over 500 hp. Imagine that in a 1,800-lb car. Experiments with headers included Zoomy-style, long equal-length headers, and large collector headers.

The CERV I was very fast for its day. Duntov lapped Daytona at 167 mph and hit 172 mph on the Sebring straight. Finally, in '64, using a Hillborn injected 377 and a modified body, Zora drove the CERV-I to a lap speed of 206 mph at GM's Milford test track.

CERV I was a definite stretch for the Corvette R&D team. What it really did was keep racing in the life blood of Corvettes. There's nothing quite like seeing a fast race car, knowing that the hardware in that racer is very much like your machine. Racing builds brand loyalty.

The CERV-I now resides in Mike Yeager's My Garage Museum, in Effingham, Illinois.

1964 CERV-II
"Duntov's 4WD GT40 Killer"

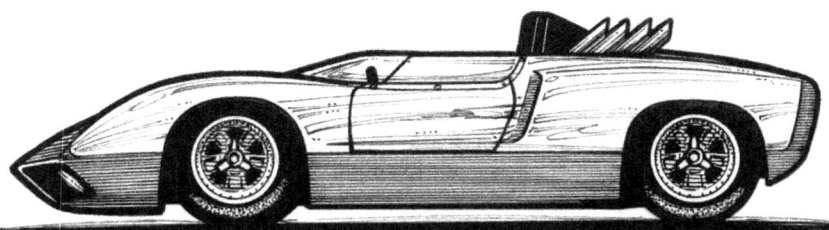

CERV II was Zora Arkus-Duntov's most exotic experimental car. Unlike the CERV I, that although was built to Indy car size specs (excluding the 327-ci engine), and was never seriously intended for racing, the CERV-II was Zora's answer to the Ford GT40. Ford had attempted to buy Ferrari so that a Ford-powered Ferrari could have a shot at the World Manufacturing Championship. Enzo Ferrari would have no part of the Ford buyout, so the deal was dead. Ford then contracted the assistance of Lola to help them build their GT40. In the sports prototype class, engine size wasn't limited, so a bored and stroked to 377-ci small-block-powered CERV-II would have made a formidable opponent to the GT40.

The original plan was to build six cars, three for competition and three spares. The construction of the car was truly ahead of its time. With the assistance of fellow engineer, Walt Zetye, Zora made sure there were plenty of the advanced features, including; four-wheel drive using a Powerglide torque converter for each end of the car, side-mounted fuel cells, a monocoque frame, low profile Firestone racing tires, and a 377 ci all aluminum V-8 using Hilborn injection, single overhead cams, making 500 horsepower. Zora had a good relationship with Firestone, so the CERV-II was wearing the widest Firestone racing tires on 15x9.5-inch wheels on all four corners.

The body was styled by Larry Shinoda and Tom Lapine. Unlike the Grand Sport, the CERV II was stable at speeds over 200 mph. It only needed a small spoiler on the rear deck. The wheelbase was only 90 inches, front and rear tracks were 53.5 inches, making the CERV II a short, wide car.

The CERV-II's first outing was in March '64. Jim Hall and Roger Penske both liked the car's unique handling and driver's position. Roger reported that he had no sensation that the front and rear wheels were being driven. Roger and Jim were also part of Zora's driving team for his Grand Sport program. When pushed to the limit, the CERV II would go into a very fast, flat spin. Tire technology made great advances in the '60s, so Duntov's patented drive system would only have gotten better. Much of the CERV II's technology was later used in the Chaparral 2D. Lessons learned on the CERV II were applied to the more complete Corvette prototype, the mid-engine XP-882.

For many years, Duntov's little rocket car held the Milford Proving Ground track record with an average speed of 206 mph! With short gearing, the CERV II would run 0-to-60 in 2.8 seconds! And with Duntov's patented 4WD power train, the car wanted to be driven faster and faster through the curves, a common characteristic of 4WD racers. This system had tremendous potential. It is a little mentioned fact that Duntov wasn't all that thrilled with the C3 Shark. Being a mechanical man and racer first, he saw no real improvement with the Shark, as it was using the complete drive train and suspension of the '63-'67 cars. Imagine if the C3 had been postponed until '70 and the new Shark came with four-wheel-drive. Now that would have made for an interesting combination - a racing L88 Corvette with 4WD... WOW!

In 1970 a ZL-1 engine was fitted into the car for some "tire testing." Later, in 1989, the car was valued at over $1.5 million. Those dragster headers must have sounded awesome! The CERV II was eventually donated to the Briggs Cunningham Museum, in Costa Mesa, California.

1989 CERV-III Corvette
"Over The Top Design"

It is quite common for car designers to start the next generation of a car just as the new version hits the showroom. In '85 work started on a new Corvette concept called the Corvette Indy. Electronics and turbocharging was the wave of the future and GM's VP of Design, Chuck Jordan wanted cutting edge technology built into future Corvettes. Designer Tom Peters came up with a curvaceous concept rendering and Jordan commissioned Cecomp of Italy to make a full-size clay model. Sufficiently impressed with the model, a running version was built by the end of '86 that would serve as the starting point for the fully-functional CERV III

The CERV III was a real-world version of the Corvette Indy show car. The Corporate Engineering Research Vehicle III (CERV III) was more than pretty show car; it would be the most advanced Corvette study to date. Chief of Chevy III Studio, Jerry Palmer, handled the styling details while Dick Balsey was the engineer on the project. The objective was to showcase the Chevrolet design team and Lotus' advanced racing experience. This was no easy task, by any means. Models and even running prototypes are one thing, a produceable real car is another.

The nose of the Indy had to be shortened and the side windows flattened out so that they could go down into the doors. The wheel openings had to be opened up to allow 3.5 inches of travel and the rocker panels reshaped to accommodate side-mounted fuel cells. Also, the overall height had to be increased a few inches.

The CERV III's hardware was just as exciting as the body shape. To start, the yet to be released LT5 engine that would eventually power the '90-'95 ZR-1 was treated to two Garrett T3 turbochargers that bumped the horsepower up to 650 and the torque to 655 lb-ft. The 3,400-pound CERV III ran 0 to 60 in 3.9 seconds, had a top speed of 225 mph, and had 1.1gs of lateral acceleration! This is C6 ZR1 territory.

Since the car was completely built by race car builders Lotus in England, carbon fiber was used everywhere possible. The underbody was carbon fiber with a fiberglass-finish coating. The classic Lotus backbone chassis was made of carbon fiber and weighed only 38 pounds. Although the suspension looked normal, the springs and A-arms were made of titanium. Actuators were used in place of shock absorbers and were connected to a state-of-the-art computer-controlled active suspension system. ABS braking and traction control was also part of the package. Active suspension was futuristic stuff in the late '80s. The transverse-mounted engine used a six-speed automatic transmission for all-wheel drive and four-wheel steering.

So what happened, why wasn't the C5 based on the CERV III? Detroit was in a major slump and Corvette sales were almost half that of '85 figures. And seems that it was never Chevrolet's intention to take the CERV III into production. This was a pure research vehicle - a test bed for advanced electro-mechanical designs, that's why production specifications were put into the design. Designing cars in an electro-mechanical world is more than sculpting sexy-looking shapes.

Numbers were crunched on the CERV III as it was shown to the public. Customers would have been looking at a $300,000 to $400,000 car - on par with the Ferrari F40 and the Porsche 959. CERV III was the last mid-engine Corvette prototype ever built.

CHAPTER 2: EXPERIMENTAL AND PROTOTYPE CORVETTES

Frank Winchell's Mid-Engine Corvettes
"Chevrolet Engineering's Other Mid-Engine Vettes"

When it comes to early Corvette history, men such as Bill Mitchell, Ed Cole, and Zora Arkus-Duntov cast very long shadows. But they did not design every aspect of the car. While Duntov got the lion's share of attention for pushing the mid-engine effort, there was another power player who was all but invisible to the public: Chevrolet Chief of Engineering Frank Winchell.

Unlike Duntov, Winchell was comfortable being a low-profile corporate man. It was said that Duntov managed with love and enthusiasm, but nobody worked "with" Winchell; they worked "for" him. Duntov and Winchell respected each other, but they often locked horns. Winchell guided the designs of three unique mid-engine concept Corvettes.

Jim Hall of Chaparral Cars ran one of GM's unofficial road-racing outfits. Their first effort produced a slick-looking car that unfortunately had lots of front-end lift. Their second effort, called the Corvette GS-II, had a much more nose-down attitude. Hall and Winchell worked out the chassis design in thin steel, then an aluminum version was created with an ultra-thin fiberglass body, a small-block Chevy engine, and an automatic transmission. The total weight was just 1,450 lbs, and the car had a top speed of 198 mph.

Hall used the basic design for his Chaparral race cars. Many were suspicious of the aluminum chassis, but Hall called it "an eyeball jiggler" because it was so rigid. After a GS-IIb version was created, work on the project ended.

Winchell's next mid-engine car was a result of an argument with Duntov. Winchell contended that if you put an aluminum engine behind the rear axle, and had the correct suspension with oversized rear tires, the car would offer superior handling. Duntov disagreed. After a layout was established, stylist Larry Shinoda "made it look pretty." Considering that there was a engine hanging off the rear axle, the car didn't look bad. The running prototype handled great - up to the tire's breaking point, when it would oversteer wildly. The car ultimately crashed in testing when production-size tires were tried on a wet track. The pieces were then sent to Smokey Yunick's shop to be used for a new race car he wanted to build, but never did. The pile of scrap was later discovered by some Corvette enthusiasts who recognized the body parts. They bought the basket case and refurbished it with a cast-iron small-block Chevy. Reportedly, it does excellent wheelies!

By '68, mid-engine mania had gripped Ford and even American Motors. When Chevrolet officials learned that Ford was developing the Mach II mid-engine Mustang, they had to do something. Of all the mid-engine Corvette concepts Winchell dreamed up, the XP-880 was the closest to a production design yet. This time, an L36 427 was placed ahead of the rear axle and turned 180 degrees so the accessory parts would hang off the back of the engine. A steel backbone frame was created, with fuel tanks placed inside the center backbone. Production suspension and brake components were off-the-shelf Camaro and Corvette pieces. The two-speed automatic transaxle from a '63 Tempest was a glaring weak point. Stylists did a great job of making the XP-880 look like a Corvette. The roof looked like the new C3, and the front and rear fender humps definitely said "Corvette." Track testing proved real potential. This time, Winchell got it right.

The car was painted Fire Frost Blue, dressed up with "Astro II" badges, and sent off to the '68 New York International Car Show. Many said that the XP-880 seriously upstaged the Mach II. Ultimately, the concept was rejected because tooling costs would have added too much to the sales price. Besides, the new '68 Corvette was selling just fine. It wasn't broke, so Chevrolet wasn't about to fix it.

1970 XP-882 Corvette
"Mid-Engine Experimental Corvette - Bad Timing"

It was a great day for Corvette fans at the New York Auto Show on April 2, 1970, because no one knew that Chevrolet was proposing a new mid-engine Corvette. The XP-882 mid-engine experimental Corvette show car had almost everything a Vette lover would want... drop-dead looks, and the transverse engine located in the middle of the car - exactly where an exotic car's engine should be. Ford and AMC never knew what hit them.

Duntov's design team started working out the mechanical challenges for the XP-882 in '68. The two prototype cars were build around small-block Chevy engines, but plans were worked out for big-block power and eventually 4-wheel-drive. Zora had been playing with 4WD since his experimental '64 mid-engine CERV II. Styling penned up a new look that screamed "Corvette," especially the stinger rear roofline. It was crisp, edgy, low-slung, yet it "looked" like a Corvette.

In August '69 new Chevy General Manager, John Z. DeLorean stopped work on the XP-882 to pursue making Corvettes based on the new, inexpensive Camaro chassis. DeLorean was met with fierce resistance from styling, engineering, and sales to NOT take the car in that direction. Then Duntov was stunned when he learned that Ford decided to buy the Italian carmaker, DeTomaso and market their new mid-engine sports car as a Ford. And, to make matters worse, Zora also learned that little AMC had designed a mid-engine car that was to be made by Italian carmaker Bizzarrini, plus Mercedes was working on their C111 mid-engine car.

Zora showed GM's chief of styling, Bill Mitchell and Chevy's chief of engineering, Alex Miar his XP-882 car that had been in storage. The decision was immediate - "Get the car into the New York show!" The XP-882 was quickly painted silver and dressed as a show car. Because there were no press releases, attendees were shocked, especially Ford and AMC. The car magazines were all over it, initiating a feeding frenzy of speculation.

Duntov's surprise exotic Corvette was powered by a transverse-mounted, 400-ci small-block engine coupled with a silent chain-drive to an Olds Toranado Turbo 400 transmission fitted with bevel gears, connected to a stock Corvette rear. Wheels were spun-aluminum, with vent slots, and tires were E60x15 on the front and G60x15 on the rear. Aside from the unique drive, the rest of the suspension was made from production parts. The interior of the car was basic prototype fashion, no frills and no real design at that point. But we all know how the story ended; they didn't come close to making the car. Forward thinking just couldn't overcome bad timing.

After the overwhelmingly positive reception of the XP-882, Delorean approved the funds to develop a big-block, 4-speed version of the car. But, a few things came up along the way. GM's president, Ed Cole had purchased a license to develop the Wankel rotary engine and charged Duntov with the responsibility of developing a high-performance rotary engine for possible use in a Corvette. Duntov handed over one of the two XP-882 chassis to Mitchell to work out a new look for the 4-rotor-powered proposal. This eventually became the 4-Rotor concept that was first shown in 1973. The other XP-882 chassis was used to research the use of an all-aluminum body and chassis. The car became known as the Reynolds Aluminum Corvette, an interesting car that weighed 500 pounds less than a standard Corvette.

Mid-engine sports cars were the stuff of small, exotic, European car makers. But between the first Arab Oil Embargo, a recession, the rotary-engine interruption, and the sales success of the production Corvette, the XP-882 or any other mid-engine Corvettes didn't stand a chance. But for a time, it sure was exciting.

1973 XP-892 Corvette
"The Mid-Engine, Twin-Rotor, Wankel Corvette?"

The XP-892 just flat-out caught everyone short. It didn't "look" like a Corvette, and used an engine that most of us had never heard of. "What's a Wankel?" Despite its unusual styling, it was a very well done prototype. However, due to the Corvette's sales success, GM was in no hurry to make an all-new car.

GM was hot on the new Wankel rotary engine, and was scheduled to offer the rotor-motor in the Vega for '75. GM acquired a license to develop the Wankel engine in '70. This was the pet project of GM President, Ed Cole. Because the engine has so few moving parts, on paper, the rotary engine looked very promising. Since 1953, people inside of GM have wanted to make the Corvette something else - smaller, bigger, a four-seater, etc. So a Wankel-powered prototype was ordered. Actually, two prototypes were made, the XP-892 two-rotor design, shown here, and a four-rotor design using the chassis from the '70, mid-engine, V-8 powered XP-882.

The XP-892 was small - about the same size as a Dino Ferrari or a Datsun 240Z. But when pressed for inside information as to the possibility of this being the next Corvette, the ever cagey Duntov was quoted as saying, "Maybe, but there are no plans to produce it."

The problem was that at 2,600 pounds, with only 180-to-250 hp, performance wouldn't be anywhere close to Corvette standards. Since the Wankel engine had serious heat problems, the XP-892 was more of a study to see if the engine was feasible for a small sports car. Power-to-weight ratio aside, everyone was very pleased with the way the car turned out.

The XP-892 was designed by Chevrolet and built by Pininfarina. Unlike a production Corvette, the XP-892 was a steel, unit-body construction. Duntov referred to the McPherson strut, independent suspension, and disc brakes as "run of the mill." The 266-ci engine had a single Rochester four-barrel carburetor, and was mated to a modified Hydramatic transmission. Duntov clearly wanted more when he said, "Add three more inches of wheelbase... and maybe a 300-ci engine, and we'd have a good car." As always, he had "something else" up his sleeve, the larger, four-rotor version.

For a prototype, the XP-892 had a very well designed and finished interior. The seats were fixed while the seat backs, steering wheel, and pedals were all adjustable. Between the engine and interior there was a 8.1 cubic foot storage space. The spare tire was under the front hood. It seems that the press never drove the car, as there was never a mention of how the car performed.

GM wasn't the only car company that seriously looked into the Wankel engine. Mercedes created the mid-engine C111, and by '75, Mazda was offering a Wankel-engine pickup truck. Sometimes, ideas that look good on paper don't work out so well. Mazda took the Wankel to the next level in '79 with the RX-7. While the car got rave reviews as a sports car, two inherent issues cast a shadow on the little rotor-motor - namely emissions and gas mileage. As emission standards increased over the years, it was more difficult for the Wankel to perform and was eventually dropped in '02.

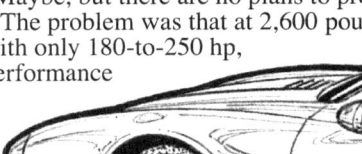

Sometimes, "interesting ideas" are best left on paper. GM privately showed the XP-892 and the V-8 powered XP-882 to potential Corvette buyers in '72. The test groups wanted to see something in between. Duntov's opinion was, "When we finally decide what the new Corvette will be, it will be for our own reasons." You saved us on that one Zora.

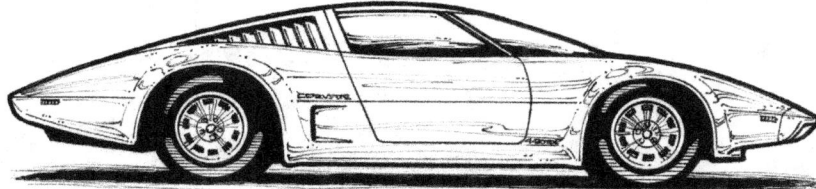

1973 4-Rotor Mid-Engine Corvette
"148-MPH Prototype Corvette"

Zora Arkus-Duntov had that rare blend of a deep understanding of engineering and a passion for speed. Aesthetics did little for Duntov, unless it helped the car's performance. Concerning the Four-Rotor Corvette, Duntov was quoted, "Looking back on my 20-year association with styling, this is the best design ever produced."

From '68 to '73, Chevrolet R&D made five unique mid-engine prototypes. So, what happened? The mid-engine Corvette dream never made it into production because of the Corvette's sales success through the '70s. Production was at an all-time high in '73, and Chevrolet returned 8,200 orders to dealers because they couldn't make enough cars! So, strictly from a business standpoint, "We're selling all we can make, don't change it!"

Another interesting situation was going on inside of Chevrolet. Four power-players were approaching the end of their careers, and they all wanted a spectacular replacement for the Corvette. Duntov from engineering, Bill Mitchell from styling, Joe Pike from sales, and GM President Ed Cole, were powerful Corvette allies. But in business, the bottom line is king.

Styling was directed by Mitchell and penned out by Henry Haga. Chuck Jordan, executive in charge of Chevrolet exterior design, gave the 4-Rotor some of its flair. Starting with the bumper height datum line, Mitchell's instructions were to "make it sleek." The long tapers on the front and rear, and a steep-back windshield, made the drag coefficient only 0.325. Gull-wing bi-fold doors, rear-deck cooling vents, louvers, scoops, and lots of show car trim made the 4-Rotor Corvette nearly perfect from every angle of view. The a-pillars were hidden and the louvers behind the b-pillar provided excellent over-the-shoulder visibility. Slightly longer, lower, and wider than a production '74 Corvette, it looked like "the future." But more importantly and unlike the 2-Rotor car, the 4-Rotor prototype "looked" like a Corvette.

On a one-mile check track, GM president Ed Cole and Duntov clicked off 148 mph in the 4-rotor Corvette. The car started out with a throaty roar and hit top speed, belching flames and making an ear piercing scream. It was actually faster than a '73 454 Corvette! But not even powerful friends in high places could get this prototype into production. Eventually, the body design came back in '77 as the Aero-Vette. Before his retirement in '77, Bill Mitchell championed the car as his Corvette legacy. For a brief time, the Aero-Vette was scheduled to be the '80 C4 Corvette. But new Corvette engineer chief, Dave McLellan had little interest in the design. Mid-engine cars were notoriously poor-selling cars. The mid-engine Corvette concept would go dormant for ten years until the arrival of the Corvette Indy concept that later became the experimental CERV III.

The 2-Rotor car was nice, but more power was obviously needed. So a bold plan was presented to get the job done. Using the chassis from one of the two '70 XP-882 cars, two 292.5-ci rotary engines joined together inside a stress member case. The 585-ci engine made close to 420 hp. The transmission was a Turbo Hydramatic 425 from a Toranado, with a Morse Hy-Vo chain and bevel gears.

CHAPTER 2: EXPERIMENTAL AND PROTOTYPE CORVETTES

1973 XP-895 Corvette
"Reynolds Aluminum Prototype Corvette"

Despite the dark clouds on the automotive horizon in the early '70s, it was a heady time and the Corvette R&D group was thinking way out of the box. The all-aluminum Corvette was the third fully functional prototype to show up in '73.

Before carbon fiber, aluminum was the darling of high-tech automotive development. After all, aluminum was the material of cutting-edge jet aircraft, space craft, and exotic race cars. An aluminum bodied car wasn't a new idea, since many European exotics had aluminum bodies, as well as Shelby's Cobra. But an aluminum "production" car is another matter.

Like aircraft and space craft, weight was the motivator for this feasibility study. Since the early '60s Detroit had been offering "off-road" aluminum parts intended for NASCAR, drag, and droad racing, but these were limited to bolt-on bumpers, fenders, hoods, doors, and mounting hardware. Mass producing an entire car body would require many assembly and durability considerations that had not yet been sorted out. But the prospect of reducing body weight by 40 percent was very appealing.

Using the same chassis and basic body shape of the 2-Rotor Corvette prototype, Reynolds Aluminum used their new 2036-T4 allow to make this all-aluminum Corvette. Except for the bumpers, tires, and interior parts everything else is aluminum. Chevrolet supplied stress analysis and Reynolds engineers worked out the details. The main constraint was that the body would have to be spot-welded like a production car. To compensate for aluminum's lower modulus of elasticity, many of the parts and attaching flanges had to be thicker. Two-part epoxy was also used for added strength and to eliminate crevices that would trap salts and dirt.

The Reynolds Aluminum car had minor body differences from the 2-Rotor prototype and used a 400-cid small-block mated to a Hydro-Matic automatic transmission. Side-by-side, the Reynolds car weighed over 400 pounds less than the steel bodied 2-Rotor prototype. But weighed against the Corvette's sales success of the early '70s, GM was in no mood to make an aluminum Corvette.

Things sure have changed since the XP-895. For decades, weight reduction was the shortest path to increased performance. Modern electronic-controlled engines are so efficient and powerful, weight isn't the big concern it used to be. That's why so many of today's new muscle cars are quite hefty. Thanks to carbonfiber, titanium, and aluminum, a C6 Z06 weighing in around 3,150-pounds, is one of the lightest performance cars on the market today.

1991 ZR-2 454 Corvette
"Chevrolet's Big Doggie!"

"Big Doggie" was most likely the last time a big-block Corvette was even remotely considered as a possible production option. Actually, it was more like a, "let's see if we can do this," kind of effort. Although it only had a snowball's chance, it

was pretty cool that it was even made.

Some Corvette engineers have all the fun. In the mid '80s, Scott Leon was a Corvette Project Coordinator at the GM Proving ground in Arizona. Although the new C4 Corvette was a success, there were those that missed that old-time big-block Corvette torque and horsepower. But Scott Leon had a plan.

One night after work, Leon and his crew decided to see if a big-block engine would fit into the frame rails of a C4 Corvette. Using an old '84 mule Corvette, the crew was surprised to find that with only a few chassis modifications, the big rat motor fit.

The engine was a real squeeze, but it worked. Remember that the C2 Corvettes were not designed from the beginning for the big-block, and stuffing the larger engine was more complicated that one would think. Producing a big-block C4 would have been equally as challenging. But Leon wanted the car to be modern, so they cobbled together a tuned-port fuel injection unit with a modified aftermarket tunnel-ram intake manifold. With a little welding and a set of Buick Grand National injectors, the system worked.

The crude engineering study was enough for Leon to get management to agree to building a 454 prototype using a '86 Corvette Coupe with an automatic transmission. Later, another prototype was made using a '89 Roadster with a 6-speed transmission and a Z51 suspension. Now things were starting to get real interesting.

The final version of Big Doggie was a very impressive machine. To get started, Leon chose one of Chevy's marine 454 short-blocks and added a set of L88 aluminum heads. The engine assembly was modified so that all production accessories would bolt on. The only modifications to the chassis was to the floor pan and the right side of the frame rail - forward of the fire wall. Aside from the large raised hood, the package looked like a production Vette. Even under the hood, everything looks like it came off the assembly line.

The ZR-2's 454 engine was never dyno tested, but was estimated at 385 horsepower, about the same as a ZR-1, but with a big difference. Big Doggie had much more low-end torque than a ZR-1 and pulled like a freight train. With the Z51 suspension parts and a 6-speed transmission, the car was a hoot to drive. To save weight, Leon used the optional hard top and removed the convertible mechanism.

In the olden days, the easiest way to mega-horsepower was through cubic inches. The sledgehammer approach had been replaced with finesse and computers. Besides, Chevrolet had too many of its eggs in the ZR-1 basket and the big-block engine didn't meet federal fuel standards. For a time, there was talk of offering a retro kit. But ZR-1 performance at a fraction of the cost wasn't what GM was interested in. Ah, it could have been cool.

CHAPTER 2: EXPERIMENTAL AND PROTOTYPE CORVETTES

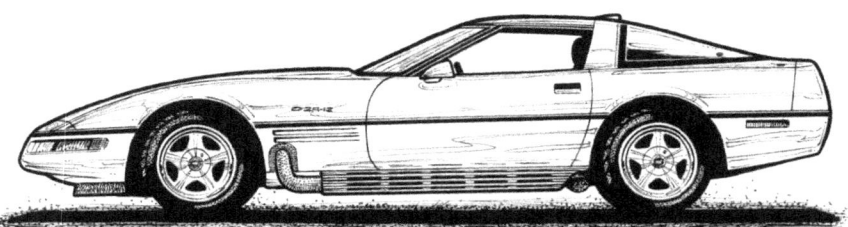

1992 V-12 Falconer Corvette
"The Conan Corvette"

When the Dodge Viper debuted at the North American International Auto Show in January 1989, no one knew what hit them. The Viper was new and fresh, yet it had a definite connection to the Shelby Cobra. Advanced orders were flooding in and you know that Corvette designers were going back to the office saying, "DAMN!"

The Corvette team was working on three fronts: improving the production Corvette, getting the LT5 (ZR-1) ready for production, and honing the CERV III prototype as a possible C5 Corvette. But the economy wasn't good and the reality of a CERV III-based car seemed dim at best. Meanwhile, Chrysler was going into production with the V-10-powered Viper. This posed a serious threat to the Corvette's "America's Only True Sports Car" status.

Under the guise of a "chassis development" program, the Corvette team came up with the idea of trumping the V-10 Viper with a V-12 Corvette prototype. Enter Ryan Falconer.

Falconer got his start in the early '60s working for Andy Granatelli's Novi engine-powered Indy racers. Later he joined in the Shelby American team and worked on the GT40 and racing Cobras. Two years later, Ryan started his own company, building his own racing engines. His associates reads like a "who's who" of auto racing legends, including Parnelli Jones, Al Unser, Mario Andretti, Jackie Stewart, and many others.

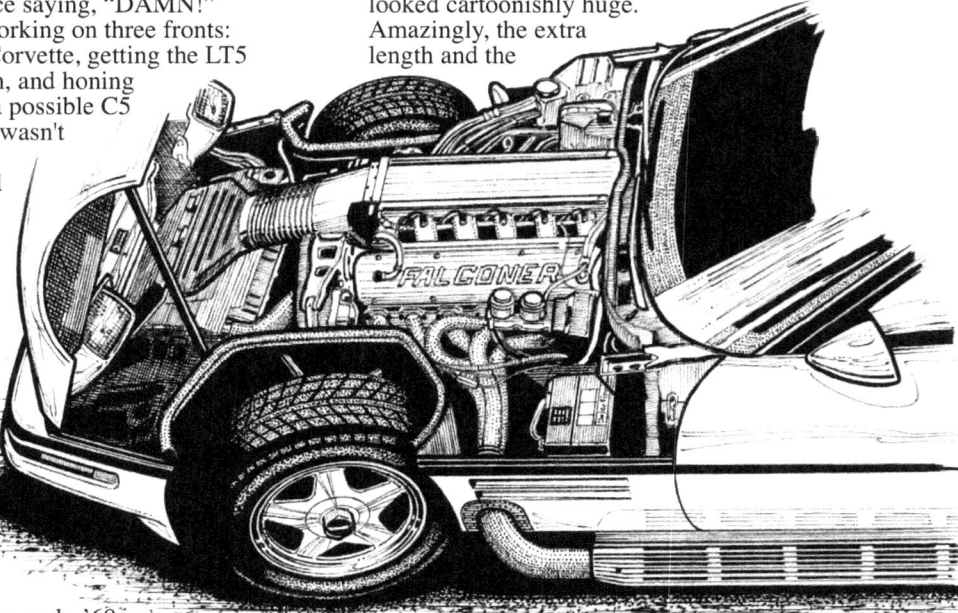

So when the Corvette team decided to one-up the Viper with two extra cylinders, they decided on one of Ryan Falconer's stunning, all aluminum V-12 racing engines. Since the Corvette would have to be stretched, this was the perfect time for a "chassis study."

Since the Falconer V-12 packed a 680-horsepower kick, the obvious place to begin was with a production ZR-1. The biggest challenge was the fact that the all-aluminum V-12 engine was 8.8-inches longer than the production Corvette engine. So the front end of the ZR-1 would have to be stretched 8 inches. SportsFab of Wixom, Michigan, was contracted to do the stretching. The extra length is barely noticeable, but the '60s-styled side pipes sure are. Those were straight-through pipes directly off the tuned headers with no mufflers! With the hood up, the engine looked cartoonishly huge.

Amazingly, the extra length and the larger engine only added 100 pounds to the overall weight of the car. The engine used electronic fuel injection with a short-runner intake manifold and the aluminum block had pressed in cast iron sleeves, similar to the famous ZL1.

Actual performance figures were never published, as this was just a "chassis study." But you can figure out the power-to-weight ratio. What was certain was that at $45,000 per engine, plus the chassis and body modifications, there was no chance this car would ever get into production. Nicknamed "Conan" because of the huge V-12 engine, the ZR-12 was without a doubt, the one of the baddest engineering study Corvettes ever.

Chapter 3
Corvette Show Cars

Over the years, Chevrolet kept the faithful stoked with dozens of spectacular show car Corvettes. Show cars are usually the realm of the stylists. Some are slightly enhanced production cars and others are used to test the public's response to new concepts and designs. Many corvette show cars have become legendary in the world of automotive design.

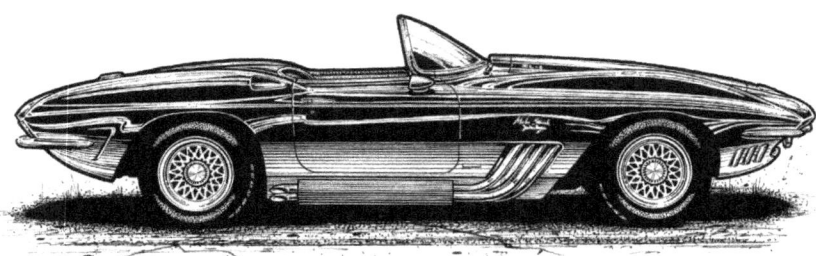

Bill Mitchell's Mako Shark Corvettes
"Shark Obsession"

Corvettes have always been about guts and glamour. Duntov provided the guts, and Styling V.P., Bill Mitchell, provided the glamour. But inside the Chevrolet design center, a war was being waged between these two men.

Mitchell joined GM in '35 and was heir to the throne of GM designer Harley Earl. Duntov was hired in '53, and by '57 was promoted to director of high-performance sales at Chevrolet. In Mitchell's world, everything was about style and he used to say, "Engineering never sold a damn thing." Duntov, on the other hand, was a mechanical man. The glue that kept these two men together was their passion for fast cars, especially Corvettes.

Starting with the aborted Q-Corvette, Bill enlisted the help of stylist Larry Shinoda to make the Q-Corvette into a roadster body that would be fitted to the mule chassis from the Corvette SS racer. Mitchell had two objectives. First, he wanted to go racing, and second, he wanted to test the public's response to the new shape. Named "Sting Ray," Mitchell raced on his own dime, and won the 1960 SCCA C/Modified Championship. The public loved the new design, making is clear - the Sting Ray would be the next Corvette.

Duntov did not like it and let Mitchell know. Zora saw the long hood/short deck styling as being stuck in the '30s. Mitchell was outraged that an engineer would dare to question his design. Mitchell called Duntov "Zorro," and Duntov called Mitchell "a red-faced baboon," but Mitchell won the day. Later when Duntov was testing the '63 Z06, he let select drivers sample the racer kit, but not Mitchell. So, Bill built his own hot-rod Corvette.

Named the Mako Shark, after a shark Bill caught while on vacation in Bimini, the car was a street version of his Stingray racer. Larry Shinoda was charged with working out the styling. Based on a '61 Vette, every surface was stylized. The car had supercharged 327, a double-bubble Plexiglas roof, side pipes, gills for front cornering lights, vents, scoops, a rear-view periscope, wire wheels, and iridescent blue paint that faded into white along the lower edge. The car was shown at Elkhart Lake in the summer of 1961 and was a smash hit. No sooner had the '63 Corvette been released, Mitchell was designing the next Corvette. Again, Larry Shinoda and a small staff were brought in to assist. But this time, Mitchell had an unusual design mandate.

Mitchell wanted to see a radical design with a tapered tail, a blending of the upper and lower portions, and prominent fenders that were separate from the body, yet grafted to it. When shown in April '65, The Mako Shark II, jaws dropped. A functioning show car was built and work began on the production "Mako Shark" Corvette. Duntov was not happy, but management liked it because there was little hard tooling to create. Zora saw is as a move away from his dream of a mid-engine Corvette.

In '69 Bill restyled the car and called it "Manta Ray." It had a long tapered tail, scooped-out roof, side pipes, and a ZL1 engine. As great as the Sting Ray was, the shark design would forever define the look of the Corvette. Despite their differences, both Mitchell and Duntov had deep respect for one another. As Mitchell liked to say, they both had gasoline in their veins. Thanks to Duntov and Mitchell, Corvettes would always have glamour and guts.

1967 F&SO 427/435 Corvette
"Bob Wingate's V.I.P. Special"

In the '50s and '60s, GM's presidents, VIPs, and high-level managers often got new cars that were specially made. These were generically called "SO" - for "Special Order" or "F&SO," for "Fleet & Special Order." However, it was unusual for a car salesman to get one. But Bob Wingate of Clippinger Chevrolet, in Covina, California, wasn't just a good car salesman. He was "Mr. Corvette."

Wingate started at Clippinger Chevrolet in 1955 as a prep guy - the fellow who cleans the cars prior to delivery. The young Corvette guy worked his way into sales, and before long, he was selling more Corvettes than anyone else in California. One day, Wingate ordered 100 '62 Corvettes for the dealership and Chevrolet management wondered, "Who is this guy?" But Chevy's Joe Pike believed in Wingate and was not disappointed. Wingate went on to become the highest volume Corvette salesman in '62 and by '66 had sold more Corvettes than any other salesman, winning him the "Legion of Leaders" award. Then, Ford's Lee Iacocca offered him a job doing the same kind of work for Mustang and Cobra sales. Wingate declined, and when Joe Pike found out, Bob got a raise and an F&SO Corvette. He was told, "Pick what you want."

Most people know about the car shown here, but there was another car before this one. In the fall of 1966, Bob got a heavily customized pearl green '67 427 Coupe. Soon Wingate's customers began asking if they could get their Vettes tricked out like his. The car created a problem because Bob's customers wanted Corvettes like his, so it was replaced with something a little more tame.

The replacement car was just as stunning. Painted Greenwood Green, it had a white stripe that started on top of the 427 hood scoop and ran over the top and back. Six taillights adorned the back, and the front bumpers were removed. Torq-Thrust mag with Goodyear Blue Streak tires and white brake calipers filled the stock wheelwells. The hood had hand-applied "427" numbering, and a Nardi steering wheel dressed up the black interior. Factory options included the L71 427/435 engine, power windows and brakes, an AM/FM radio, tinted glass, a shoulder harness, side pipes, a wide-ratio 4-speed, and a 3.55:1 Posi-traction rear. Wingate recalls the body being "perfect."

With a Clippinger logo and Bob's name painted on the door, for the next year, when he wasn't selling Corvettes, he was touring the Southwest, attending car shows, autocross races, and drag races, promoting Clippinger.

While the car was owned by the dealership, Wingate's deal was that he could sell the car and keep the money as his yearend bonus. So he sold the car to a young fellow who promptly blew up the engine. Later, Wingate learned that his F&SO Vette had been smashed when a truck ran into it while it was parked on I-10 after running out of gas. Oh well.

Twenty-five years later, Californian Bob Radke found a '67 coupe in very bad condition and bought it as a hot rod project. When he checked the tank sticker, he noticed "COPO/F&SO" and the notation "Build Per FSO." Radke had a very rare machine. After some research, he learned that the original owner had been Bob Wingate, the "Corvette Guy." Radke's seven-year resto took the car back to when it was delivered to Wingate, the day before Thanksgiving 1966.

VIP Corvettes have become hot collector cars, and Radke hasn't indicated that he's anywhere close to being ready to part with this beauty.

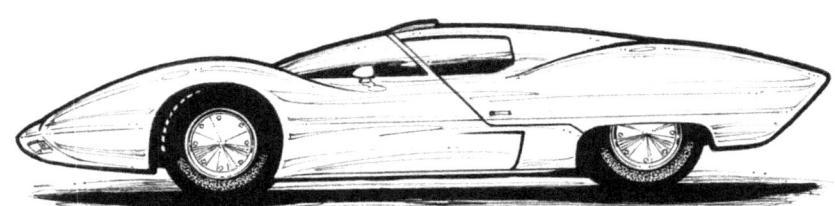

1968 Astro-1 Mid-Engine Experimental Car
"A High-Performance Corvair-Powered Corvette?"

Almost from the beginning, there have been those at Chevrolet who wanted the Corvette to be "something else." Along the way there have been proposals to soften the Corvette, add a back seat, and to use steel for the body. The surprise about this car is that it wasn't supposed to be a possible future Corvette.

The "official" purpose of the Astro I was to study aerodynamics and new features. However, according to insider, Roy Lonberger, one of the designers that worked in Hank Hagga's Chevy-2 Studio, they had "race car" in mind. This ultra-light, monocoque chassis design with an aluminum, flat-opposed-six Corvair engine wasn't all that unlike the prototype Porsche racers of the day. So, the concept wasn't that far outside the parameters of reality. After the racing program was canceled, the car was made into a show car - a common experience for many Chevrolet experimentals.

While GM's chief of styling Bill Mitchell and Larry Shinoda are generally credited with the design, according to Lonberger, Mitchell selected a sketch he had created and charged Shinoda for making sure the young designer's car was completed on time with Mitchell's approval. Roy got lucky on this one because it was one of the few concept cars that went from a designer's sketch to a running prototype with no significant changes.

Engineers had long known that frontal area and shape were major factors in how slippery a car is in high-speed air. Much of what we take for granted in aerodynamics was new territory in the mid '60s. For this study, function followed form. To keep the front profile as low as possible, a modified, flat, opposed-six Corvair engine was placed behind the rear wheels. Although a far cry from the rip-snort'n 427s of the day, the little 176-ci engine was made of alloy aluminum with steel cylinder sleeves and featured single-overhead cams, hemi heads, Weber-like carburetors, and made 240 horsepower. That's 1.36 hp per cubic inch! From a per-cubic-inch ratio perspective, that kind of power was on par with the L88 and ZL1 engines. The flat aluminum engine helped create a center of gravity that was unattainable with a production-based Corvette.

The unibody construction had large boxed side sill members that added stiffness as well as housing a fuel cell on the passenger side. The bulkhead behind the driver and the forged aluminum windshield header provided rollover protection.

The front and rear suspension used double wishbones and four-wheel disc brakes. Wheels and tires hadn't gotten fat yet, so 5.5 inch and 7.0 inch wheels were used front and back.

Note the absence of any normal door lines. The entire canopy hinged up from a pivot point behind the rear wheels. Since the car was 35.5 inches tall, 12.3 inches shorter than a '68 Corvette, the seats were fixed to the canopy and actually raised up so that you could step into the interior. This was not a rainy day car.

The Astro I had many styling tricks that were standard for GM study cars; a closet at the base of the windshield for wipers, pop-up spoiler brake lights, access panels on the hood for servicing fluids, and periscope rear view mirrors. The interior had the gauges, warning lights, and twin-grip steering control device. The powerful wheel humps and the stinger rear roof line definitely screamed, "CORVETTE." Trick stuff in 1967.

At only 35.5 inches tall, the Astro I was as low as a Countach, 15 years earlier. By '67 the Corvair had a swirl of controversy around it, although engineering had fixed all of the car's suspension problems, but it was too late. If the Astro I had been packing a big 427 engine, it would have gotten a lot more attention from the automotive press. This unusual concept/show car is still around and sometimes shows up at Corvette car shows. The ropes around the car are to keep visitors from tripping over the car.

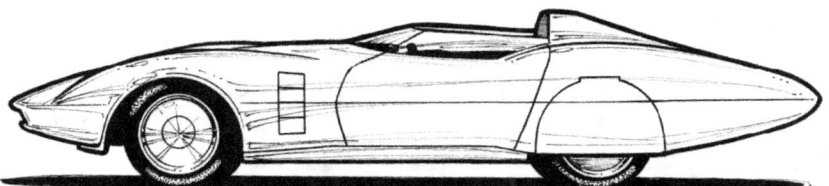

1968 Astro-Vette Show Car "Moby Dick"

By the late '60s, automotive stylists and engineers were seriously looking at aerodynamics. Race cars were using all sorts of exotic wings and spoilers. Even hot street cars were using chin spoilers and rear deck spoilers or wings. C2 Corvettes always had a front end lift problem at high speeds. The new '68 Corvette had a small chin spoiler and a slight up-lip at the back end, but the car still had front-end lift problems.

Chevrolet seemed to be bingeing on show cars and concept cars in the late '60s. The Astro-Vette was one of what seemed like a continuous stream of concept show cars. Styling created this car as an aerodynamic study to see how slippery the then-new Shark Corvette could be made. Although some criticized the car as being pure schmaltz, two notable styling features were picked up.

In 1968 Pontiac started offering "Endura" soft front bumpers on the GTO, so it looks like designers may have been thinking in that direction. Designers will often take a new shape concept and over-design it about 120 percent. Then when they're told to "tone it down" a 10 to 15 percent reduction will get them where they wanted to be to begin with.

What they probably were not thinking about in 1968 was 5 mph front and rear bumpers. In 1973, when most cars got huge, chrome, front bumpers, Corvettes got the Astro-Vette treatment. Then in 1974, the tail end was restyled, a la Astro-Vette. So, all wasn't lost on the Astro-Vette project. Designers went with the sex-appeal of a roadster. If they had really been serious, a coupe version with a low, teardrop, similar to the roof line of the Astro-I would have been very interesting.

In September '67, a new International Blue '68 Corvette was delivered to the Design Studio to be the starting point for the new aerodynamic study. The obvious features on the Astro-Vette were the extended nose, roadster windshield, closed rear wheel openings and extended tail. The nose was extended considerably and the grille opening was kept to a minimum. The long hood has a very subtle bulge to cover the 427 engine and the then-new windshield wiper closet door was gone. Scribe lines on the front fenders were to be pressure-actuated flaps that opened if underhood pressure was too high. Designers took advantage of the B-pillar hoop by reducing its height and crafting an airfoil to minimize air drag. Taking cues from the hot cars of the '30s, the Astro-Vette had smooth wheel disks on very narrow tires, and rear fender skirts were

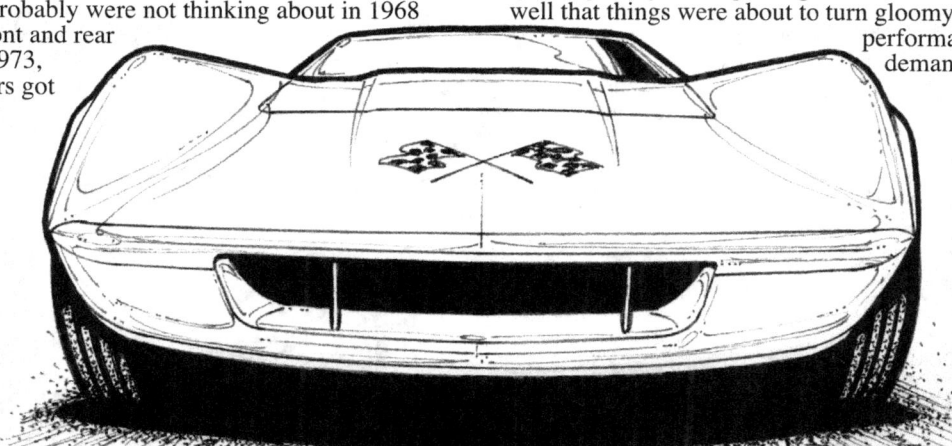

hinged at the top for tire access. Like the front, the back end was extended and tapered. Designers even added partial front and rear belly pans to smooth underside airflow. The interior was medium blue and stock, except for the racing steering wheel.

Most folks didn't know what to make of the Astro-Vette. Chevy insiders named it, "Moby Dick," in essence calling it a big, white whale. But the timing of this car wasn't quite right. By the beginning of '69, insiders knew full well that things were about to turn gloomy for performance cars. New demands were being placed on designers and engineers for safety, emissions, and fuel economy that had previously been of minimal concern. Had the times been different, an L88 or ZL-1-powered Astro-Vette would have made for an interesting Bonneville speed car. Corvettes had become regulars at the Bonneville event, so a racing Astro-Vette would have been very interesting.

The Astro-Vette faded away, but it made its mark on Corvette styling. The Astro-Vette now resides at the National Corvette Museum.

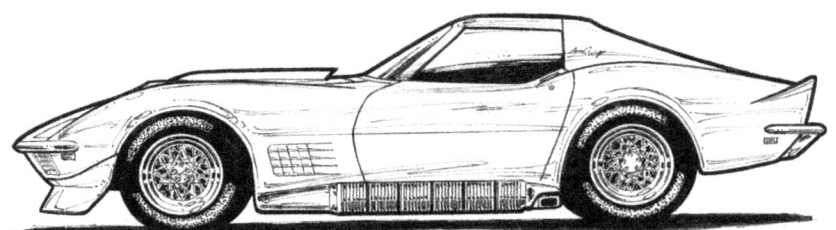

Bill Mitchell's 1970 Aero Coupe
"It's Good To Be Sr. V.P."

Being the Senior V.P. of Design at General Motors sure had its perks for Bill Mitchell. Since his earliest days as chief of design, Bill always had a hot Corvette to drive to and from work. This particular Corvette had three lives and was Mitchell's favorite "perk car" while working at GM. The actual car that was made into the "Aero Coupe" was born as an off-the-assembly line 1968, small-block Corvette. Over the next seven years the car lived through three incarnations: the "Aero Coupe," the "Scirocco," and the "Mulsanne."

The first thing that Mitchell's Design Staff did was to remove the 327 small-block and drop in one of the new ZL1, all-aluminum Can-Am engines. For several years the ZL1 used an experimental Rochester fuel-injection unit and an prototype, four-speed Hydra-Matic transmission. The ZL1 was awesome, but the four-speed automatic was replaced with a Turbo 400 unit. And what Bill Mitchell show car wouldn't be complete without side-mounted exhausts? Mitchell aptly described the Fuelie 427 ZL1 Aero Coupe as a "real bear!"

With plenty of power under Bill's right foot, the Design Staff started work on the body. It may have been slightly overdone, but that's what show cars were supposed to be. Officially called a "Research and Development Vehicle," the Aero Coupe had many interesting styling cues. The egg-crate front grille and side vents were previews of the refreshed '70 Corvette. The front end had a deep, "shovel-style" front spoiler that wrapped around its chin. At the rear, there was a matching, wrap-around spoiler similar to the '70-1/2 Z-28 Camaro, but graphed into body and angled back more than the Camaro version. The side pipe covers were similar to the optional, production side pipes, except the section under the doors had six groups of vertical scribe lines. The windshield and roof were interesting. The A-pillars were curved at the top corners, allowing the glass and roof to have a smooth, continuous curved line. The removable roof panel was a single piece and hinged at the back. Another Mitchell pet design element was the periscope rearview mirror system. Since the car was using Chevrolet's 427 ZL1, the RPO ZL2 hood option (same as used on the L88) was used. And continuing with the Can-Am influence, fat Goodyear tires were mounted on wide, Chaparral-style "lace" alloy wheels.

The interior was very plush for a Corvette, reflecting a new marketing position for the '70s Corvettes. It was completely trimmed in tan leather and deep-cut carpet. Years later a crude digital unit was added to the dash that projected the car's speed on to the windshield - a prehistoric version of today's heads-up display feature.

The Aero Coupe was completed with a deep, candy apple red paint with heavy gold metalflake, gold striping, trimmed with Corvette, and ZL-1 badges.

This very special Corvette went on to delight Corvette fans for years, with each version getting more wild. The Scirocco version was repainted bright red with gold feather-like pinstripping and a red painted front bumper. The hood was styled somewhat like the regular small-block hood, but the point was extended into the front clip and there was a grille-vent at the back edge of the hood. When the car finally became the Mulsane in '74, only insiders knew that it was really a '68 small-block Vette on steroids.

Being the Senior V.P. of Design at General Motors sure had its perks for Bill Mitchell. When the car wasn't on-duty at car shows, it was either pacing Can-Am races or was Bill's personal ride. What a job!

1974 Mulsanne Corvette Show Car
"Bill Mitchell's Best Stingray Ever!"

Only Bill Mitchell could get away with this. Bill always managed to have a hot daily ride. Engineering prototypes that weren't street-legal stayed behind the fence, but many of the show car Corvettes managed to go home with Bill. His usual statement on his "design study" cars was, "This thing runs like a bear!" For the Mulsanne, Bill added, "This is the best Stingray ever." Considering what was under the hood, it SHOULD have run like a bear!

The Mulsanne actually had three previous lives. Born as a stock 350 '68 Corvette, the car was originally the '69 "Aero Coupe" show car used to preview the '70-1/2 styling changes. The bright red metalflake with gold pinstriping had a 427 ZL-1 all-aluminum engine and a prototype four-speed automatic.

A short time later the Aero Coupe got its second makeover and received the slim, Manta Ray-style side-pipe covers, a new hood and front end, a new red paint job with the front bumper-grille assembly painted body color, elaborate pinstripping on the hood and flanks, and was renamed the "Scirocco." For the next four years the car worked as a pace car at Can-Am races. These were the days of heavy ZL-1 powered McLaren dominance. Mitchell thought it was cool that his Mulsanne pace car had the same basic engine as the McLarens.

The third and last incarnation for the car was the '74 Mulsanne, named after the long 3.7-mile Mulsanne Straight where the Le Mans racers often hit speed of well over 200 mph! Like all of the Mitchell show cars, the Mulsanne had a large crowd around it at the '75 New York Automobile Show. Bill didn't pen every line on the Corvette, but his style was always present.

Painted bright metallic silver, the Corvette Mulsanne wore '74-style front and rear bumper covers - the version without the small bumperettes. The pop-up headlights were replaced with four rectangular lamps under body-fitting clear plastic covers. The new hood had a raised center section with recessed, functional scoops on both sides. The curved A-pillar, high-mounted racing mirrors, periscope rearview mirror system, and electric rear window were all carry-overs from the previous Scirocco exercise.

The interior was completely trimmed in leather with fixed seats and adjustable pedals and steering wheel. Mitchell wanted the speedometer to look like a gunner's site. So a roller-type speedometer reflected speed numbers on to the windshield. This was so that the driver could watch the road while "blasting" past lesser cars.

Since the Mulsanne was made to be a pace car, Mitchell wanted to make sure his Mulsanne had enough grunt. Bill couldn't have a "stock" ZL1, this engine was bored out to 454-cid and wore an experimental Rochester fuel injection system. Chaparral lace wheels and flames exiting the fender vents added show car splash.

The Mulsanne Corvette was the last of the Mitchell Corvette show cars before he retired in '77, after 42 years of service to General Motors. Immediately after retirement from GM, Bill started William L. Mitchell Design and worked as a design consultant until 1984. In an interview after leaving GM, Mitchell lamented over the cookie-cutter designs of most of GM's cars by the early '80s, "They all look alike!" he retorted. Bill wasn't the only person to take issue with the styling of GM's platform cars. For a man that spent his life creating uniquely styled automobiles, this must have been difficult to see. Former Sr. V.P. of GM Design, Chuck Jordan said, "The man had flair!" William L. Mitchell passed in 1988.

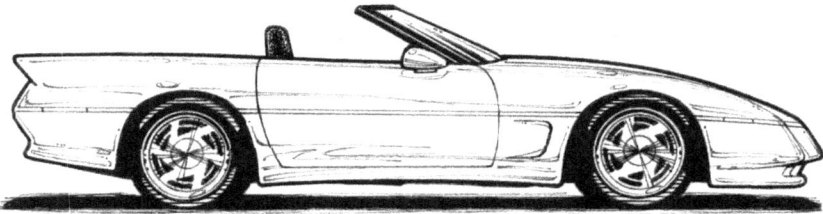

1988 ASC Geneve Corvette
"A Well-Received Study"

Aside from the Corvette Indy concept car and the CERV III, there weren't many Corvette show cars during the '80s. Cars had become astonishingly complex from the heydays of the '60s when there was a constant flow of Corvette concept cars, show cars, and refurbished race cars. Designers and engineers had enough to do just keeping up with the latest crash and emission standards. But deep inside the design studios of Chevrolet, new ideas were being flushed out around the clock, only a few ideas got out the door for public viewing.

ASC (American Sunroof Corporation) of South Gate, Michigan, was founded in 1963 by Heinz Prechter and specialized in sunroof and convertible conversions, lift-out roof panels, and custom interiors. Prechter worked with all of the Detroit car companies, many European car manufacturers, and some of George Barris' custom cars. The company designed all of the parts, mechinisms, electrical components. ASC began a Corvette convertible development program in 1984 that eventually arrived in Chevrolet showrooms as the '86 Corvette convertible.

As an R&D developer for Chevrolet, the ASC team was aware of the Corvette Indy project. Armed with this knowledge, ASC did their own styling analysis of what an Indy-inspired C4 Corvette might look like. The concept drawings were blessed by Design VP Chuck Jordan and Sr. Designer John Cafaro, and ASC had the green light to build a prototype.

ASC began the Geneve project early in 1987 with a stock, 230 hp Corvette that would serve as an armature for the new body parts. This wasn't an add-on body kit, it was a reskin of the existing C4. The Corvette Indy could be characterized as "smooth and sleek." The ASC team set out to emulate that aspect of the Corvette Indy.

The front auxiliary lights were mounted under the bumper and integrated with the new front spoiler. The hood dome was simplified with a single bulge instead of the twin bulges of the stock design. Front and rear wheel openings were reshaped to incorporate new side sills that flared out and were integrated with the rest of the body, with front fender vents looked somewhat like those used on the C5. The rear end design had a low top deck spoiler that jutted out, as well as a lower spoiler. LED taillight lenses were flush mounted, and the side marker lights were integrated into the body side molding. Side-view mirrors were faired into the A-pillars. The interior featured custom seats with open headrests, charcoal suede leather inserts and black leather trim. With the blood red paint and new 17-inch, 12-slot wheels that came with the Z51 and Z52 suspension packages, the car looked fantastic, like a contender for a near-future production Corvette.

Concept cars are always "far-out." Prototype and show cars are much closer to real cars. ASC looked at the Corvette Indy and asked, "What would this styling look like on an existing Corvette?" The Corvette Indy had wild proportions and applying those styling cues to an existing Corvette would be quite a challenge. When ASC's version of a Indy-style C4 was finally completed, it had subtle hints from the Corvette Indy concept car, but it looked like a real production car.

At the 1988 Geneva Car Show, Jordan and Cafaro were very impressed and ordered new exterior, interior, and power top styling studies. The ASC Geneve was a hit.

Before the car went to Geneva, spy photos showed up in the magazines as the "The Next Corvette!" The automotive press has always been hungry for Corvette appetizers, and the Geneve Corvette show car was a very tasty treat.

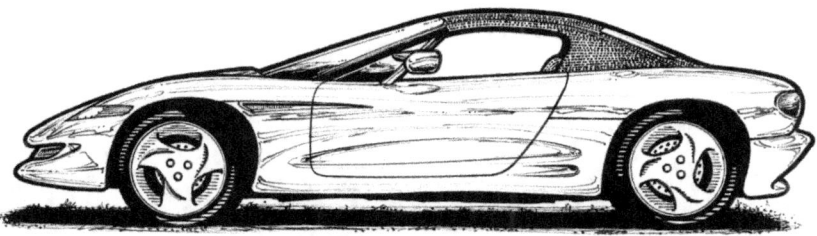

1990 Sting Ray III
"California-Style Corvette"

Designing the "next Corvette" is a never-ending job for the elite Corvette Design Department. It's also one of the most challenging design tasks in Detroit. Between egos, budget concerns, and turn wars, it's amazing it ever gets completed.

The late '80s and early '90s were some of the worst economic times GM had ever experienced to that date. The management chess game was mind boggeling. Dave McLellan was never interested in fulfilling Duntov's vision of a mid-engine Corvette and retired in '92. The ZR-1 would be his crowning achievement. GM's new president, Bob Stemple put the C5 project on hold while the GM cash-crunch was solved. No one was sure of when the next Corvette would hit the road, despite many attempts to define the new design.

The taskmaster for the new Corvette was V.P. of Design, Chuck Jordan, know as the "Chrome Cobra." Jordan secretly staged a 3-way C5 internal competition between John Schinella's Advanced Concepts Center, Tom Peters' Advanced 4 Studio, and John Cafaro's Chevy 3 group. Jordan would be retiring in '92 and wanted the next Corvette to have his mark on it.

Wanting to be "out there," Chuck determined that the car should have a Porsche-like character and be powered by a high-tech, lightweight V-6 engine. Jordan didn't want the C5 to be simply a reskin (like the Shark cars), he wanted to see a fundamental change, not just a new fashion statement. The designs were unique and the competition was fierce. Schinella's California-based studio concept, the "Sting Ray III" with its deep, black cherry paint was the first design completed and was well received at the '92 Detroit International Auto Show. However, the Detroit-based design groups were less than thrilled with the car.

After the structure and drivetrain placements were determined, a long series of styling sketches were made, presented, debated, and finalized. Next a full-size clay model was built to work out the styling details. The completed shape had to look "new," yet had to have traditional Corvette styling elements. The curves and fender budges were reminiscent of the Mako Shark II cars of the mid '60s. Once the shape was completed, a running prototype was built.

The backbone chassis and the engine-transaxle placement determined the proportions of the car. With the heavy side rails gone, interior access was much improved. The wheelbase was a 6.8 inches longer, the length decreased by 2 inches, the width grew by .9 inch, and the height was .8 inches taller than a stock Corvette. Most notable was the long, slopped windshield, the narrow feline-like fixed headlights and the roadster-only roof design. The unusual side-view mirrors were swept back and attached to the top of the door and the door frame.

The front suspension used coil-over-shocks and the transaxle was moved back. Unfortunately, there was a V-6 under the hood, which may have been one of the reasons why the design was never seriously considered as the C5 Corvette. Usually, interiors are designed by different groups, but Jordan insisted that the interior layout reflect the design group's thinking. As is the case with most show cars, the seats were in a fixed position and the steering column and pedals were adjustable. Instruments and controls were all grouped to the left and right of the steering wheel, forming a fighter cockpit-like look.

Wheels and tires hadn't yet gotten huge, like today, so the car's 18x10-inch front and 19x10-inch rims on 285/35ZR-18 and 303/35ZR-19 wheel/tire combo filled the wheelwells nicely.

The Sting Ray III never came close to production, although the oval taillights and transaxle were used on the C5 and new C6 now has fixed headlights. But a good design is never wasted. The basic shape became the Cavalier convertible. But I'm sure that's not what Schinella had in mind. The Sting Ray III was the last of the all-out Corvette concept-show cars of the '90s.

CHAPTER 3: CORVETTE SHOW CARS

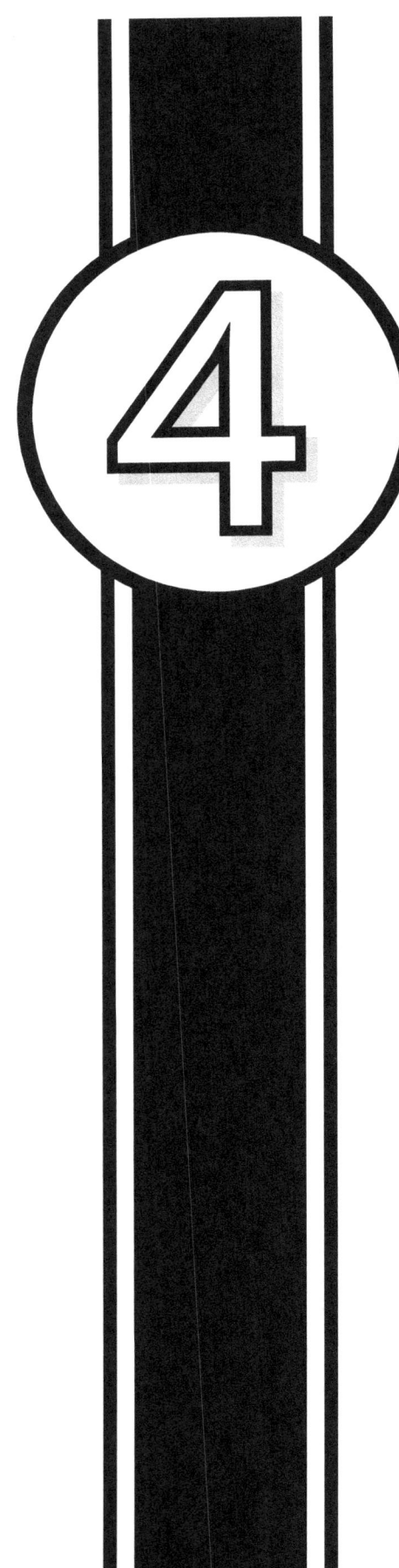

Chapter 4
Racing Corvettes

Were it not for hot racing success, the Corvette surely would have faded after a few years. Good looks might sell a car for a few years, but successful racing will elevate a car to legendary status. From the live-axle C1 to the high-tech C6.R racers, Corvettes have been everything from the underdog to the dominator. Always loud, fast, and fun to watch.

1956 265 V-8 Corvette
"Duntov's Daytona Flyer"

The C6.R is arguably the finest Corvette racing machine to date - a wonder of aluminum, titanium, carbon fiber, and computers. By contrast, the '56 Daytona Speed Weeks Corvette was born of cast iron, steel, fiberglass, and pure guts - lots of guts!.

Appearance aside, the first-generation Vette was far from a true sports car. The car's steel perimeter frame was essentially the same as a regular Chevy sedan. When Duntov started test driving the Corvette, he quickly learned two things; without a steel body, the Chevy sedan frame was quite flexible, and the car understeered a lot. Thanks to the arrival of the '55 Thunderbird, the Corvette was given a second chance for '56 with a completely restyled body, inspired by the '54 Mercedes 300SL. Chevy's 265-ci V-8, new in '55, gave the Corvette a much-needed power boost.

To demonstrate the new V-8's power, Duntov drove a modified '56 Chevy in the Pikes Peak hillclimb event and set a record time of 17 minutes, 24.05 seconds. During a party after the event, Zora told Chevy's, Ed Cole that a race-prepared Corvettes could perhaps touch 150 mph. Cole liked the idea and made Duntov his Corvette-racing field commander.

Duntov started with a '54 Corvette as his test mule. He knew that he needed an additional 30-hp and better aerodynamics. First, he revised the V-8's camshaft to provide the required performance boost. This was the beginning of the famous "Duntov Cam" option. Then he added a tonneau cover to the passenger side, a fairing behind the driver's head, and a full belly-pan. At GM's Phoenix test track, Zora drove the mule to a top speed of 163-mph. In December '55, Duntov took his mule car, fitted it with '56 body panels, and blasted the Daytona beach with a 150.583-mph run. In February '56, he arrived with three race-prepared Corvettes - the mule car and two slightly modified stockers, all painted white with blue stripes and side coves. The mule had cone fairings over the headlights, taping over most of the front grille and fender vents. The other two cars were also equipped, with tonneau covers and taped-up fender vents. Each Vette was powered by a 265 small-block with the Duntov Cam, special 10.3:1 compression heads, and an output of 255 hp. But here's the kicker: Because they were running on packed beach sand, the cars were equipped with snow tires!

Duntov drove the mule, and John Fitch and Betty Skelton drove the two other cars. In the standing mile, Duntov, was the fastest in the modified class with a 89.753-mph run. Chuck Dalgh's T-Bird came in second with a 86.872 mph, and Fitch came in third. But the real bragging rights went to the top-speed event. The Dalgh T-Bird didn't compete, and the Corvettes romped. Fitch won the production-sports-car class with a speed of 145.543-mph, and Skelton came in Second with a 137.773-mph run. Duntov had the fastest time in the modified class with a 147.300-mph run. Strong headwinds kept the Corvettes from passing the 150-mph mark.

The event was so successful, GM gave Duntov the go-ahead to build three more cars and six weeks later, the cars raced at the 12-hours at Sebring. The Corvettes had problems, but managed to finish their first major competition, setting the stage for bigger things to come. And that's how the Corvette racing legend began.

CHAPTER 4: RACING CORVETTES

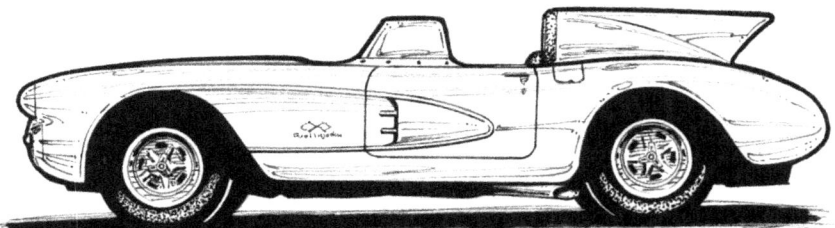

1956 SR-2 Corvette
"Special Racing Corvettes"

The '56 Corvette was so well received that GM executives felt comfortable enough to indulge themselves with special racer versions of their new darling sports car. It all started in the Spring of '56, when Harley Earl's son, Jerry, wanted to race a Ferrari. Harley would have no part of that, so he offered to have his Chevrolet team build Jerry a hot Corvette, and by June, Jerry had his Corvette racer.

Ultimately, three SR-2 Corvettes were built. On the first SR-2 made for Earl, one immediately notices the custom body. Remember, Jerry really wanted a Ferrari. The nose was extended, it had scoops on the doors, twin cut-down windscreens, and a short fin mounted in the center of the trunk lid. The interior had extra instruments, power windows and stock seats. There also was a fire extinguisher, a wood-trimmed steering wheel and a radio. Power came from a basically stock 265, dual-quad stock engine with exhausts exiting just in front of the rear wheels. The Chevrolet R&D guys really weren't race car builders.

Bill Mitchell was Harley Earl's No. 1 man and upon learning of Earl's car, wanted his own SR-2. However Bill's SR-2 was much more involved. From the outside, the most obvious difference was the much taller fin mounted behind the driver, like the Sebring cars from earlier in the year. Also, Bill's SR-2 was 3 inches wider and the body was hand-laid, lightweight fiberglass. The doors were gutted and the handles were replaced with pull-cords. The interior had full carpeting, an

I.D. plate that read, "Chevrolet SR-2 Corvette," and there was a steering column-mounted tachometer. Mitchell's SR-2 also had a 45-gallon fuel tank. Bill had a cleared sense of what a race car needed.

To make sure the SR-2 had the highest blessing, a third car was built for GM's president, Harlow Curtice. This SR-2 was strictly a custom cruiser. It had the low center fin, extended nose, and lots of special touches. The hood had louvers similar to the Sebring cars, but had to be heavily reenforced. The car had blue leather seats, whitewall tires on Dayton wire wheels and a special stainless steel removable top. The total cost of the Curtice SR-2 was $50,000 in '56. A year later, he sold the car to a neighbor.

The entire SR-2 adventure only lasted a year and a half. By December '57 all three cars were sold off. During that time they were all retrofitted with 283 Fuelie engines and 4-speed transmissions. Jerry Earl quickly learned that his car was way too heavy, so it was sent back to Chevrolet for some serious weight reduction. All nonessential hardware was removed and replaced with lighter materials. Jerry liked Mitchell's "high fin" so a similar version was added to his SR-2.

The Mitchell and Earl SR-2's both saw real racing action. Mitchell took his SR-2 to Daytona in February '57 with Buck Baker driving and Smokey Yunick wrenching, the SR-2 took top honors in the modified class with a average speed of 93.047 mph. Later, the car ran second behind a Jaguar D-Type in the flying mile with a speed of 152.866 mph. At the Nassau Tourist Trophy Race in December '57, with NASCAR driver Curtis Turner driving and Smokey Yunick spinning his wrenches, Earl's SR-2 won an early heat, but blew its engine in a second race. Earl then sold the car to Jim Jeffords of Nickey Chevrolet racing team and it raced with the "Purple People Eater" paint scheme and won the SCCA B/Production title in '58. Obviously, the Nickey team effort was more serious, but it showed the car's real potential.

All three SR-2 Corvettes were bought and sold many times. Happily these interesting pieces of early Corvette history are still around.

1957 RPO 684 Corvette
"The First Corvette Racer Kit"

Aside from Corvette racing buffs and historians like me, few Vette fans are aware that from '57 to '62, Chevy's sports car was a dominant force in SCCA racing. So how did a beauty queen in '55 turned into a brute on the race track? Thank Zora Arkus-Duntov. With actual racing experience at Le Mans, he was the only man for the job.

The 265-CID small-block engine arrived just in time for the Corvette. Of the 700 '55 Vettes, only seven had the old "Blue Flame Six" six-cylinder engine. Then, in '56, the Vette got an extensive face-lift. Duntov was already at work on a

souped-up, topless '56 that would go on to blast the beach at Daytona with a 147.300-mph run. The team followed that effort by finishing their first sports car competition at the 12-hour Sebring race. Chevy's ad men took maximum advantage of Duntov's racing exploits by running a full-page print ad showing the '56 racer in the pits of Sebring, with the headline, "THE REAL McCOY." Chevy didn't have a racing reputation then so they were "the new kid on the block," gunning for Fords. Corvette buyers were stoked with the hot-looking new car in full battle regalia.

Duntov and his team took all the lessons they learned at the track and created "heavy duty" parts that were readily available at any Chevrolet dealer. For new '57 Corvette buyers that wanted to race, there were four essential options to get. For $726, RPO 579E got you the racing version of the "Ram Jet" 283 FI engine. The fuelie unit was connected to a fiberglass box mounted to the inside fender well, that was ducted to the front grille. Sales literature described this as "not intended for pleasure driving." The second essential option was the new, $188 Borg-Warner T-10 four-speed transmission. This was a fully synchronized gearbox that required no double clutching. For $15, RPO 276 got you the new "wide" 15 x 5.5-inch steel wheels. The final essential option was RPO 684, the Heavy Duty Racing Suspension. This was the setup that pulled it all together and helped create the Corvette's dominance in SCCA racing in those days. The $780 package included heavy-duty front coil springs, five-leaf rear springs, a larger front sway bar, larger, stiffer shocks, 16.3:1-ratio steering, and heavy-duty brakes with finned aluminum drums and Bendix Cerametallix pads. The rear brake cooling system had ducts running from behind the headlights, down the inside of the rocker panels, and into scoops on the inboard side of each brake's backing plate. Inside each drum was a small metal turbine that pulled hot air out of the drums. Like the L88 that followed it, RPO 684 also deleted the radio and heater and was available from '57 to '59.

The base price of the '57 Vette was $3,176. When you added on $1,727 of racing options, you were looking at a nearly $5,000 car. Keep in mind that a '57 Bel Air Sport Coupe hardtop cost a mere $2,299. Only 43 '57 Corvettes were outfitted with the three main options. RPO 684 would be the first of many racer kits. As for how many of these cars remain, no one knows for sure.

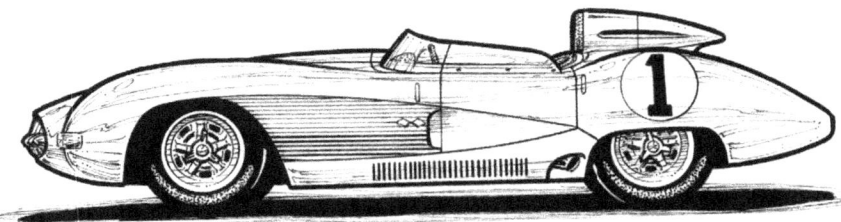

1957 SS Corvette
"Duntov's Le Mans Racer"

The Corvette SS was the first in a long line of great "what if" cars from Chevrolet. The idea of using racing to inspire sales was relatively new to Chevrolet in the mid-'50s. After great press with the '56 Sebring racers and a new fuel injected engine ready for racing battle, Duntov felt it was time to take on Europe's finest and race at Le Mans.

The D-type Jaguar was "the" car to beat in '56. Harley Earl shook up everyone by bringing into the design studio a D-Type Jaguar - the same kind of car the Briggs Cunningham took third place at the '56 Sebring race. No one knows if Earl was really serious, but his suggestion was to rebuild the car with right hand drive, install a Chevy engine, and restyle the car as a Corvette!

Zora Arkus-Duntov was outraged and began his own plan for a Le Mans racer. Zora's plan was quickly approved and the Corvette SS racer was born. But time was not on their side. It was summer of '56 and a Sebring debut was only nine months away. Duntov hand picked his crew and began working day and night. Since his crew had never built such a car, Duntov bought a Mercedes 300SL tube frame to use as a model for the chassis. Duntov only had approval to build one car, but managed to order enough R&D parts to build a mule car at the same time. After all, parts had to tested for fit and function. When the finished car and the mule arrived at Sebring in March '57, the official racer was still being worked on in the transporter. Although not as refined as it looked due to little track development time, the car was stunning.

The steel blue racer looked like an exotic European. Although most of the parts were off the shelf or bought, the entire car was handmade and parts were cast in aluminum wherever possible. Power came from a 283 Fuelie with aluminum heads, 9:1 compression, and long tube headers. The body was even made out of ultra-light magnesium, which turned out to be a major problem. The Corvette SS weighed in at 1850, 100 pounds less that the D-type Jag. But things went badly on the track due to a lack of time. The rough mule car actually ran better than the finished car. The new braking system never got sorted out and the magnesium body made the interior unbearably hot.

The untested car had many problems and only ran 23 laps before it had to retire due to a failed rubber bushing on the rear suspension. Driver, John Fitch felt cheated, lamenting that the effort didn't have another month to sort the car out. In May '57 GM ordered the racing department at Chevrolet (Duntov) to stop all work on the SS racer. By the end of the month it is decided that the SS Corvette would be cleaned up and made into a show car. The following month, plans for the construction of three more SS Corvettes is canceled. GM's official position was that they would adhere to the AMA ban on factory-supported racing. The same month, Duntov is promoted to director of high-performance Chevrolet vehicles. Perhaps a wink and a bone, from GM's management.

But Zora the hot rodder wasn't finished with the SS. After the car was cleaned up and refurbished, in December '58 he took the one-of-a-kind racer out on the GM Phoenix test track and hit 183-mph in the little racer. The same month, Bill Mitchell bought the SS mule chassis and started work on his Sting Ray racer. The following month Zora drove the car at the 2.5-mile Daytona track and got it up to 155-mph. Today, both the Corvette SS and the Sting Ray racer are alive and well.

1959 Stingray Racer
"Executive Privilege"

In December of 1958, one era ended and another began. The legendary Harley Earl retired and 46-year-old William L. Mitchell was the new head of GM's Styling. To mark his territory, Mitchell changed the name of the studio from "Styling" to "Design." Bill had always been a car guy with a passion for performance. Aside from his brief stint with his SR-2, he had never actually campaigned a racer. With a VP's salary and inside connections, Bill had a race car built that thrilled thousands and shaped the Corvette's history.

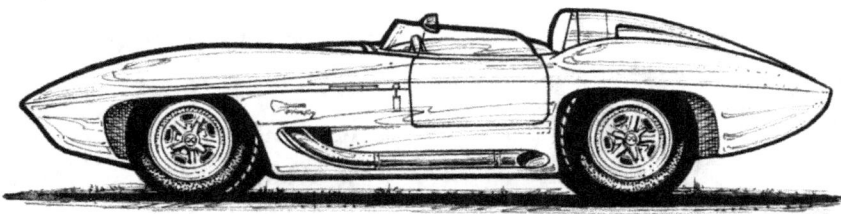

The '57 Corvette SS racer had been put out to pasture as a show car and the Corvette SS mule chassis was placed in storage. Within weeks of taking over as chief of design, Mitchell bought the mule chassis for $1 and brought in stylist Larry Shinoda to create a roadster version of the Q-Corvette body design by Pete Brock and Bob Veryzer, to be used on the Corvette SS mule chassis. Larry gave the roadster a teardrop fairing around the rollbar and a single, short windscreen, similar to the 1956 SR-1 Corvette. When completed, it was totally original and drop-dead gorgeous. An instant classic.

Even though Bill Mitchell officially raced his Sting Ray out of his own pocket, he had ample resources from within Chevrolet. The main problem with the SS Racer's chassis was the braking system. This was due to the complex double-booster setup. Later in the first season, a single Hydrovac power assist system was installed. A disc brake system was ruled out due to cost. Power came from a slightly modified production 283 Fuelie with open headers.

yet thought about chin spoilers. The car's top speed was around 155 mph and was always a very shaky ride.

By April 1959, Mitchell's Sting Ray racer was ready for battle. The first season was a shake out time, something the SS Corvette never had the opportunity to experience. There were several wins and a few crashes. Driver Dick Thompson was suspended 90 days after the first race because of aggressive driving. By October '59, the body had been damaged and repaired enough that it was time for a new skin. The first body was as thick as a production Corvette, but the new version was ultra-thin and used balsa wood for reinforcement.

The 1960 season was the Sting Ray's year to shine and by October Dick Thompson won the points championship. This was a major accomplishment for the Corvette and Duntov. It proved the worth of the basic layout, chassis, suspension, and engine combination that Zora envision in late '56 when work started on the Corvette SS racer.

Later in the month of October '60, Mitchell returned the Sting Ray racer to Chevrolet where the car was cleaned up, refurbished, and decorated with official "Corvette" and "Fuel Injection" badges. From there, it was out to pasture, along with the SS Corvette, as a show car. It's first gig as a show car was at the '61 Chicago Auto Show as a SCCA B/Production champion. Fans were thrilled.

The most challenging aspect of the race car was the Sting Ray's aerodynamics. Designers thought that by making the body flat on the top and rounded on the bottom, they would create an inverted airfoil, a huge air wing that would push the car down onto the track. What actually happened was just the opposite. At speed, the 2,154-pound car would sometimes lift the front wheels off the ground. This was corrected by raising the back end, thus raking the overall stance. Too bad they had not

The Sting Ray racer was even once a movie star and can be seen in the Elvis Presley film, "Clambake." It's arguably the best part of the film.

The Sting Ray racer is still around and received a complete restoration in 2005, except the seats. It was reasoned that because so many famous people sat in and drove the car, the natural patina in the leather should be maintained. If you ever get to see the car in person, you'll be taken back at just how small the car really is, it just looks big.

CHAPTER 4: RACING CORVETTES

1960 Fuel Injected Corvette Racer
"Briggs Cunningham's Le Mans Assault"

Thirty-nine years before the '99 C5-Rs arrived at Le Mans, there was another Corvette team that took the French track by storm. GM's official position was, "We don't race," but that didn't stop Duntov from making hot parts for racers to use on their Vettes. Briggs Swift Cunningham was a wealthy financier, and since the '30s he'd poured millions of dollars into racing his cars and yachts. He racked up dozens of sports-car wins in the '50s and took the America's Cup sailing title in 1958. He had a passion for creating racing teams and competed with the finest European sports cars. But when the big V-8 Corvettes started winning races, Cunningham took notice.

Back in Detroit, Duntov was looking for people to race his Corvettes. In '60, the rules for the GT 5000 class allowed big-engine cars to race at Le Mans. Cunningham loved speed, and Duntov loved seeing Corvettes raced. Briggs built a three-car team, and Lloyd Casner fielded a similar-looking Corvette. Lined up before the race, the four white Corvettes were an imposing sight to the Europeans.

Compared with the modern C5-R and C6.R, the Cunningham and Casner Vettes were amazingly stock. The cars were prepared by Alfred Momo, with help from Duntov, Frank Burrell, and a few other Corvette engineers. All used a lightly modified 283/290hp Fuelie engine with cast-iron manifolds, side-exit exhausts, and an oil cooler. Racing drum brakes were installed, along with Halibrand magnesium knock-off wheels and racing tires. An oversized gas tank was added and fitted with a center-mounted, quick-fill cap. The interior had a roll bar, special instruments, racing bucket seats, and an adjustable steering column. All of the cars were fitted with a bolted-on hardtop and painted white with blue stripes.

Le Mans is all about speed and endurance. Car No. 1 crashed and burned after three hours of racing. At the 17th hour, the Fuelie engine in car No. 2 expired. At hour 22, car No. 3, with Bob Grossman and John Fitch driving, suffered a broken radiator cap that led to a blown head gasket. The engine was packed with ice, and the car finished the race in Eighth overall and First in the GT 5000 class. The Casner car finished Twenty-first overall. The fastest of the Corvettes hit 151 mph on the Mulsanne Straight and recorded a 4:26.2 lap time.

Production Vettes wouldn't see 150 mph until the arrival of the big-blocks. Briggs Cunningham knew how to build fast endurance cars, and Duntov was all too happy to provide unofficial assistance from Chevrolet. This was the juicy stuff of legends.

Gulf One '62 Corvette
"The Most Successful C1 Racer?"

The Grady Davis' Gulf Oil '62 Fuelie is one of the most successful single C1 Corvette race cars ever. In 1962, the car competed in the SCCA's A/Production class with Dr. Dick Thompson behind the wheel and won 12 out of 14 races-an 85.7 percent win rate. We're not slighting the huge success of the C5-R or C6.R Corvettes, but those wins were achieved by a two-car team.

It's amazing how close this car is to a street Corvette. When Gulf Oil executive ordered the car, he specified four options. RPO 582 got him the 327/360hp fuelie engine, RPO 685 added a Borg-Warner T-10 four-speed transmission, RPO 687 added the heavy-duty brakes and special steering, and RPO 675 brought a Positraction rear. The total cost for a car such as this was around $5,300 - a lot of money in '62.

After the car was purchased, it was driven to Yenko Chevrolet for race prep. Don Yenko's team had a lot of experience in turning Corvettes into race cars, so the car was well prepared. Almost all of the prep work was bolted on and easily removable, as we'll see later.

Davis' Corvette got the standard prep treatment. The front and rear bumpers were removed, and vents and a deflector were added to the hood. A 37-gallon fuel tank was added, and the rear glass was modified to accommodated a quick-fill gas cap. Plexiglas replaced the side windows, and an aluminum racing seat replaced the stock bucket. Stewart-Warner gauges were added, along with a Motorola two-way radio. A roll bar was installed, and the interior carpeting was replaced with rubber mats. Chromed-steel lift bars were added to the front and rear to assist in pit stops. The engine was essentially stock, with the factory cast-iron exhaust manifolds connected to 2-1/4-inch exhaust pipes that exited just ahead of the rear wheels. Koni shocks were used, and Goodyear Blue Streak 7.00-15 tires were mounted on the stock steel wheels. FIA-required marker lights were added to the roof and passenger side, and the stock Ermine White body was treated to a blue racing stripe with matching side coves, and identification numbers. From there, it was off to the races.

At its first race, at Daytona in January, the Gulf Oil Corvette came in Second. The next month, the car took First Place at the Daytona Continental. In March, the team took another First Place win at Sebring. At the Washington Marlboro Governor's race, the car did not finish. Then, from the Virginia International President's Cup race in April to the final race at the Watkins Glen Grand Prix, Davis' Fuelie won every time to take the A/Production Championship.

Davis sold his Fuelie to Tony Denman in favor of a new '63 Z06. But the '62 was still potent enough to take the pole position at Daytona in January of 1963. Denman raced the car a few times, then converted it back to a street car. For the next 16 years, the car's owners didn't have a clue that they were driving a former A/Production champion, until Reverend Mike Ernst bought the Vette off of a used-car lot for $3,500 in 1979. Ernst researched its past, and restored the car to its former glory. Since then, the car has had several owners and restorations. In August 2008, at the Pebble Beach Concours d'Elegance, the Gulf Oil '62 Corvette sold for $1,485,000. Lots of cars have sold for over $1 million at vintage car auctions, but when it's an old Chevy racer that cost $5,300 new, people take notice.

CHAPTER 4: RACING CORVETTES

1963 ZR-1 Corvette
"The Original ZR-1"

Corvette racers never had a better friend than Zora Arkus-Duntov. For the most part, Zora was good at sidestepping GM's "we don't race" edict. For those who knew what to look for, there were always plenty of "heavy-duty" and "off-road" options for Corvettes. As the new Sting Ray was being prepared for the '63 launch, Duntov assembled the most advanced Corvette racer kit to that date - the Z06.

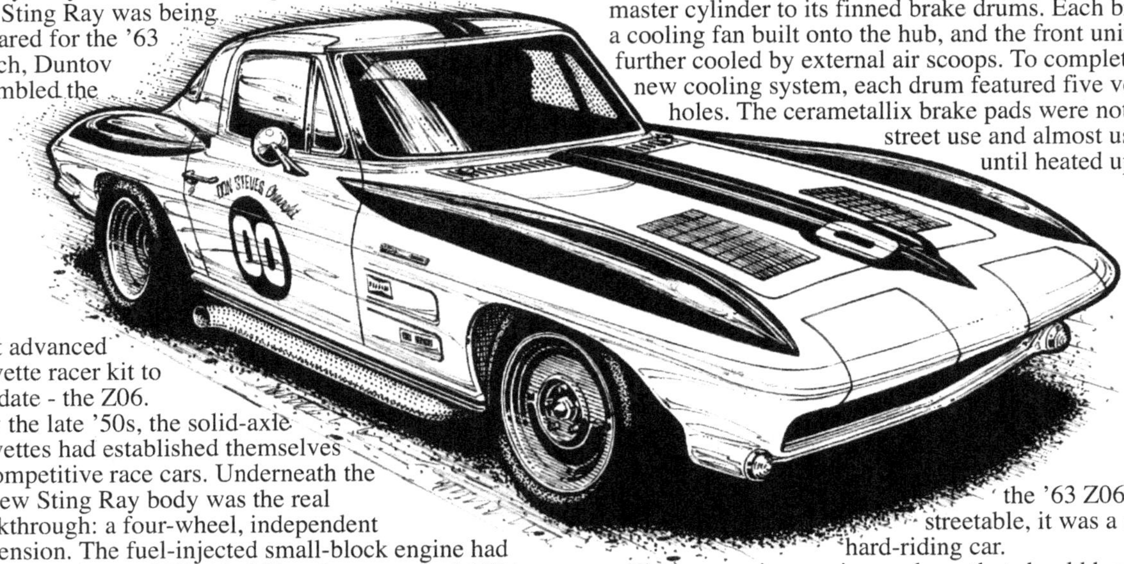

By the late '50s, the solid-axle Corvettes had established themselves as competitive race cars. Underneath the all-new Sting Ray body was the real breakthrough: a four-wheel, independent suspension. The fuel-injected small-block engine had been opened up to 327-ci in '62 and now packed 360 hp. The all-new suspension of the Sting Ray was essential to better use the extra power on the race track.

The Z06 package was the most expensive Corvette option offered to that date. Costing $1,818, the Z06 option was very pricey. Plus, there were other options that were mandatory for the Z06, including; the L84 Fuel-Injected 327, the close-ratio 4-speed transmission, and the positraction rear axle. These goodies added an extra $661, for a complete price of $2,479, on top of the $4,252 base price of the car. Buyers were looking at a $7,000 Corvette in 1963! You could buy a loaded '63 SS Impala for just over $3,000.

The hardware included in the Z06 package was amazingly advanced for its time. With plenty of power on tap, most of the Z06 extras were designed to enhance the suspension and brakes. The front suspension had stiffer shocks, beefier springs, and a thicker, .94-inch stabilized bar. The rear suspension had a 7-leaf transverse spring - two more than the stock setup. To fit the larger 7.75 x 15 racing tires, the rear inner wheelwells were wider. The knock-off alloy wheels were an on, and off, and on again part of the Z06 package. Not all Z06 cars had the knockoff wheels. To reduce the number of pit stops, a 36.5-gallon fiberglass gas tank was included.

But the real advancement could be found in the car's race-designed braking system. Many of the older Corvette race cars had less than inadequate brakes. The system was completely new, from its vacuum-assisted, dual-circuit master cylinder to its finned brake drums. Each brake had a cooling fan built onto the hub, and the front units were further cooled by external air scoops. To complete the new cooling system, each drum featured five vent holes. The cerametallix brake pads were not for street use and almost useless until heated up. While the '63 Z06 was streetable, it was a noisy, hard-riding car.

This was an impressive package that should have propelled the new Sting Ray into the winner's circle. Unfortunately, there was another race machine being built at the time by a Texas chicken farmer/racer named Carroll Shelby. Shelby's little Cobra had as much power as the Corvette and weighed 1,000 pounds less. But because they were both considered "production cars," the Vette and the Cobra competed in the same class. Mickey Thompson raced one of the first six Z06 cars and won the L.A. Times Three Hour International in October, 1963. It was a default win, however, as the leading Shelby Cobra broke.

The Z06 package had no external markings, so it never developed the kind of status enjoyed by the L88. Until the arrival of the '01 Z06, the '63 Z06 Vettes were mostly forgotten. But the Cobra problem aside, Z06 equipped Corvettes did rack up wins. The official Z06 production count was 199 units, making the Z06 one of the rarest Vettes ever offered.

Meanwhile, back in his private skunkworks, Duntov was working on a Cobra-killer. It was called the "Grand Sport."

1963 Grand Sport Corvette
"Chevy's Cobra Killer"

The '63 Grand Sport is arguably the ultimate "could-have-been" Corvette. Had GM not pulled the plug, and given the car some development time, this 2,100 pound monster could have been a true snake-killer. But it wasn't to be.

Grand Sport's problem wasn't a lack of hardware or technical assistance, it was political. The problem began with the '57 Automobile Manufactures Association ban on factory supported racing. At first, Ford, GM and Chrysler complied, but by 1960 Ford and Pontiac were developing racing programs despite the AMA ban. In June of '62, Ford and Chrysler announced that they would ignore the AMA ban and openly develop racing programs. Then Ford backed the Shelby Cobras that all but obliterated the new Z06 Sting Ray's chances of success. But Duntov had a powerful ally, Chevrolet division head, Semon Knudsen.

Zora figured that if Pontiac was developing the Super Duty program and other groups in Chevrolet were developing the Mark II Mystery Motor, he should be working on a real racing version of the 1963 Stingray. In June '62 Knudsen approved the construction of 125 lightweight Grand Sport Corvettes - 25 for Chevrolet and 100 to be sold to privateers. This would homologate the cars as official GT Class production automobiles.

Five pilot cars based on the new Sting Ray were built in order to sort out the design and production of the remaining 120 cars. The bar was set high with a target weight of just 1,900 lbs, using an all-aluminum 377-ci small-block, making 550 horsepower! The production steel frame was replaced with a lightweight tube frame that utilized near-production suspension parts. This was to be a 180-mph Corvette. Everything was strictly racing! The body was made of very thin fiberglass and almost stock except for the nose and rear window. After its initial outing in '63 the GS grew all sorts of flairs, scoops and bulges. The interior looked stock, except for the racing bucket seats, roll cage, and 200 mph speedometer! Initial tests were promising and Duntov was confident that the GS had a good shot at the Cobras.

The car's best effort was its first race at the Nassau Speed Week in November of '63. It just so happened that Duntov and a small team of his engineers were on vacation at Nassau that very same week! When the team of three Grand Sports arrived at the track looking lean and tough, Carroll Shelby was NOT happy. The Cobras got a good thrashing, as the Corvettes took all three races. Duntov and his team were elated!

When the cars were returned to Michigan, Duntov had a long list of improvements for his team to complete before the next race. That's when Zora lost his ally. Kundsen got a dressing down for approving the program and was ordered to dispose of the five cars. Fortunately, the cars were sold to the men that drove them at Nassau and were raced independently from '64 to '66. Without factory support, the Grand Sports never lived up to their potential. But fans never forgot and the Grand Sports became the ultimate Corvette legends.

CHAPTER 4: RACING CORVETTES

Gulf One 1963 Z06 Corvette
"The $1.113 Million Sting Ray"

In January '09, attendees of the Mecum Muscle Cars & More Auction got to witness the historic '63 "Gulf One" racing Z06 Corvette sell for $1.113 million. While that's not the highest price ever paid for a Corvette at auction, the audience went wild. After all, any time an old race car that cost around $6,000 new, sells for over a $1 million, it's an exciting thing. Plus, there were three surprises that came out of the auction itself.

The first came in the form of the man who spent more time behind the wheel of the car than any other driver, 88-year-old Dr. Dick "The Flying Dentist" Thompson. It was great to see Mr. Thompson there and he's a man of few words. When asked about the car, he simply said, "I enjoyed driving this car very much. It sure looks a lot better now than when I was racing. A little work's been done on it. I had hoped to drive this car at Le Mans, but it didn't work out that way. It would have done real well, I think. It was a great car to drive."

Did he say, "Le Mans"? That was the second big surprise. Z06 authority Eric Gill presented an internal Chevrolet document indicating that the Gulf One Z06 was to be raced at Le Mans in '63. In the end GM decided to enforce its ban on racing and killed the trip.

The last surprise was the car's selling price. In August '08 the Gulf One No. 2 '62 racer sold at auction for a whopping $1.485 million. The owners were hoping for more, but still, it was the first '63 Z06 to sell for over $1 million.

Let's have a look at what made this car so special. The '63 Z06 option was a "racer kit" and was never intended to be used on the street. But like the L88 kits from '67 to '69, a few of these cars were used as street drivers. Of the 199 Z06s built in 1963, only 124 had the radio/defroster delete option, and only 63 had the oversized 36-gallon fuel tank. The $1.818 Z06 option on top of the $4,257 baseprice brought the total to $6,075. For a little perspective, a '63 SS Impala could be purchased for around $3,200. Later in '63, it was discovered that the Z06's new cast-aluminum knockoff wheels were having problems holding tire pressure. They were removed from the package, lowering the option's price to $1,293.

Duntov designed the Z06 package to take advantage of the Sting Ray's new chassis and four-wheel independent suspension. The option provided a platform upon which a racer could, with good preparation, have a competitive Corvette race car. It included the 360-hp L84 "Fuelie" 327 engine, an M-20 four-speed transmission, higher-rate front and rear springs, heavy-duty shocks and stabilizer bars, a 36-gallon fuel tank, and finned aluminum knock-off wheels. Most elaborate was the braking system, which included finned aluminum drums, internal cooling fans, vented back plates, cerametallic linings, and a dual-circuit master cylinder.

The Z06 racer kit was supposed to keep the Corvette in the winner's circle, but there was the Shelby Cobra issue. The power-to-weight ratio difference was simply too great. Actually, the two cars shouldn't have been in the same class.

Corvettes wouldn't get their edge back until the arrival of the L88's in '67. Like most race cars, the Gulf One '63 was bought and sold many times. Interest in the '63 Z06s was pretty much gone until the moniker came back in 2001. Today, the Gulf One '63 takes its place in the survivors' club of Corvette-racing history.

1963 Grand Sport Corvette Roadster
"The Cobra Killer's Last Chance"

Road racing in America went through a tremendous growth period during the mid '60s. A competitive race car could be obsolete in only two years. Duntov and his crew quietly started building five Grand Sports in June '62 1962. Three of the Grand Sport Coupes got plenty attention at their debut race in Nassau, such that GM brass ordered the program halted. "We don't race!"

One race certainly isn't enough to sort out a race car, but it was obvious that three GS cars needed help. It was well known that roadsters had less wind resistance, so Duntov ordered two of the GS cars to be made into roadsters with short, cut down windshields, for "evaluation." The three coupes were sold in 1964 and the two roadsters were supposed to be sent to the crusher. Somehow, Duntov managed to avoid that fate. In 1965 one of the roadsters surfaced at a car show at Notre Dame University. Someone in the press quipped that a Grand Sport with the new 427 NASCAR engine might be an interesting race car. Enter Roger Penske.

Penske was planning to race a 427 Coupe that year and was offered the two remaining Grand Sport Roadsters to add to his team. Assisting in the preparations was veteran Corvette racer, Dick Guldstrand. The team knew that the Grand Sport was getting tired, but it was too tempting to pass up. Guldstrand supervised the complete rebuilding of one of the roadsters and the necessary changes required for the Traco Engineering-built, 500-horsepower, big-block 427 engine.

By the time the Grand Sport Roadster made it to Sebring in March 1966, the four-year-old car was seriously outdated. But it was a valiant effort that might have had a chance with some factory support. The biggest problem was still the suspension and it's infamous front end lift.

Driver Delmo Johnson was quoted as saying, "As far as I'm concerned, if any driver ever says he had complete control of that car, he's lying to you." Between the front end lift and the power from the 427, Roger Penske said, "It was so light in the front end that when you really stood on the gas, the front end would come off the ground like a dragster."

Power was not a problem for the roadster. During practice, Guldstrand reported that he could easily blow off even the Ford Mark II cars. A. J. Foyt got dusted and was quoted as saying, "What's in that damn dinosaur? It went by me like I was stopped." During actual racing, the car was embarrassingly inadequate. It's really quite unfortunate because all the car needed was a little suspension work. Although based on a lightweight tube frame, the suspension was essentially the same as the later highly successful L88 racing Corvettes.

Penske sold roadster 001 to John Mecam and roadster 002 to George Wintersteen who raced the car and later sold it for $6,700. George still regrets the sale. But, racers race cars, they don't save them, and no one knew how valuable they'd become many decades later.

The Grand Sports were the ultimate "could have been" racing Corvettes. Completely lost in the '70s, they have all been found, restored, and are now some of the most valuable Corvettes ever made. Today, Grand Sport replicas are quite popular and bloody fast.

Roger Penske's 1966 L-88 Corvette
"The First L-88 Racer"

Roger Penske began racing in '58 at the Marlboro Motor Raceway in Maryland. By 1960 he'd won the Sports Illustrated SCCA Driver of the Year award. Zora Duntov recognized Roger's skills and hired him as a driver for the '63 Grand Sport Nassau assault and a lasting friendship was formed. Race cars were becoming brutally fast, and many talented drivers were being injured or killed. In '65 Penske hung up his helmet and focused on his new Cadillac dealership. Then one day, Duntov called.

Zora was working on a new weapon to take on the 427 Cobras, called the "L88." Duntov asked if Roger was interested in a pre-production L88 to use for a little "field testing."

In '62, Chevrolet began work on a replacement for the 348/409 truck engine. A few prototypes were let out the back door to be used for NASCAR evaluation. Car magazines called the new engine "Chevy's Mystery Motor." The big-block finally made it into production in '65 as a 396, with a 427 version following a year later. Ever the fox, Zora had an even more radical plan in mind.

Corvette racer kits had been available since '57, but this was like no other. At center stage was the L88 engine that was basically an L72 427 on steroids. Packing 12.5:1 compression, solid lifters, a racing camshaft, a big 850 cfm Holley carb with no choke, an aluminum intake manifold, and a TI ignition, this was not a street-car engine. Also included were the J56 heavy-duty brakes, a 36-gallon fuel tank, the F41 heavy-duty suspension, a prototype Positraction differential with 2.73 gearing, an M-22 rock crusher transmission, off-road exhaust, a teakwood steering wheel with telescoping column, heater and radio deletes, and a prototype cowl-induction hood. Needless to say, Penske accepted Duntov's offer.

Penske worked out a one-race sponsorship deal with Sunoco and assembled a team to run in the 24 Hours at Daytona. California Corvette racer Dick Guldstrand was hired to help prep the L88 and co-drive with George Winterseen. Dick picked up the L88 beast at the St. Louis assembly plant and drove 800 miles to Penske's Pennsylvania shop, in January, with no heater and just a furniture blanket to keep warm.

Once in the shop, 100 pounds were removed through the use of aluminum replacement parts. Magnesium racing wheels with wide tires necessitated small aluminum flares on the wheel wells. The rear fenders were also bulged out, and the trailing arms were notched. Suspension bushings were replaced with aluminum spacers, dual electric pumps and an engine-oil cooler were added, and extra-large header side pipes were installed. The interior got a roll bar, racing gauges, and shut-off switches. Racing headlights with clear covers were added, and every nut and bolt was safety wired. The team worked around the clock up to the day of the event.

The competition was very tough. In the middle of the night, the Corvette t-boned a slower car, losing most of its front end. The team wired the body together and taped flashlights to the front fenders for light! Despite this handicap, the team won First in the GT class, 11th overall, and hit 168 mph on the Daytona back stretch!

Sunoco was so pleased with Penske's performance, they extended his sponsorship to cover the 12 Hours at Sebring, where the L88 won the GT class and came in Ninth overall. Roger Penske's new career as a team owner had officially begun. Penske sold the car after Sebring, and subsequently it was raced in many different forms. It was even converted into a street machine at one point. The car's current owner, Kevin Mackay, did a total restoration in 2001 and has since earned the NCRS American Heritage Award. Today, the L88 prototype is completely functional and considered by many to be one of the finest examples of Corvette racing history in existence.

THE ILLUSTRATED CORVETTE SERIES

1967 427 L-88 Drag Racer Corvette
"In Memory of Astoria-Chas"

From its earliest days, drag racing was the little guy's motorsport. Guys wrenched on their street cars during the week and raced at their local drag strip on the weekend. The tale of Charlie Snyder's "KO Motion" L88 '67 Corvette reads like the Buddy Holly story of drag racing.

During the late '60s, Long Island, New York, was a hotbed of muscle car activity. Motion Performance owner Joel Rosen had a sweet deal with the owners of the local Chevy dealer, Baldwin Chevrolet. Rosen was building brand-new Chevy Phase III supercars while his business partner and friend, Marty Schorr, then editor of CARS magazine, kept Chevy fans drooling with road tests and photo features of Motion's activities. These were exciting times for high performance street cars.

Charlie "Chas" Snyder was a local guy who lived in Astoria, New York, not far from Rosen's operation. In February '67, the 19-year-old Snyder took delivery of a new Marlboro Maroon 427 Corvette roadster. He took the car straight to Rosen's shop for some serious tweaking. It wasn't long before Snyder's Vette was winning at both the local strip and the late-night street-racing scene on Connecting Highway in Queens.

But Rosen's tuning proved to be more than the Sting Ray's steel frame was ever designed for. The twisted frame was replaced with a new gusset-welded unit, and a fresh L88 427 engine was installed.

Shortly later, Snyder, by then 20, was drafted into the Army, so racing took a back seat his Army duties. Soon Rosen had the KO Motion car running low 11s. Then Snyder volunteered for Airborne Ranger training and was sent to Vietnam in the spring of '68. One month after his arrival, he was killed by a mortar round.

The Snyder family and his friends at Motion Performance were devastated. A year later, Chas' mother gave Rosen and driver John Mahler permission to race the car with the goal of setting the national record for Chas. When Rosen was ready for the AHRA record run, the L88 was chock-full of the hottest parts from Chevrolet and the after market. The L88 was balanced and blueprinted, and its bottom end was beefed up. Modified aluminum heads, a performance camshaft, an 850-cfm Holley double-pumper, Hooker headers, 4.88 rear gears, a Hurst shifter, and 10-inch slicks were added. With Bill Foster at the wheel, Snyder's L88 took the AHRA A/Sport Production national record with an 11.04 e.t. @ 129-mph. The official listing in the record book reads, "In Memory of Astoria Chas." Later, John Mahler ran a 10.47 at a local track.

The car was then trailered to Snyder's sister's house, garaged, and covered for the next 31 years! Long Island businessman Glen Spielberg was just eight years old when he first saw the KO Motion car and knew he had to have it some day. After three decades, the Snyder family finally agreed to sell the car to Spielberg on the condition that he would not restore or modify it. Today, the car is as it was the last day it was raced. The Buddy Holly of Corvettes lives on.

1967 - 1969 L88 Corvette
"L88s Go On The Attack!"

From '56 to '75. Duntov created a foundation of uncompromising performance for the GM's flagship sports car. Were it not for his personal racing experience and his never-ending push for improvement, GM surely would have axed the car early on.

The '63 Sting Ray should have put the Corvette ahead of the competition, but with the advent of the Shelby Cobra and the death of the Grand Sport, the Vette remained outgunned until the arrival of Duntov's stealth bomber, the '67 L88.

While an L88 Corvette was some 900 pounds heavier than a '63 Grand Sport, Duntov took the car as far as he could. The L88 Vettes were one tick away from being all-out race cars. As everyday drivers, they were all but unusable, just the way Duntov wanted it. Here's why.

By the mid-'60s hot-rodders and wannabe racers were buying anything with big power numbers. While the big-block Chevys were beasts for the street, the L88 was designed for one thing: racing. In the brochure, the L88 looked like a second-rate performer, rated at just 430-HP, five less than the 427/435 L71! Luxury options? Fuggetaboutit! The L88 had a special "delete option" that removed items such as the heater, the radio, the A/C, and the radiator shroud. The engine had aluminum heads, a radical cam, a huge four-barrel carb, 12:1 compression, a 103-octane fuel requirement, and a 2,000-rpm idle. With open headers and a sharp tune, an L88 could generate over 600 hp.

The L88's suspension also race-ready. The F41 suspension included stiffer shocks and springs, front and rear anti-sway bars, and racing brakes. Fender flares to cover racing tires were included in the trunk. With the $947 L88, and other required options, buyers were looking at a 50-percent increase over the base price, making the L88 package the most expensive Corvette to date. This was a low-profile package and no badges were added. During the three years the option was offered, '67 through '69, only 216 L88s were ordered.

Sunray Oil Company sponsored a pre-production '67 L88 Corvette with the help of Don Yenko. Three weeks after Yenko took delivery, the car was on the starting grid for the 12 Hours of Sebring. Driven by Yenko and Dave Morgan, the Sunray Oil Vette smashed the GT class track record, won First in class, and Tenth overall. At the '68 24 Hours at Daytona race, the car ran 194 mph on the high-banked track.

The James Garner American International Racing team took delivery of three '68 L88 Corvettes that were prepared by Dick Guldstrand. Two of the cars raced at the 24 Hours at Daytona. Car No. 44 finished the race but was sold when the team switched to Lola T70 Mk II coupes. Many years and many racers later, the car was completely restored and sometimes runs at historic races.

The most successful of the L88 Corvettes was the Owen-Corning Fiberglass car of Tony DeLorenzo and Jerry Thompson. Although not a numbers-matching L88 car, this all-out A/Production racer racked up 22 straight class wins, qualified

on the pole at most of its races, and won two national championships. At the end of '71, OCF decided that they had gotten enough out of racing and pulled the sponsorship.

Duntov envisioned a much lighter car, but the L88 package proved that with 600-plus hp and suspension parts to back it up, the Corvette once again had a fighting chance on the race track.

1970-1/2 - 1972 ZR-1 Corvette
"The Original ZR-1"

By '70, the Detroit performance party was largely over due to concerns over leaded gasoline and insurance rates for muscle cars. While the GM brass was putting the kibosh on speed, Duntov was working to keep it alive.

In February of '69, as the new general manager at Chevrolet, John DeLorean and his product planners were working on a new theme for the Vette: the luxury sports car. The $158 Custom Interior Trim option was just the beginning of the added creature comforts that would define the Corvettes of the '70s.

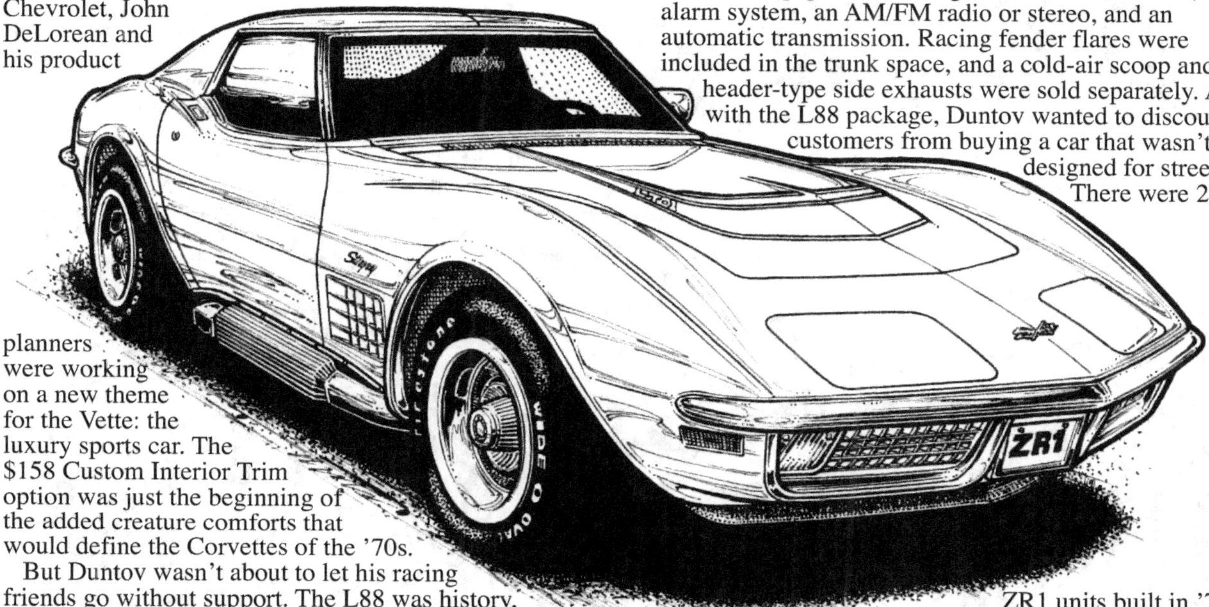

But Duntov wasn't about to let his racing friends go without support. The L88 was history, and the ZL1 was a crate motor. The hot new engines were the LT1 350 and the LS5 454. For the racers, there was the LT1–based ZR1 option, and the planned LS7-based ZR2. Unfortunately, the ZR2 never made it into production in '70, but it did make a brief appearance in '71 with the detuned LS6 454. Only 12 of the $1,747 ZL2 cars were made. This was the base car for big-block road racers in the '70s.

The ZR1 and the ZR2 were officially designated as "off road," which translated to "racing only." Like the '67 to '69 L88 cars, the ZR Corvettes were not happy on the street, but they did provide an excellent base on which to build SCCA Class A or Class B racers. The '70 ZR1 package cost $968 and included the following: the solid-lifter, 370-horsepower LT-1 engine; an M22 four-speed transmission, heavy-duty power brakes, a transistor ignition, a special aluminum radiator, a metal radiator shroud, special springs and shocks, and front and rear stabilized bars. Not available with the ZR-1 was power windows, a rear-window defroster, air conditioning, power steering, deluxe wheel covers, an alarm system, an AM/FM radio or stereo, and an automatic transmission. Racing fender flares were included in the trunk space, and a cold-air scoop and header-type side exhausts were sold separately. As with the L88 package, Duntov wanted to discourage customers from buying a car that wasn't designed for street use.

There were 25 ZR1 units built in '70, 8 units built in '71, and 20 units built in '72. When the 454 ZR2 option was released in '71, only 12 units were built. All of the ZR Corvettes were built by Chevrolet's "Repair Department" in St. Louis.

The '70-1/2 Vette received a minor makeover. There was the revised, egg-crate grille and matching side vents, square front turn-signal lights, rectangular exhaust tips, and flares on the back edges of the wheel openings. Positraction and tinted glass were now standard. The LT-1 and ZR1 option included the big-block hood with pinstriping and "LT-1" lettering.

It would be 18 years before the ZR1 name would resurface in '90, and another 19 years before the '09 version showed up. It was definitely worth the wait!

CHAPTER 4: RACING CORVETTES

John Greenwood's 1972 ZL-1 Corvette
"B. F. Goodrich Street-Tire Racer"

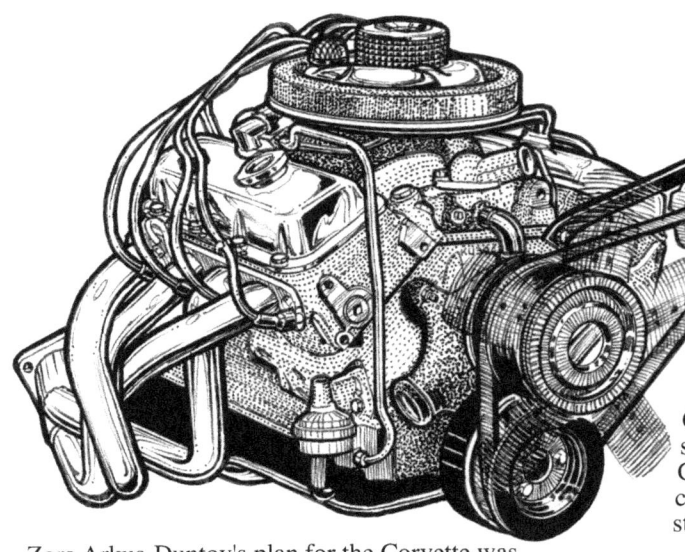

Zora Arkus-Duntov's plan for the Corvette was two-fold. First, he wanted to make the Corvette the kind of car that was capable of being driven at 100-percent by 10-percent of the Corvette drivers. And second, if the stock Corvette wasn't up to delivering what the customer wanted, he could buy all of the go fast

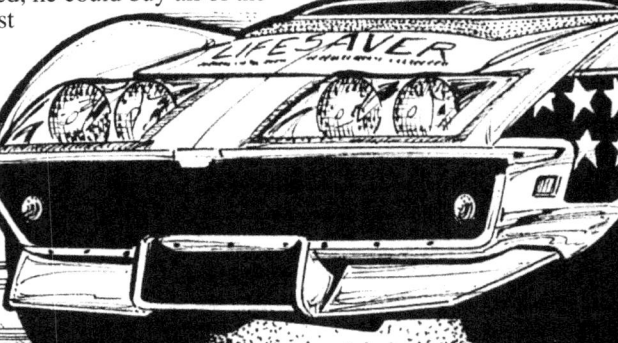

parts he needed from his local Chevy Parts Department. This basic plan not only helped win races, but helped make legends.

John Greenwood was a typical drag racing guy in the '60s. At his wife's suggestion, John discovered the fun of gymkhana competition at a local supermarket parking lot in his '68 427 L88 Corvette. Having been bitten by the road racing bug, he went to road racing school to get his SCCA driver's license. John already knew

how to goose a big-block Chevy for more power and by 1970, he was racing an A/Production, 427 Corvette.

In short order, John defeated the Owens-Corning Corvette team of Tony DeLorenzo and Jerry Thompson after they'd won 22 straight races. Driving with comic Dick Smothers, John then went on to win the American Road Race Championship in '70 and '71. Greenwood was beginning to get a lot of attention. BF Goodrich had a racing marketing program and financed Greenwood with over 6-figures to race on their new, high-performance street radial tires. This was a radical plan, but the cash was great.

With great financing and sponsors like Briggs Chevrolet, John was racing big-time. Although racing on street tires put the car at a slight disadvantage, Greenwood's strategy was to race the long courses where cornering power wasn't as critical as speed on the straights.

The plan sort of worked. Greenwood's cars always qualified well and often set records. At Le Mans his ZL-1 powered car was clocked at over 200 mph! But hardware woes hurt the team for two years, and BF Goodrich ended their sponsorship after the '73 season.

In '71 John created "John Greenwood Sales" in partnership with Briggs Chevrolet. Here's where John really made his mark in Corvette history. By using his skills as a parts developer, John made and sold go-fast hardware. Racers could get everything from body parts and tube chassis, to suspension systems and window nets. Everything was race tested and proven.

John may not have won as many races as he wanted to, but he sure helped a lot of other guys make their Corvettes winners.

1972 L-88 Corvette
"Heinz & Johnson Le Mans Racer"

One of the most important aspects of the Corvette story is its racing heritage. Were it not for Duntov's insistence that Corvette customers have access to well-engineered performance parts for their Corvettes, there would have been very few successful Corvette race cars.

Over the years, Corvettes had not done well at the 24 Hours of Le Mans. It had been 12 years since the Briggs Cunningham Le Mans assault. Many Corvettes had raced at Le Mans with astonishing lap times and top speed blasts down the Mulsanne Straight, only to have some minor part break, forcing the cars out of the race. But that's what endurance racing is all about. Although it is known as the "Heinz & Johnson" racer, the car was owned by Toye English and worked on by his son, Dave. After taking first in GT class at the 24 Hours of Daytona and the 12 Hours of Sebring, the team decided to race the car at Le Mans.

When they arrived at the race, they weren't allowed to race because they did not have an invitation! Luigi Chinetti, an importer of Ferraris, had entered only two cars and agreed to let the Toye English team use his third invitation, as long as they repainted the car to look like Chinetti's Ferraris: red with a blue and white stripe, and wearing the N.A.R.T. decal. A small price to pay after taking the car and crew all the way to Le Mans, France.

The racer could not have performed better. For the entire 24 hours all the Corvette needed was a driver change every hour, gas, tires, and oil. On the very long Mulsanne Straight, the car big-block Vette topped out at 210 mph! Only the prototype cars were faster.

The Corvettes were the biggest and heaviest cars in the GT Class, prompting many to ask, "What's in that dinosaur?" Oh, just good, strong, Chevy parts, thanks to Duntov and crew. The car is basically a '68 L88 model. Under the hood, the L88 was balanced and blueprinted, with an 850 Holley carb on an aluminum high-rise manifold, and header-side exhausts that helped crank out over 560 horsepower. The suspension used heavy-duty L88 parts, along with solid suspension bushings, heavy-duty springs, anti-roll bars, and double-adjustable Koni shocks. A standard M22 transmission and heavy-duty Posi unit were used as well.

Racing body work included factory L88 fender flares, L88 hood with the cowl-induction, plexi racing headlight covers, and the factory hardtop. A front spoiler helped keep the front end down on the 3.7-mile Mulsanne Straight. The interior had a full compliment of gauges, a bolt-on eight-point roll cage and a Vega steering wheel. American Torque-Thrust aluminum wheels and Goodyear racing tires gave the car a distinctly American musclecar, tough guy look. This is exactly what Zora had in mind with his "for racing only" parts program. With the right parts, carefully assembled, and Dave Heinz and Bob Johnson behind the wheel, an independent team had a chance. Completing the 24 Hours of Le Mans is an amazing achievement for any car, let alone a production car with over-the-counter, bolt-on factory parts.

CHAPTER 4: RACING CORVETTES

John Greenwood's 1976 Wide-Body IMSA Corvette
"The Batmobile"

John Greenwood was described as "the perfect Corvette guy." He was well financed, blue-collar, and liked getting dirty working on his race car. Also, he was good at building very powerful big-block Chevy engines. In a field of factory-supported SCCA A/Production and Trans-Am cars, Greenwood was a classic underdog, the Grumpy Jenkins of road racing. John had been beating up Porsches and BMWs since the early '70s with his homemade, 8,000 rpm ZL1 Corvettes. His "Spirit of Sebring '76" Corvette was to be the wildest race car ride of his career.

Although the car was called a "tube framed" car, John started with a stock Corvette steel birdcage frame that was first gusseted for added strength, with the tube frame then welded on. The front suspension used stock mounting points, but was lowered using 25 percent stiffer springs, adjustable Koni shocks, and various size sway bars. The rear suspension used coilover shocks, twin A-arms, and sway bars to eliminate squat. For those long, high-speed straights, Greenwood used 2.73:1 rear gearing. Hurst-Airheart NASCAR disc brakes with dual master cylinders provided excellent braking. With the huge factory-option pontoon fenders, John was able to use Sterling alloy wheels 11" x 15" in the front and 17" x 15" in the rear, with Goodyear Blue Streak tires 24.5 x 10-15 on the front and 28.0 x 17-15 on the rear. Corvette race cars had long since progressed past the racer kit option. Duntov enlisted Greenwood's help in developing the body kit for the new ultra-wide racing tires that were being used on IMSA and Trans-Am Corvettes. Corvette race cars were always tough-looking, but this was over the top.

Greenwood's ZL1 engine was bored to 467 ci and made over 700 hp @6,800 rpm and 620 ft-lb of torque at 4000 rpm. The engine used a stock crank, Carillo rods, Isky roller rockers, a dry-sump oil system, and a Lucas fuel injection on a magnesium cross-ram manifold. Transmission was a blueprinted M22 rock crusher. Ready-to-race, Greenwood's Batmobile the car weighed 2,885 lbs.

John wanted to make a street version of this car. But federal regulations, safety, and liability concerns of the day prevented him.

In '76, Greenwood and Dick Smothers won Sebring and took the pole position at Le Mans, but engine trouble took them out of the race. John's Corvette hit 211 mph on the Mulsanne Straight! Not bad for a street racer from Detroit.

1985 - 1988
Showroom Stock Racers
"Too Fast For Their Own Good"

Racing Corvettes had a tough time in the '70s. They were fast and loud, but had trouble finishing races. While never short on power, their frame and suspension was designed in 1960! Corvettes were simply outdated. But that all changed when the new C4 arrived in the Fall of '83.

The C4 Corvette had several design features that lent itself to

becoming a successful racer. A balanced and blueprinted L98 350 engine with open headers could easily and reliably make 350 hp. The backbone frame, steel birdcage, advanced rear suspension, and forged aluminum front suspension formed the basis of a design that would totally dominate Showroom Stock racing for four years straight!

The series began when Nelson Ledges racetrack manager John McGill wondered that since the 24-hour motorcycle races did so well, would there be any interest in a 24-hour series for cars? At first the series attracted Rabbits, Pintos, and small Chrysler cars. Since the track isn't far from Detroit, it didn't take long before the motor city types were bringing their Camaros, Firebirds, Mustangs, and Porsches to race. When Dick Guldstrand got the SCCA to back the series, things really began to take off.

The Z51 performance option helped to create the perfect showroom stock racer. It's a good thing, because when the first Z51 C4 Vettes finally hit the road, it was obvious how in the quest for a racer-like suspension, the package was almost impossible to live with on the street. It was this characteristic that helped make the early C4s the dominant force in Showroom Stock. Here's what was included in the $600 option: A stiffer monoleaf rear spring, heavy-duty shocks, harder suspension bushings, a 25-mm front antiroll bar, 13:1 quick-ratio steering, an engine oil cooler, an extra radiator fan, and P255/50VR-16 tires on 16x8.5-inch front wheels and 16x9.5-inch rear wheels.

The term "stock" is a bit of a misnomer. Aside from a full roll-cage for safety concerns, the only changes allowed were heavy-duty shocks, and two-way radios. Stock catalytic converters tend to melt due to the stresses of long distance racing, so it was legal to remove them. This also helped open up the breathing of the engine.

From '84 to '87 Corvettes from various Chevrolet supported teams won every race entered - 17 victories in 17 races! One team was so fierce that Chevy asked them not to race so that newer teams could have a chance. Not since the big-block days had Corvettes been so tough.

Other racers weren't so thrilled. By the end of the 1987 season, Corvettes were banned from Showroom Stock racing to "preserve the integrity of the series." Thus began the 1988-'89 "Corvette Challenge Series." Chevy supplied the parts, and customers reaped the benefits. Corvettes and racing - perfect together.

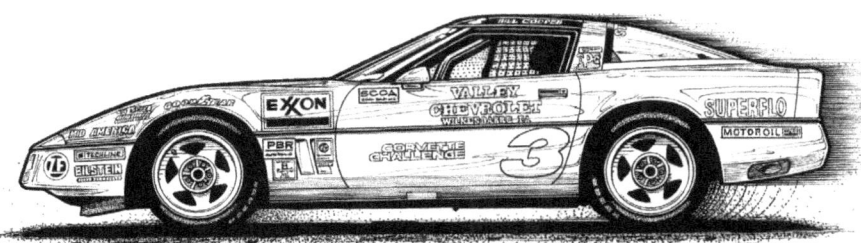

1988 Corvette Challenge Racers
"Factory-Built Sportsman Racers"

For decades General Motors had a strange attitude towards racing. Obviously, many people raced Corvettes, but GM would never officially stand behind their efforts. All that changed in 1988 with the beginning of the "Corvette Challenge Series."

It was a banner year for the Corvette. There was the 35th Anniversary Special, the high-output Callaway option, an awesome GTO body kit, and the production of 56 specially prepared, street-legal Corvette race cars. The series was an outgrowth of the Corvette's total dominance of the Showroom Stock series from '85 to '87. Since Corvettes were banned from the series for '88, someone had to come up with a plan. Thanks to someone with connections, a Corvette-only race was created.

Toronto racing promoter John Powel pitched the idea to Chevrolet with a plan to sign on sponsors to create a million dollar, 10 race series with equally prepared, performance Corvettes. Chevrolet agreed and began building cars that used every performance part available for the race cars. A total of 56 cars were built then each car was retrofitted with a full rollcage and other safety items. The engine and running gear of each car was balanced, blueprinted, and sealed by the Protofab engineering. To keep things on the up-and-up, a special tamper-proof green paint was applied to hold-down bolts of each 5.7-liter Tuner Port Injection L98 engine to assure that the engines wouldn't be tweaked.

The races were supporting events for CART and IMSA, but had full and extensive coverage on ESPN with on-screen information from real-time telemetry from the cars. Although common today, this was very cool racing coverage. The Vettes were equalized to the point where every car raced used gas from the same tanker. The "racing" all came down to the driver's skill behind the wheel. This was the same model used in the IROC (International Race of Champion) series that was developed in the early '70s and popularized by the IROC Camaros of the mid '80s.

The series was very popular with the fans and most of the drivers enjoyed the experience as well. When the '89 season began, the country was in a recession and sponsorship money became a problem. Chevrolet ended up financing the series for the million dollar purse. More importantly, Dave McLellan's Corvette engineers gained R&D information from 50 Corvettes racing ten races in '88 and twelve races in '89. Nearly all of the adjustments and parts improvements went directly into production Corvettes. That's what you call, high-profile field testing.

The cars could do over 160-mph, but speed has never been cheap. A Corvette Challenge car cost over $35,000 and was officially street-legal. Even though the Corvette Challenge cars were powered by well-assembled stock engines, make no doubt, these were racing Corvettes. A few articles were published about the cars and they were described as rough-riding, harsh machines. The series concluded at the end of '89.

What started out as a zero-cost deal for Chevrolet ended up costing quite a lot, but they did get their money's worth in field testing. Also, SCCA reported that other manufacturers were ready to take on the Corvettes again in '90 in the Escort World Challenge Series. The competition had two years to catch up, so the Corvettes didn't run away with the series, but they did win 50 percent of the 10 races entered.

1990 ZR-1 Corvette
"ZR-1 Corvette Shatters A 50-Year Speed Record With a 175.885 MPH Run"

Racing Corvettes used to have a long history of durability issues. There are many accounts of Corvette racers setting track records and winning pole positions, only to have parts breakage put their cars out of the race. The success of the Showroom Stock and the Corvette Challenge cars proved that the new C4s had what it took to win long races. So it was only a matter of time before someone tested the new ZR-1 under racing conditions. Enter Morrison Motorsports.

On March 1 and 2, 1990, the Morrison Motorsports prepared ZR-1 Corvette shattered the 50-year old, 24-hour speed record with an astonishing average speed of 175.885 mph with a "near-stock" ZR-1 Corvette! The details of the ZR-1 speed machine are a genuine testimonial to the quality of the new ZR-1.

In 1940, David, "Ab" Jenkins set the 24-hour speed record with his "Mormon Meteor III" racer. The huge 5,000-pound machine was designed by Augie Duesenberg and used a 850-hp, 27.5-litre aircraft engine! In 1940 Ab nailed the record with an average 24-hour speed of 161.18 mph. The record stood for 50 years. Many attempted to break the record, and all failed... until the ZR-1 arrived.

The ZR-1 speed record attempt was the idea of Pete Mills, a west coast automotive writer. Mills saw potential in the new ZR-1 and pitched the idea to Corvette racer Stu Hayner. Corporate connections can be helpful. Hayner talked with Chevy's John Heinricy who pitched the idea to the right people inside GM. Tommy Morrison was also brought on board with the plan and the project was approved by the GM brass. The only change to the plan was to also run a stock L98 Coupe.

The FIA rules mandated that a speed record car must carry "non-consumable" spare parts in the event of a breakdown and the driver wasn't able to get back to the pits for repairs. Consequently, the ZR-1 had to carry an additional 300 pounds of spare parts in two suit cases lashed to the rear roll bar supports of the full roll cage! Drivers were expected to be able to fix the car if something broke.

The ZR-1 was essentially stock, with the exception of racing wheels and slicks, an EDS telemetry system, a 45-gallon fuel cell, and other assorted racing and safety parts. The suspension was stock, minus the anti-roll bars and the rear used a 3.07:1 gear set. Extra oil coolers and differential coolers were added and the headlights were replaced with racing lights. The stock L98 Coupe was similarly prepared.

The 7.71-mile Firestone test track in Arizona was chosen for the speed record assault. The track had 1.5-mile long straights and 2.35-mile curves that allowed the car to be driven nearly flat-out. There were three lanes to the track and no guard rails, making driving at high speed a concentration challenge. The L98 coupe ran for 6 hours before it was pulled so that it could be shipped to a car show in Geneva.

The ZR-1 ran nearly flawlessly for 24 hours with only one minor repair. At the end of the day, the 8-driver team broke 3 world records and set 4 FIA records. After breaking the records, Tommy Morrison took a 2-lap victory run at full-throttle! The ZR-1 Corvette was proven to be a solid performer. How sweet it was!

1999 C5-R Corvette
"Factory-Backed Corvette Racer"

Almost from the beginning, Corvettes have been the ultimate American "could have been" race cars. Whereas its domestic rivals operated factory-supported racing programs, GM chose a different approach. The company built hot cars and parts, and sometimes even helped selected racers via an unofficial "back door" policy, but it always avoided an all-out racing program. That is, until the C5 Corvette was released.

Zora Arkus-Duntov gave us the legendary '57 SS project, the '63 Grand Sport, and the 427 L-88 racers, while Dave McLellan championed the '88-'89 Corvette Challenge cars. Dave Hill's efforts culminated in birth the all-new '97 C5. By the end of '98, it was obvious the new car was a sales success, posting nearly triple the sales from the previous (abbreviated) season. With the financial bottom line firmly in place, it was time to go racing!

In the fall of 1998, a fully backed GT racing effort was blessed and christened the "C5-R." The new team was to be managed by Doug Fehan and Ken Brown, engine work was assigned to Joe Negri, and race-car builders Pratt & Miller Fabrication would manage chassis development and car construction.

GT rules required that mostly stock parts be used. This gave the newly redesigned Corvette a competitive advantage. The hydro-formed steel main rails, front and rear chassis cradles, and LS1 engine were nearly track-ready in stock form. From there, it was simply a matter of adding selected race-spec parts to build an all-out competition Corvette.

To hit the 2,500-pound target weight, the C5-R was put on a weight-reduction plan, gaining carbon-fiber body panels and other lightweight pieces. Retained stock parts included the rack-and-pinion steering, front and rear control arms, windshield, auxiliary and driving lights, and basic block design. The modified LS1 engine displaced 427-cid, had 12.5:1 compression, and produced over 600-hp and 500 ft-lb of torque. The new body panels were designed for maximum stability at 200 mph. Since the basic shape was already excellent, improvements were limited to add-on appendages and underbody treatments.

Two race cars were built by members of GM Motorsports, Chevrolet Race Shop, Pratt & Miller Fabrication, and Riley & Scott Race Car Engineering. The driving team consisted of Ron Fellows, Andy Pilgrim, John Heinricy, Chris Kneifel, Scott Sharp, and John Paul Jr. After a thorough test session in Sebring in November '98, the team was ready for its maiden race, the 24 Hours of Daytona in January '99.

Both Vettes finished the race, outlasting 36 other entries, and one of the cars came in Third in class. The crew, drivers, and machines showed stunning potential for a debut effort. Yes, some minor parts broke, but the Corvette finally had the backing it had deserved since 1953. This was just the beginning of what would become the finest Corvette racing team ever.

112 THE ILLUSTRATED CORVETTE SERIES

2001 C5-R Corvette
"Victory at Le Mans"

Had it not been for Zora Arkus-Duntov, there never would have been a C5-R. The Corvette's first chief of engineering knew firsthand the value of racing. In 1952 and '53 he co-drove an Allard sports car at Le Mans. Then, in '54 and '55, he drove a 1,000-cc Porsche Spyder to a class win. While Duntov never got to see all-out factory support for a Corvette racing team, his passion for

motorsports lived on in the hearts of the C5 design team. With the car having proved more successful than anyone in GM's upper management could have imagined, '99 seemed like the perfect year to introduce a factory-supported Corvette racing program.

GT endurance competition is arguably one of the most difficult forms of auto racing. Cars have to be fast, powerful, and durable. Drivers must have stamina, and teams need to work together perfectly. And, of course, there's always the luck factor. Fortunately, the C5 came with all the basic elements a racing engineer could want, giving the C5-R a great platform from which to start.

The 24 Hours of Le Mans is the ultimate victory for sports-car manufacturers. The 8.45-mile course is mostly made up of two-lane country roads. By the third season the cars and the team was primed for victory. The '01 C5-Rs were called the "wide body" cars because they had been built to the maximum allowable width for the GTS class. GTS cars actually had to be crash-tested as part of the certification process.

As noted, luck can play an important part in endurance racing. Vicious rain started just 10 minutes after the green flag. Most cars had to quickly pit to exchange their racing slicks for rain tires. Rain caused two of the four Vipers to crash, and a third had to drop out of the race due to electrical problems. The three controversial S7R Saleen cars all broke. For decades the Corvettes had borne the brunt of the bad luck and durability problems. This race was C5-R's time to shine.

Through the night the No. 63 and No. 64 C5-Rs swapped the lead several times. At one point, the No. 64 car made a 15-minute pit stop to fix a broken starter. Then, the car spun out two times in as many laps, putting it far back from the leaders. One hour before the end of the race, it poured again, and the pace car had to come out. When this happens, hard-fought leads shrink, as cars can catch up with, but not pass one another. When the checkered flag came down, C5-R No. 63 crossed the finish line with C5-R No. 64 slightly behind.

The '99 C5-R made a very good showing in its first five races, even taking Second at Laguna Seca. The '00 season got off to a good start, with the Vettes taking Second place at Daytona. The year ended with two wins, three seconds, and a credible Third place in the GTS class at Le Mans. 2001 proved to be the best year yet, bringing the Corvette's first-ever overall win at the 24 Hours at Daytona. The stage was set for Le Mans.

The team finished first and second in the GTS class and 8th place overall. Car 63, driven by Ron Fellows, Johnny O'Connell, and Scott Pruett, ran 278 laps totaling 2,349 miles. Car 64, driven by Frank Feron, Andy Pilgrim, and Kelly Collins, ran 271 laps totaling 2,289 miles.

Speedvision said it best, "Nobody at Le Mans knows the Corvettes won at Daytona, but everyone at Daytona knows that Corvettes won at Le Mans!"

2005 C6.R Corvette
"Continued Racing Success"

By the beginning of 2004, the Corvette team was busy getting the new Vette ready for production. Around the same time, C5-R builders Pratt & Miller were brought in to begin development work on the first C6.R.

From '99 through '03, the Corvette Racing team won its class in 25 of 44 races entered. Class wins at Le Mans came in '01 and '02, followed by a Second Place showing in '03. In '04, the team won all 10 races entered and scooped up its third Le Mans victory. For the new C6.R, the pressure was on.

GT-class racing is popular because the cars are closely related to production sports cars. Pratt & Miller initially built two C6.R racers based on the upcoming C6 Corvette. With the wheelbase being 1 inch shorter, and the body itself being 5 inches shorter, this wasn't going to be a mere re-skin of the C5-R.

Since many of the C6's chassis details had been worked out from racing the C5-R, the new C6.R was already ahead of its predecessor. The car used the same hydro-formed frame rails, slick shape, and flush headlights as the '05 production Vette. And with the addition of a large rear wing and a deep front spoiler, the C6.R had a superior lift-to-drag ratio.

The car's LS7.R powerplant was such a gem that at the end of the '05 racing season, it was honored with the Global Motorsports Engine of the Year Award. The all-aluminum fuel-injected, 427-ci small-block was equipped with a dry-sump oil system, CNC-ported cylinder heads, titanium valves and connecting rods, a forged steel crankshaft, and plate-honed cylinder bores.

The C6.R used the same driver's air-conditioning system as the C5-R cars. The unit pumped cool air into the driver's suit and helmet to combat heat exhaustion. Other noteworthy features included a small, flat-screen monitor connected to a rear-mounted video camera; sensors and electrical plug-in receivers to remotely monitor engine functions; and a light-activated sensor to measure side-slip while racing.

The 12 Hours at Sebring was the only race of the '05 season in which a C6.R didn't win First in class. The cars took Second and Third, not too shabby for a debut outing. Were if not for two minor tire problems, the team would have taken Sebring as well.

But Le Mans is always the big prize, and here, the C6.Rs did not disappoint. The Aston-Martin DBR9s qualified Nos. 1 and 2 in class, with the Vettes qualifying Nos. 3 and 5. The strategy was simple: run consistent, 3:55 laps and don't breaking anything.

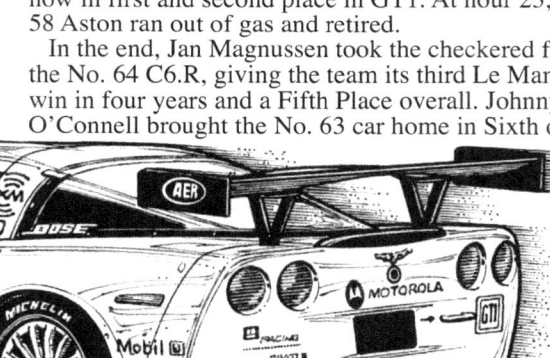

The race started at 4 p.m., and soon the Astons and C6.Rs were swapping the GT1 lead. In the second hour, C6.R No. 64 experienced two left-rear tire failures, but it remained within striking distance of the Astons. At hour 17, the top three cars were within 4.5 seconds of each other, and the heat was climbing into the 90s. Hour 19 sealed the deal for the C6.Rs when the No. 59 Aston pitted for heavy repairs. The Corvettes were now in first and second place in GT1. At hour 23, the No. 58 Aston ran out of gas and retired.

In the end, Jan Magnussen took the checkered flag in the No. 64 C6.R, giving the team its third Le Mans class win in four years and a Fifth Place overall. Johnny O'Connell brought the No. 63 car home in Sixth overall and Second in class. The Third Place Aston was 16 laps and 136 miles behind the winning C6.R.

We should also mention the brilliant work of the Corvette Racing pit crew. In '05, the team only experienced two crashes, one at Sebring and the other at Lime Rock. In both instances, the cars were driven back to the pits, repaired, and re-entered in the race. The C6.R went on to win its class in 10 out of 11 races in '05. When the Z06 was released in '06, the family connection to the C6.R was obvious. While the Corvette Racing Team racked up victories, C6 buyers were the winners.

Chapter 5
Special Editions and Tuner Corvettes

Chevrolet got into the special edition game in '78 with the arrival of the 25th Anniversary Special and The Pace Car Special. Since then, we have had a steady stream of production 'Vettes with extra goodies direct from the factory. For some, hot factory 'Vettes weren't hot enough. That's why there are "tuner" Corvettes. There's a small community of creative people who love nothing more than taking a perfectly good Corvette and making it into a supercar. Tuner Corvettes often live hard lives, and many have become legends.

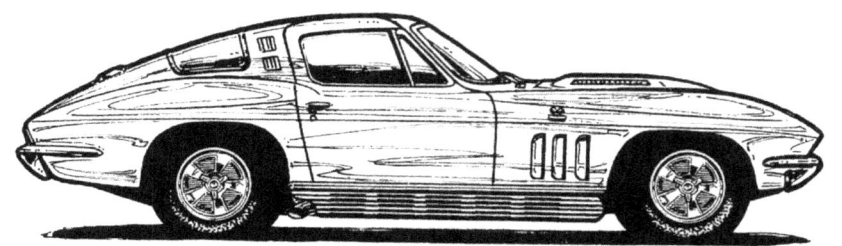

1965 396 Big-Block Corvette
"Simply Raw Power"

In the mid 1950s, Detroit was hot with racing fever and NASCAR racing was uniquely "American." Ford and Chrysler completely disregarded the 1957 AMA ban of factory supported racing. GM, on the other hand, officially observed the ban and was "not in racing." While they had their backdoor program for preferred racers, because they couldn't really get behind any particular team, GM cars were often playing catch-up.

The 1962 NASCAR "427 Mystery Motor" was a 500-plus horsepower experimental engine design that would eventually make its way into the Corvette by '65. Corvette Chief Engineer, Zora Arkus-Duntov was not altogether happy with this idea. Duntov had worked hard to make sure the Corvette's weight had a 50/50 front-to-back balance. Adding 150 pounds to the front of a rear driven car seemed like a bad move to him. For years Zora had been trying to get the engine in the middle of the Corvette for added traction and superior balance. After all, Indy car and the exotic road racing Chaparrals and Porsches were mid-engine layouts. The upside to the big-block was gobs of easy, raw horsepower

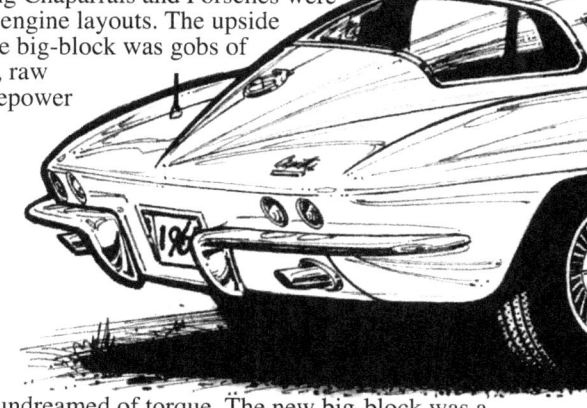

and undreamed of torque. The new big-block was a genuine stump puller! Although he didn't like it, Zora made sure the big-block Vette was as good as he could make it. Customers and racers definitely liked it!

The Mark IV 396 Corvette hit the streets in April of 1965, and no one was ready for the personality change. The high-revving big-block Sting Ray was now a street monster! Officially known as the L78, the new all-cast-iron 396-ci engine cranked out 425-hp at 6,400 rpm with 415 lb-ft of torque at 4,000 rpm. Truth be told, the published horsepower rating was at least 25 hp short. Best of all, the L78 option was only $292.70, compared to $538 for the Fuel Injected 327. The larger engine required extra hood clearance, so a beautiful hood dome was designed with functional cooling vents. Everything was heavy-duty with the 396 and included the K66 ignition, a larger fan and radiator, a close-ratio M20 four-speed gearbox, and the G81 Positraction differential. Stiffer springs and a larger stabilizer bar held up the front end, while beefed up U-joints and half-shafts kept the drive train together. 1965 was also the first year for four-wheel disc brakes. The new Vette had ample stopping power to go with its increase in horsepower. With the new optional side pipes, with their 2.75-inch diameter, chambered design, the 396 sounded like a roaring bear.

Sales for 1965 were up slightly from '64, with 23,564 units sold compared to 22,229 in 1964. But 2,157 of the '65 Corvettes were ordered with the 396. 1965 big-block Corvettes were the rarest of the Sting Ray big-blocks. In '66, 10,374 big-blocks were sold and 9,687 in '67. Even though the '65 big-blocks are by far much more rare, it's the '67 big-blocks that commands the most money today. It should also be noted that the 396 option wasn't available until March '65 and production ran through to August '65. Plus, there was the usual "wait and see" attitude with customers.

Behind the scenes, the silver fox, Duntov, was working on the initial phases of a racing big-block variant that would become the legendary L88. The L88 wouldn't be available until '67.

1969 ZL1 Corvette
"The $10,000 Megabuck Corvette"

Imagine having a new Corvette with more power than a big-block, and the weight of a small-block. Tantalizing notion, isn't it? That was the basic idea behind the all-aluminum, 427 ZL1 Corvette. The idea of an all-aluminum engine for the Corvette was first outlined in 1957 as part of the "Q-Corvette" project. What finally emerged was more than anyone ever expected.

While everyone loved the 427's power, Duntov was not happy to have 51-percent of the Corvette's weight over the front wheels. Some calculating showed that if the engine was completely made of aluminum, the weight would be close to a small-block. So it was decided to go-for-broke and make the ZL1 a monster.

Thinking "race car tough," Duntov started with a stock L88 and added an aluminum block that was fitted for a dry-sump oil system, larger main bearing bulkheads, extra cylinder head bolts, 12:1 compression pistons, a new camshaft, and open-chamber aluminum heads. Cast-iron sleeves were installed in the piston bores to solve the wear problem with the aluminum alloy block. With a set of headers, the ZL1 made over 585 horsepower at 6,600 rpm!

Of course, an engine designed for racing needs to be field tested.

Since Chevrolet didn't officially race cars, Duntov and his team built a ZL1 as a race car. Zora started off with a production L88 and did what any racer would do - start removing anything that didn't look like a race car. So, out went the headlights, bumpers, heater, upholstery, spare tire mount, and other various small items. In went header side-pipes, racing wheels and tires, L88 fender flares, riveted headlight covers and a small lip across the leading edge of the hood to keep it from blowing off at high speed. This was Zora's quasi racer. An easy 1/4-mile blast netted a 12.1 et and the racing tires and brakes generated 1-g of stopping power. Keep in mind, this was not a flushed-out racer, just a working mule car. John Greenwood's ZL-1 racer hit 210 on the Mulsanne Straight at the '72 Le Mans race.

The big hitch for the ZL1 was its price. Zora was asked, "What kind of a man would buy a ZL1 Corvette," he answered, "First, he'll have a lot of money." The ZL1 option alone cost $3,000 on top of the L88 option. That made the ZL1's total cost over $10,000 in 1969! That was almost twice the cost of a normal 427 street Corvette

All this makes for great magazine copy, but for the street, the ZL1 was a waste. Only two ZL1 Corvettes were officially produced, making them some of the rarest Corvettes ever made. However, a small, but unknown quantity of ZL1 Corvettes were built for evaluation and road testing by select magazine journalists and editors. *CARS* Magazine editor, Marty Schorr got to drive a street ZL1 and was underwhelmed with the real-world, on the street performance of the ZL1.

The ZL1 was a starting point and an extra tool for Corvette racers. The two official ZL1 cars are the Roger Judski yellow-with-black striped car and the Kevin Suydam white-with-black striped car. Then there's John Maher's orange roadster that was ordered through Yenko Chevrolet. Why the official count remains "2" is not known. What is known for certain is this was really Chevrolet's all-out racing Corvette!

1969 Baldwin-Motion Phase III GT Corvette
"Joel Rosen Builds a Grand Touring Corvette"

The term "GT" is arguably one of the most misused automotive designations. The term is an abbreviation for "grand touring." A GT car is a road-going, lightweight, semi-luxurious coupe built on a high-performance chassis, for long trips, you need a car with plenty of power, a strong chassis, and loads of creature comforts to make the journey pleasant. Most high-priced European car companies all offered GT cars for their affluent customers.

In the '60s, Detroit carmakers started to use the GT term on pony and mid-size cars. Many enthusiasts wanted more and sought the help of specialty shops to build a package car. The original Shelby Mustangs were turn-key supercars. But at a small shop in Baldwin, New York, Joel Rosen was making his own machines called the Baldwin-Motion SS and Phase III Supercars.

Rosen was a successful racer and tuner with a proven reputation for building dependable, high-horsepower big-block Chevy engines. He partnered with local dealer, Baldwin Chevrolet, to build brand-new, fully-warranted, enhanced versions of Chevy muscle cars. Rosen's cars were extreme and he was the only guy back then building Corvette supercars.

Phase III Supercars were reasonably priced and guaranteed to run 11.5s (or quicker) in the quarter-mile. Meanwhile, Rosen was dreaming of his own GT car to take on Europe's best. Joel began where the regular Phase III Corvette ended. Since every car was built to the customer's specs, we'll look at Rosen's prototype '68 Corvette. First, the engine was disassembled and blueprinted. A low-restriction air filter was used with a 1,050-cfm Holley four-barrel carb on an aluminum high-rise manifold. The engine had tube headers, a Motion Super/Spark CD ignition, and M/T finned valve covers. The exhaust was a factory side-pipe system with chambered pipes. Horsepower was rated at 500 on Rosen's dyno. The suspension received special shocks, bushings, and springs, along with a single traction bar. The wheels were 15-inch slotted alloys mounted with wide Goodyear Polyglas tires.

At the '69 New York International Auto Show, people were stunned by the GT's, muscular good looks. The Monza Red '68 prototype had the distinctive Motion striping package. All four wheelwells were flared to cover the wide tires, the side vents were reversed, and remote-controlled mirrors were used. The fastback rear window opened up the rear storage area and the rear deck had a Le Mans quick-fill gas cap.

Zora Arkus-Duntov was at the show and gave the GT his blessings. The starting price was $10,500 - over double the cost of a stock '69 Vette. Production GTs had fixed headlights and the stock taillights were replaced with two sets of three slotted lamps.

The Phase III GT Corvettes were built from '69 through '71 and approximately 12 cars were made. No two were alike. No doubt the mega-buck price was a major factor. A loaded '70 Phase III GT turned out to be one of the most expensive of the Phase III GT Vettes, costing a mind-bending (at the time) $13,000. Only five Phase III GTs are known to still exist. Specialty Corvettes have come a long way since 1969, and many other tuners have applied Rosen's concept to their own dream machines. "Mr. Motion" was the first.

1970-1/2 LT1 Corvette
"Balance of Power"

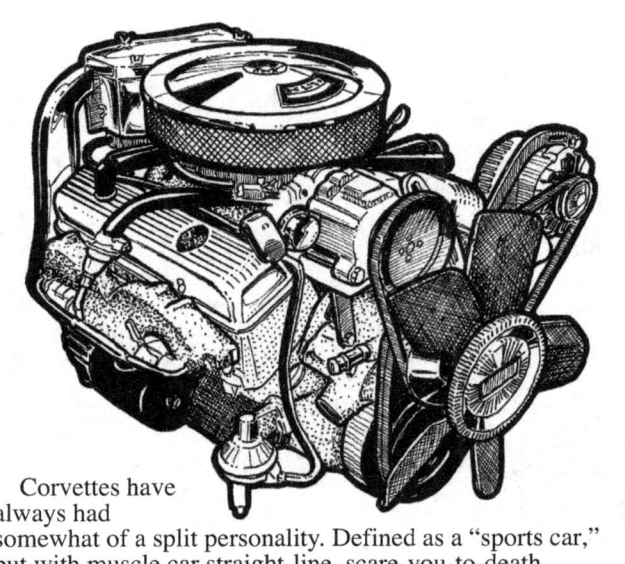

Corvettes have always had somewhat of a split personality. Defined as a "sports car," but with muscle car straight-line, scare-you-to-death acceleration. Detroit learned early in the performance game that there's no substitute for cubic inches. But the penalty is extra weight. When the Corvette went "big-block" in '65, the split widened between the sports car and muscle car groups. The '70 LT1 option gave buyers the best of both worlds - plenty of grunt and perfect balance.

Although Zora Arkus-Duntov loved the brutish big-blocks, his ideal setup for the Corvette was a balanced, mid-engine, aluminum small-block layout. After many attempts, the mid-engine Corvette just wasn't to be. His plan-B was to make a high-revving, high-performance, lightweight small-block, with a 50/50 weight distribution. The resulting LT1 option just blew everyone away.

The LT1 engine had about every trick part a production car could have. Designed as a high-rpm performer, everything was stout. The cast-iron block had four-bolt main caps and a forged crankshaft at the bottom end. The connecting rods and pistons were forged steel and had 11:1 compression. A dual-plane aluminum manifold and 4150 Holley four-barrel rated at 800 cfm handled the intake side. Oversized valves in performance heads and solid-lifters along with a high-lift cam gave the LT1 a lumpy, "don't mess with me" idle, and cast-iron manifolds with 2.5-inch pipes handling exhaust. The ignition system was the latest transistor Delco model. Too bad the aluminum heads just weren't ready yet.

It all added up to 370-hp at 6,000 rpm, and 380 ft-lb of torque. With the relative light weight of the small-block, the LT1 was just a tick off the straight-line performance of the 454. Quarter-mile-times were around 14.10 seconds @ 102-mph, with 0-to-60 times around 6-seconds. But the best part was that because of the balanced arrangement, the LT1 could be driven as deep into corners as Europe's finest. Some publications reported that the LT1 was as fast, if not faster, through the curves than the '70 911 Porsche!

The LT1 option wasn't cheap though. At $447.60, it was $10.50 more than the '69 L71, 427/435 engine and $157.95 more than the '70 LS5, 390-hp 454. For '70, Chevy sold 1,287 LT1 Corvettes. Interestingly, the air conditioning option was $447.65, 5-cents more than the LT1, but not available with the LT1, as was an automatic transmission.

As good as the LT1 was, Mr. Duntov made sure there was a racer kit version. The ZR1 was essentially an L88 package with the LT1 engine. This $968 option provided a base for a competitive B/Production racer. Only 25 were ordered. Many C3 fans consider the '70 LT1 to be the best of the C3 Vettes. The car offered hairy, solid-lifter grunt and 50/50 weight balance, combined with a car that had not yet been overloaded with luxury accessories, low compression, and emissions equipment. If a rough and tumble, take-no-prisoners machine is your criteria for performance, the '70 LT1 is your Corvette.

The Motion/Maco Corvettes
"Joel Rosen's Sharks"

As the '63 Corvettes were hitting the showrooms, GM Chief of Styling Bill Mitchell was dreaming up the next model. With the help of stylist Larry Shinoda and a small team of designers, the radical Mako Shark II was shown to GM management in spring of 1965. The mock-up made jaws drop and the order was given: "Build a running version!"

By October, the running version of the new design headed out to the show-car circuit, where it received rave reviews. It was obvious: The Mako Shark II had to be the next production Corvette.

Building a stunning concept car is one thing, but making it into a production car is something else. Lots of compromises were made to the overall shape that pushed the release back a year to '68. Even though the styling was much more tame, the production version was still gorgeous. With coupe and roadster versions, lots of options, and seven engines to choose from, interest in the show car quickly vanished, but not for everyone. Enter, John Silva.

Silva wanted the new Corvette to be the Mako Shark II. By the time he designed a body kit for the production Corvette, Joel Rosen had already building his Baldwin-Motion Phase III Supercars. Since Rosen's Corvettes had a considerable amount of custom fiberglass work, Silva worked out a deal with Mr. Motion. Silva produced three cars for Rosen and authorized the tuner to make molds from his parts. In '72 Joel began offering Maco Shark kits, as well as turn-key Maco Sharks packed with as much horsepower as the owner and his wallet could handle. Each was built to order, and every car was different. Motion built Macos from '72 to '78 and continued selling kits well into the '80s.

But Rosen always had another project on the back burner. In '73 he retired the Phase III GT and created his Manta Ray that offered the best of the Phase III GT and the Maco Shark. Built on a '73 Corvette, the Manta Ray had its own unique look. From the doors forward, it was a Phase III GT with '73 side vents. The roof section was pure Maco Shark, and had a very tall rear spoiler. Manta Rays were only offered in '73, and just three were produced.

Rosen's last shark was called the Moray Eel. Built on a '72 Corvette, it was part Maco Shark, part Manta Ray. The front end had provisions for hood grilles or vents, but were glassed over for a smooth look and the headlights were placed in the front grille. Only one Moray Eel was produced.

The Silva/Motion Maco Sharks used a simple formula: start off with a great car and make it your own. And it all started because John Silva wanted a Mako Shark II.

120   THE ILLUSTRATED CORVETTE SERIES

1978 Pace Car Corvette
"25th Anniversary Collectible?"

The Corvette's tough-guy legend is founded on racing and performance. By the mid-to-late '70s, Corvette high-performance and racing efforts were in the pits. Power was down, weight was up, and Porsches were eating the Corvette's lunch at the race track. The announcement that the 25th anniversary Corvette would also be the pace car at the '78 Indy 500, looked like the highlight of the decade for Corvette fans. But controversy was in the mix right from the beginning.

Initially, it looked like a triple-play for Chevrolet. First, the '78 Corvette received a sleek new fastback roof that completed the overall redesign started in '73 with the soft bumper covers. Second, all Corvettes wore the 25th Anniversary badges. And third, three special Corvettes would serve as the pace cars at the '78 Indy 500, and replicas would be available. Then the details set in.

The initial proposal was that there would be 300 pace car replicas, the same number as the '53 production run. The car would have a two-tone silver paint (for the silver anniversary), red pinstriping, and special Goodyear tires with "CORVETTE" sidewall lettering. Then the plan was to make 2,500 replicas, 100 for each year of production. But there were 6,200 dealers that all wanted at least one replica, so production went up to 6,502 units. Then two key elements were changed.

The special "CORVETTE" tires were deemed too expensive, and paint was changed to silver and black. Then there was the price issue. The RPO 1YZ8778 package cost $4,302, on top of the $9,351 base price - a 46 percent premium! Here's what came with the option: The exterior had special two-tone paint and pinstriping, unique front and rear spoilers, glass roof panels, sport mirrors, and red pin stripped aluminum wheels on P225/60R15 tires. The interior came with power windows and door locks, tilt-telescopic steering column, convenience group, silver thin-shell seats, AM/FM with a CB radio or an 8-track tape player, dual rear speakers, and a power antenna. The $525 L82 engine rated at 220-hp was not part of the package.

The controversy started right on the showroom floor. For a "premium collectible," quality was not good. On many of the cars, fender seams and slight bubbles were clearly visible. The black upper body paint only made the defects look worse. Then, there were the opportunistic dealers who tacked on surcharges that bumped the price up to between $15,000 to $22,000. One dealer was asking $75,000 for his replica. Then, there were individuals making replicas of the pace car replica, asking full price for their creations! All that, for a car with no more "grunt" than a regular Corvette.

Meanwhile, at the 62nd Indy 500 race on May 28, 1978, Jim Rathmann drove one of three Pace Car Corvettes to start the race. One of the pace cars was given to Al Unser for winning the race, another was sent to the Detroit Museum, and the last pace car was sold through a Chevy dealer to a professional baseball trainer. The '78 Pace Car Corvettes were the first pace cars to work the race with a stock drivetrain. All previous pace cars had serious performance enhancements. But the production Corvette, even though it was down on power from its earlier days, was up to the job!

In today's market, '78 Pace Car Corvettes can be purchased for between $7,000 to $30,000. Although the '78 Pace Car was always a very nice car, between the high volume and low performance, the car's value has yet to take off - over 30 years later. But imagine a '69 427/435 Corvette Pace Car instead of the '69 Camaro. Pace Car. Now you're talking!

1987 Callaway Corvette
"Chevy's Back-Door Supercar"

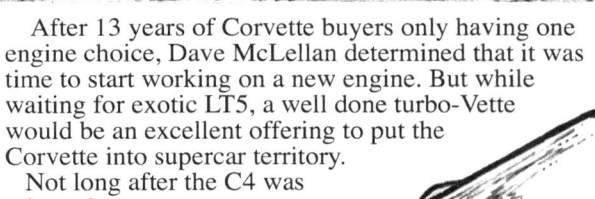

After 13 years of Corvette buyers only having one engine choice, Dave McLellan determined that it was time to start working on a new engine. But while waiting for exotic LT5, a well done turbo-Vette would be an excellent offering to put the Corvette into supercar territory.

Not long after the C4 was released, work began on a new powerplant for the Corvette. All sorts of combinations were considered, with a turbocharged V-8 finally winning out. Dave McLellan was aware of Reeves Callaway's turbo work on quality European and certain Japanese engines. McLellan thought it made sense to forge a relationship with Callaway and let the Connecticut firm develop a turbo-Vette for quick release.

After several prototype Turbo Corvettes were built, a deal was struck in June '86 that created the official 1987 Corvette option number RPO B2K as the Callaway Twin Turbo option. Cost? A hefty $19,995 on top of the $27,999 base price, plus the mandatory Z51 Handling Package for an additional $795. A completed Callaway Twin Turbo Corvette could be yours for only $48,785! However, if you wanted 345 net horsepower with 465 ft-lb of torque at 2,200 rpm, that was the price of the party. The car ran 0-60 in just 4.5 seconds and the quarter-mile in 13.2!

Performance like that far surpassed the old 427 and 454 days, but it wasn't easy. The L98 350 engine received a complete blueprint and balance rebuild, Roto Master 1H1 RHB52 twin turbos nested on both sides of the engine, and an air-to-air intercooling system was used. Special parts to accommodate the demands of the turbo installation replaced many stock parts, including; Cosworth 7.5:1 forged pistons, a high-output Melling oil pump, an auxiliary solid-state fuel enrichment system, and a heavy-duty brass and copper radiator. Hood mounted NACA ducts were considered, but it was found that ducting from under the front of the car worked better. The only visual change on the car was the elimination of the heavy stock wheels and the use of 17-inch, 9.5-inch wide light-alloy Dymag wheels and 275/40ZR-17 Goodyear Eagle tires.

All of the extra hardware added up to 100 pounds, making the Callaway Corvette weigh in at 3,600 pounds. But it really didn't matter, because the extra 105 hp turned the Corvette into a genuine stump-puller!

Only 184 Callaway Corvettes were built for '87. Despite the outsourcing of the car, Corvette buffs considered it a "real" Corvette because it was on the order sheet. The ZR-1 was a full two years away, so the Callaway was the perfect interim exotic Corvette.

THE ILLUSTRATED CORVETTE SERIES

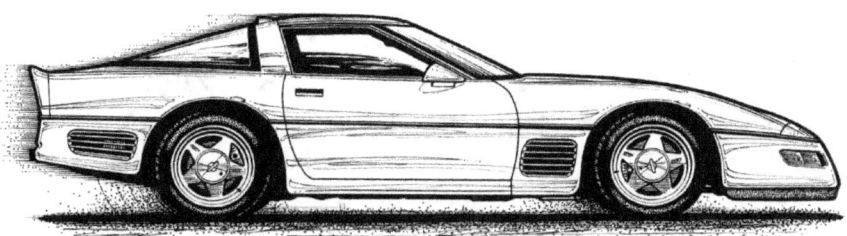

1988 Callaway Sledgehammer
"Callaway's 254.76 MPH Corvette"

While the 200 mph '09 ZR1 is receiving well-deserved kudos, nearly 20 years ago Reeves Callaway and his team smashed the record books with a street-driven twin-turbo '88 Corvette called "The Sledgehammer."

The Sledgehammer was a radical version of an '88 production Vette. This was no one-of-a-kind exotic like the Ultimate Aero, built by Shelby Supercars. The Ultimate Aero's record-setting average speed was 256.18 mph - not much more than the 254.76-mph production-based Sledgehammer.

Plans for the Sledgehammer began after a modified Callaway Twin-Turbo won the *Car & Driver* "Gathering of the Eagles" top-speed event in 1987. Reeves Callaway drove the car to a top-speed of 231 mph. The car was fast, but it was rough, hot, smelly, and difficult to drive. Corvette Chief Engineer Dave McClellan joked about Reeves 231-mph car saying, "Des Is Der Sledgehammer!" The name stuck and Reeves got busy!

Callaway wanted to build a streetable 250-mph GT. The modifications were relatively simple: a Lingenfelter engine to produce least 900 hp, suspension tweaks for high-speed stability, interior mods for safety, and a body kit to enhance aerodynamics. Deutschman Design created the body kit to be stable at 250 mph. Road-racer Carroll Smith was contracted for the suspension work, and Callaway employees Tim Good, Elmer Coy, and Dave Hendricks were assigned to oversee the project.

The 349.8-ci, 4-bolt-main Chevy Bowtie block used a cross-drilled Cosworth crankshaft, Crower rods, Jesel roller rockers, and stud girdle, and Crane roller lifters. A mild Cam Techniques camshaft kept the engine streetable. The Brodix heads were O-ringed with copper gaskets, and studs were used instead of bolts. A Barnes 10-quart dry-sump oil system was used. Compression was just 7.5:1, and the twin Turbonetics T04B-Series turbos with were set at 22 psi. The large intercoolers were mounted behind the front bumper, and the turbos were mounted behind the front grille. Callaway-made stainless-steel headers were connected to huge-diameter exhaust pipes and SuperTrapp mufflers. It all added up to 898 horsepower!

The suspension was lowered one inch, and adjustable Koni shocks controlled dampening. Special high-speed Goodyear tires were mounted on 17 x 9.5-inch Dymag magnesium wheels at the front and back. A Doug Nash five-speed gearbox was equipped with a special overdrive unit for the top-speed push. The driveline was beefed up, and a special Spicer/Dana rear was installed.

The interior was stock except for the leather-covered roll bar, a fire-suppression system, and additional monitoring equipment on the passenger side of the dash. A modified Toshiba laptop PC was used to gather and measure vital statistics.

On October 19, 1988, the team drove the car to the Transportation Research Center in Ohio. Once on the 7.5-mile track, a few bugs had to be worked out. On October 26, 1988 after some nasty weather cleared out, with John Lingenfelter driving, the Sledgehammer lived up to its name, blasting through the timers at nearly 255 mph. After some celebration, the team packed up, and the Sledgehammer was driven home to Connecticut!

The Amazing 1990 ZR-1 Corvette
"Super Corvette"

Whether it was deliberate or accidental, Chevrolet milked the automotive press and stoked Corvette fans for nearly two years with the ZR-1 Corvette! It was the biggest power increase since the introduction of the big-block engine in 1965 and the first time there was an optional engine since the last big-block in '74. But unlike the $250 optional LS4 454 engine, the ZR-1 was a total-car package deal that cost a thunderous $27,016 on top of the $31,979 base Corvette.

The ZR-1 conversion was much more involved than simply dropping a larger engine under the hood. The biggest challenge had to do with assembly line production. The original idea was to have a set of double-overhead-cam heads made that would replace the stock L98 heads. But it was soon discovered that the extra width from the new heads made it impossible to install the engine on the assembly line jigs. Changing the assembly line or the frame was not an option. Lucky for Corvette fans, the decision was made to have a completely new engine developed.

Since GM owned Lotus, work began in May of '85 by Lotus engineers to design a new engine for a super-Corvette. The new engine would be designed to fit into the Corvette assembly line, but the overall package would be far from cheap. Unlike the Cosworth Vega's DOHC bolt-on head, the new LT5 would be a fresh start.

Even though the introduction was delayed because Chevrolet wanted to get it right, the finished product was stunning. The L98 Corvette engine had 245 hp, the ZR-1 packed 375 hp! The engine had four overhead camshafts and 32 valves. Heads used a fast-burn cloverleaf chamber design with a centrally located spark plug. The intake manifold had 16-runner inlets and two Multec injectors per cylinder. It had a direct-fire ignition with camshaft sensors and used 12 quarts of oil. Even though the engine was all-aluminum, because of the engine's complex design, an assembled LT5 weighed almost 40 lbs more than the all-cast-iron L98. Just the same, the ZR-1 is a jewel of an engine.

To handle the extra power, special 315/35 ZR-17 Goodyear Z-rated tires were mounted to 11-inch wide rims. To cover the larger tires, new body panels were made to replace the stock doors, rear fenders, rear fascia, and upper rear panel. The taillights were rectangular, as were the exhaust tips. All of the Z51 suspension parts were standard.

The ZR-1 was a real bear. It ran the quarter-mile in 13.4-seconds and 0-to-60 in 4.9-seconds and top speed was 171 mph. Despite the $58,8741 price, it didn't stop 3,049 customers from buying a '90 ZR-1. During the six model-years the ZR-1s were offered, just 7,018 units were produced.

Several factors contributed to the low sales. It all came down to trying to sell a very expensive car into a very sluggish market. By '92, not only did the base Corvette look almost the same as the ZR-1, the new LT1 engine brought the performance of the base car almost to the same level as the ZR-1. But for those with deep pockets, it was all worth the price. Regardless, the ZR-1 was an instant Corvette legend.

THE ILLUSTRATED CORVETTE SERIES

Dick Guldstrand's 1995 GS90
"Guldstrand-Style Grand Sport"

Dick Guldstrand is a member of a very unique club. He is one of a dozen or so men who actually worked on and raced one of the original '63 Grand Sport Corvettes. Designed to be a Cobra-killer, only five Grand Sports were built by Zora Arkus-Duntov before GM caught wind of the plan. The axe fell, and fortunately all five cars were sold to privateers, rather than being sent to the crusher. But for Dick Guldstrand, his Grand Sport experience would stay with him for decades.

"Goldie" went on to race many other Corvettes and eventually started a business tuning competition Vettes. As one of Chevrolet's back door consultants, Guldstrand was very involved suspension development in the early days of the C4. By the late '80s Guldstrand was offering an enhanced version of the C4 called the GS80. The only problem in Dick's mind was that the car looked like a stock Corvette with custom wheels and tires. It was "Chevy's car" and he wanted "Dick's car." When the ZR-1 was released, Goldie saw an opportunity to bring back the Grand Sport... Dick Guldstrand-style.

The GS90 would prove to be the most expensive specialty Corvette ever built. Guldstrand pitched the concept of a restyled, hopped-up ZR-1 to his pals at Chevrolet. Dick asked for 15 ZR-1s and a few million dollars. He got one car and a blessing.

The GS90 was a reskinned ZR-1 Corvette with a 475-hp ZR-1 from D.K. Motorsports and a Guldstrand-modified suspension. Steve Winter styled the car as a throwback to the 1963 Ferrari GTO. The only stock Corvette body parts are the windshield and side windows. The lines are bold and muscular with a few cues from the C2 Corvette. Goldie threw every trick he knew into the GS90 from thicker anti-roll bars to coil-over shocks replacing the stock mono-leaf sprint. Then he capped it all off with 18-inch aluminum wheels from OZ in Italy and a Nassau blue paint job with a single bold white racing stripe. Performance was stunning with 0-to-60 in the low 4-second range and a top speed of over 175 mph.

The only problem was the price. The GS90 cost $134,500 over the price of a $72,208 ZR-1, for a total of $206,208! The total number of GS90 cars produced is not known, however, at least 6 GS90 Roadsters were built. Production was planned for a roadster, speedster, and lightweight GS90 to be sold through Chevy dealers. But the Grand Sport "curse" returned when GM killed the deal. As least Guldstrand made more of "Dick's car" than Zora made of the original Grand Sports.

1995 Pace Car Corvette
"Pacing the Indy 500 For the Third Time"

1995 was an unusual year for the Corvette. It was the final year for one of the most exotic and expensive production Corvettes ever made, the ZR-1. It was also the third time a Corvette was used as the pace car for the "greatest spectacle in motor racing" - the Indianapolis 500. A Corvette paced the Indy 500 in '78 and in '86. Pace Car replicas have been the subject of some wild collectibility speculation, especially in '78. But the '95 Pace car Special would prove to be a very desirable Corvette.

The '78 Pace Car special came along during the darkest days of Corvette performance history. After decades of tire-burning performance in the '50s, '60s, and early '70s, the Corvette had become a shadow of its former high-performance persona. But at least it survived the muscle car meltdown of the early '70s. So when the '78 Pace Car Special was announced, collectors and speculators went a little crazy thinking that the car would become one of the most desirable Corvettes of all-time. What was supposed to be a limited-production run of 300 turned out to be 6,501 cars. And there was a serious issue over quality control, or lack thereof. It ended up that many buyers paid way too much for their cars and the collector value never was there.

The Corvette was reborn in '84 and there was no looking back. The roadster returned in '86 and the Corvette was given the opportunity to pace the Indy 500 once again. To avoid the big collector crunch, Chevrolet decided that every Corvette Roadster would be a "Pace Car Special." This time Chevrolet produced 7,315 pace car replicas. There was also a big price increase from the '78 Pace Car replica. In '78 the 185-hp Pace Car option made the car cost $13,653 - a lot of money back then. The 230-hp '86 Pace Car cost $32,032. 1995 was like a different world. The Pace Car Special now cost $46,481, had 300-hp under the hood, was lighter, and much more refined. And with only 527 units built, it was a true collectible.

The $2,816 Indy 500 Pace Car Replica option was arguably the nicest Corvette pace car package to date and was very distinctive. The paint scheme was dark purple metallic over arctic white and a white convertible top. The new style, 5-spoke ZR-1 alloy wheels wore 275/40-17 Goodyear GSC tires. The interior had black and purple leather seats with '95 event logo embroidered on the headrests. All of the '95 Pace Car Special Corvettes were built in March and April of '95 and the first 50 cars built had all-black interiors. As mentioned previously there was no horsepower increase for 1995, but there were many subtle improvements made to the car. The only options that were not available were the lift-out roof panels, the adjustable suspension package, and the ZR-1. A fully loaded '95 Corvette Pace Car Special could cost over $51,500. The base price of a '95 Corvette was only $36,785.

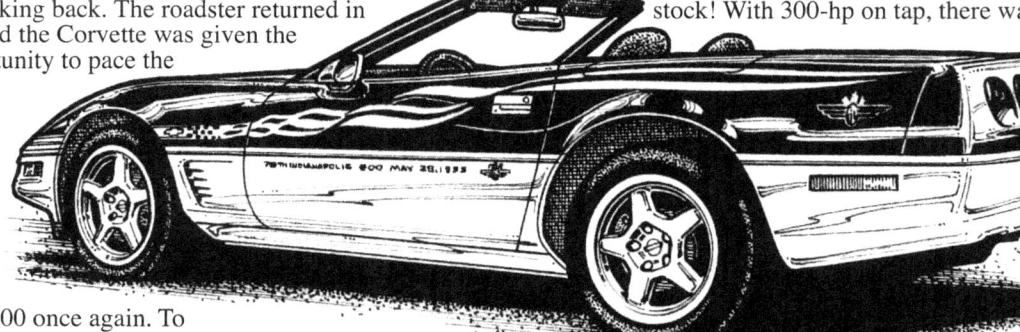

Chevrolet built three cars to pace the Indy 500 in '95. Two of the cars built had the standard 4-speed automatic transmission and the third car had a manual 6-speed gearbox. The only things added to the actual pace cars were 360-degree strobe lights, a roll bar, five-point driver and passenger harnesses, and an on-board fire suppression system. Everything else on the cars was stock! With 300-hp on tap, there was no need for any power enhancements or special performance engines. The stock '95 Corvette was more than up for the job.

Chevrolet only allotted one '95 Pace Car Special to each of the top Corvette retail dealers from '94. Since the production numbers were so low, the current value of the '95 Pace Car Special is still high, fetching between $25,000 and $38,000.

Chevrolet General Manager, Jim Perkins paced the '95 Indy 500 with the only stick version of the pace car Corvette.

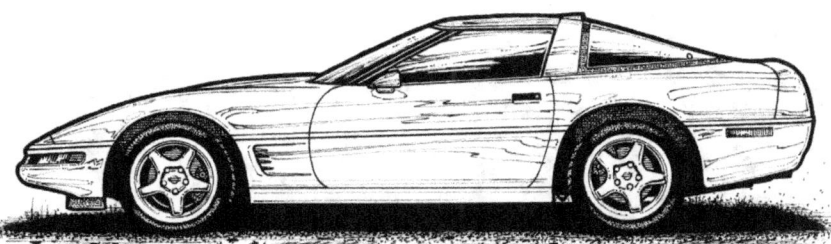

1995 ZR-1 Corvette
"The End of the Line For the ZR-1"

All good things come to an end, right? The ZR-1 was the most aggressive engineering effort ever put into production Corvettes. It's a miracle and a mystery that the Corvette is even alive in General Motors. When you hold the stodgy, bean-counting nature of GM up against the $31,258 ZR-1 option, it's even more amazing. Remember, this is a company that has put the Corvette on the chopping block many times since '53. It just goes to show you what passion, and a love of high performance automobiles can do to even the most conservative corporate decision makers. Fortunately, the C4 was a sales success, enabling greater things to come forth.

Despite the basic nature of GM, there were enough performance hounds working at top levels that saw the value of buying Lotus Engineering in the '80s. Thanks to Lotus' expertise in building and developing exotic all-aluminum engines, the Corvette team had the resources to design a state-of-the-art, world class, exotic American V-8 engine. In sports car circles, Corvettes had always carried the stigma of its "basic" pushrod Chevy engine. The ZR-1 absolutely put an end to all that nonsense.

When the ZR-1 was being planned and developed, the Chevrolet Marketing Departments optimistically projected at least 5,000 units per year. Since the entire run of ZR-1 cars from 1990 to 1995 amounted to only 6,939 units, from a business viewpoint, the ZR-1 was a dismal failure. But from a performance and status perspective, the ZR-1 was a stunning success.

In the late '80s the "collectibility" craze was in full-swing. The ZR-1 was supposed to be an '89 model option, but was delayed due to minor certification problems with the engine. All this did was stoke the magazines and the collectors. When the ZR-1 finally arrived as a '90 model, some dealers sold the cars with steep markups. Five years later, they were selling ZR-1s at steep discounts. Chevrolet engineering and marketing guru Ed Cole said, "The problem with sports cars is you have to sell all of them the first day"

Aside from the new front fender gills and a few other details in the base Corvette, the '95 ZR-1 was a carryover. To sweeten the ZR-1 package, the Z07 Selective Ride Control and the low tire pressure tire warning system options were now included. The most noticeable visual change in the '95 ZR-1 was the 17-inch, 5-spoke alloy wheels. Mercury Marine, the manufacturer of the ZR-1 engine, had completed production of ZR-1 engines in November 2003, so the '95 model still had 405 horsepower. And remember, that is "net" horsepower, not like the olden days of unrealistic "gross" horsepower ratings. The gross power rating for the ZR-1 was closer to 500 hp. This shows up in the ZR-1's 111 mph speed after a 13.1-second quarter-mile blast.

So why didn't the ZR-1 become the "to die for" Corvette of the early '90s? It boiled down to aesthetics, price, and the increasingly high standard of the base Corvette. The ZR-1 had dedicated rear body parts to cover the huge 11-inch wide rear wheels. Except for the restyled rear fascia and a slight curve on the front of the rear wheel openings, the ZR-1 looked like a regular Corvette. Then in '91, all Corvettes had similar styled tail lights. The ZR-1 almost looked like a regular Vette. Too bad some vents and a spoiled couldn't have been added.

Then there was the price issue. While no one could argue about the ZR-1 engine, a single option costing almost as much as the car was more than most buyers would accept. Yes, the ZR-1 could run with Europe's big dogs, but it didn't look exotic, it looked like a regular Corvette. And finally, as

the base car got quicker and faster, the performance gap got to the point where the price wasn't worth the performance gain. But it sure looked good with the hood open.

The ZR-1 provided valuable know-how that showed up in the '97 LS1 engine for the new C5. Also, let's not forget the Morrison Motorsports '91 record-smashing, 171.885 mph ZR-1 Corvette. The ZR-1 helped put to rest that tired, old rant from the European crowd that the Corvette was nothing more than a pretty Chevy.

CHAPTER 5: SPECIAL EDITIONS AND TUNER CORVETTES

1996 Grand Sport Corvette
"Finally, A Production Grand Sport"

The new C5 Corvette was behind schedule, but that didn't stop Dave Hill, John Heinricy, and the Corvette Design team from dishing up the stunning '96 Grand Sport option. The 1963 Grand Sport was arguably the ultimate "could have been great" Corvette. And while the '96 Grand Sport option was a long way from the 2,000-pound 1963 road racer, it was "official" and available to the public.

Included with the Grand Sport option was the $1,450 optional LT4 engine with 330 hp. The most noticeable features were the Admiral Blue paint and bold white stripe that ran over the hood, top, and tail, and the

blacked-out ZR-1, 5-spoke wheels that wore Goodyear P255/45ZR-17 tires in the front and P315/35ZR-17 tires in the rear. Rather than use the ZR-1's wide rear body parts, the rear tires were covered with fender flares designed for Japanese export Corvettes, that almost no one knew about. The roadsters all had smaller rear tires and no rear fender flares.

There were three hot-ticket options for the '96 Corvette. As an interim step for the C5 model, there was the new LT4 engine that was only available with manual transmission Corvettes. This 330-hp option put the '96 Corvette in the 13.5-second quarter-mile range. Then there was the $1,250 Collector's Edition with its Sebring Silver paint and ZR-1-style 17-inch wheels. And for the historic racing crowd, there was the Grand Sport option.

In 1963, then Chief Engineer Zora Arkus-Duntov, built five, 2,000-pound Corvette replica race cars to battle Carroll Shelby's 298 Cobras. When the GM brass found out about Duntov's back door racing program, the axe fell and the five Grand Sports were thankfully sold and not put into the crusher.

In the late '80s Corvette racer and engineer Dick Guldstrand built modified Corvettes that he called "Grand Sport 80," followed by his stunning "GS90 Corvette" in the mid '90s. But for some odd reason, Chevrolet stayed away from using the Grand Sport tag until 1996.

The Grand Sport option (RPO Z16) was available on the coupe for $3,250 and on the roadster for $2,880.

The interior could be either all black, or red and black with embroidered "Grand Sport" trim. Other GS details included black brake calipers with raised Corvette lettering and special serial number sequences, similar to the ZR-1. Red hash marks were added to the driver's side front fender as a salute to the racing '63 Grand Sports.

The new LT4 engine also saluted the Grand Sport with a bright red throttle body with "Grand Sport" lettering. All of the other Corvette performance options were available with the Grand Sport.

A loaded Grand Sport coupe cost nearly $45,000 and a roadster went for over $53,000. To insure exclusivity, only 1,000 Grand Sports were built: 810 coupes and 190 roadsters. The Grand Sport option was part of the 3-part swan song for the C4 Corvette. The Grand Sport Admiral Blue with white stripes has become a popular paint scheme that has shown up on many other generation Vettes. Zora would have been very happy.

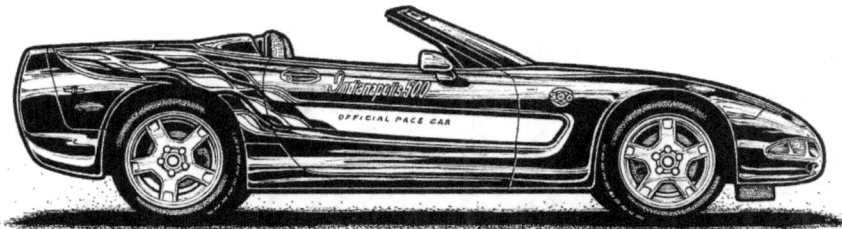

1998 Indy 500 Pace Car
"Pacing The 500... Again"

1998 was a spectacular year for Chevrolet's Corvette. Not only did sales more than triple over '97, but the convertible was back, the Vette was voted *Motor Trend's* "Car of the Year," and the car was even chosen to pace the 82nd Indianapolis 500 - its second such appearance at Indy in only four years.

The Corvette's fourth time pacing "the greatest spectacle in racing" was by far its most successful. While there were a lot of background changes - not least the race's switch from the CART series, a move

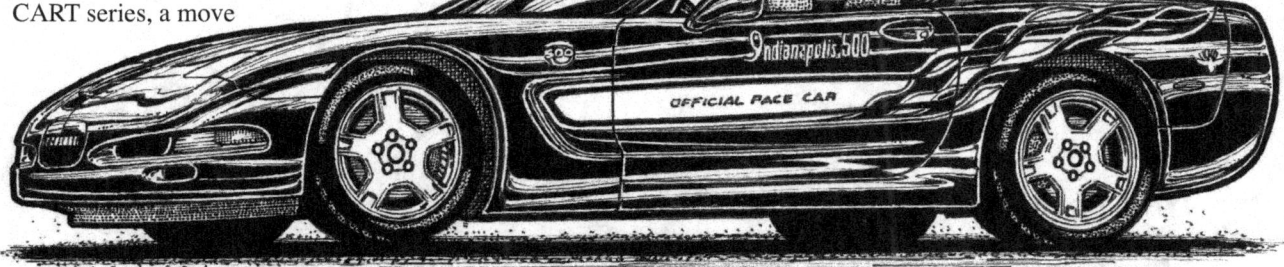

that left some purists less than thrilled - Indy was still the most watched auto racing event on the planet. Having the new C5 convertible, with its 200 mph graphics, leading a pack of 200+mph Indy racers amounted to a multi-million dollar, worldwide publicity event for Chevrolet.

Cars selected to pace the Indy 500 typically need some juicing up to handle the job, but this was not the case with the '98 Corvette. The car used to start the race was surprisingly stock. The exterior of the car was virtually the same as what any customer with $50,000 could buy at his local Chevrolet dealer, with very few exceptions. The pace car had built-in roll bars behind the seats and strobe lights integrated into the back of the tonneau cover. The Vette's intake and exhaust systems were also slightly modified, netting an additional 25 horsepower and bringing the LS1's output up to 370. The transmission was a stock 4-speed automatic.

Behind the wheel of the Corvette Pace Car was champion golfer Greg "The Shark" Norman. Some speculated that Greg was chose because of his

While the '98 Corvette Pace Car was arguably the finest of the four Corvette Pace Cars to that date, Chevrolet only built a total of 1,163 of them. The sticker price was $49,464 for the automatic version and $50,229 for the 6-speed-manual version. Of the 1,163 cars built, 616 were automatics and 547 were manual-transmission cars.

When the green light was given for the '98 convertible to pace that year's Indy 500, Corvette designers were told, "We want something that will grab people instantly. The goal of the package is to stand out." Everyone was very pleased with the design.

The car was painted "Radar Blue" - actually, more of a blue-purple. Starting from the front fender vents, a wide yellow stripe that faded to white, with thin red stripes ran back towards the doors and blended into a checkered-flag pattern that wrapped up and over the rear deck. The hood had wide twin yellow with thin red stripes that also blended into a checkered-flag design. The stock wheels were painted with the same yellow used on the graphics.

The rest of the package was more icing on the cake and included leather sport seats with yellow inserts, electronic dual-zone heating and air conditioning, an anti-theft locking system, digital clock, Delco AM/FM radio with a CD player, Bose speakers, and speed-compensated volume control. Also included were special floor mats with the Indy 500 logo, yellow stitching on the

historically appropriate nickname. Actually, Greg had been the Chevrolet trucks spokesperson since '95 and was highly visible in many of Chevy's TV ads. Prior to the race, Norman speculated about driving the Indy 500 Pace Car Corvette, saying, "Approaching the 18th green in a major tournament is exciting, but leading the pack of roaring horsepower, in that new Corvette convertible - that's going to be a special moment."

leather shifter knob, a performance axle, and fog lamps. The RPO-Z4Z Pace Car Replica option was only available on Corvette convertibles.

By 1998, Corvettes had paced the Indy 500 four times. Chevrolet built 6,502 '78 pace cars, 7,315 '86 pace cars, 527 '95 pace cars, and 1,163 '98 pace cars. While not the rarest of the Corvette pace cars, it was definitely the fastest and wildest-looking Corvette Pace Car to date.

CHAPTER 5: SPECIAL EDITIONS AND TUNER CORVETTES

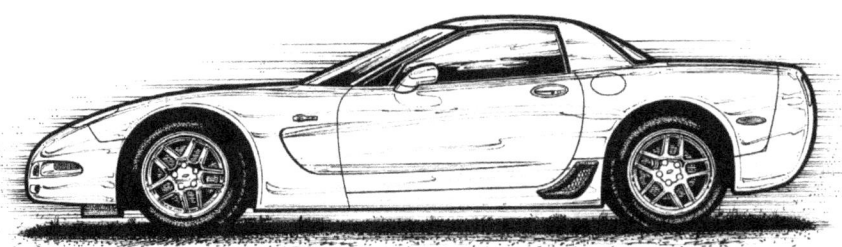

2001 Z06 Corvette
"The INCREDIBLE Z06"

This was the Corvette to die for. When we think of really hot Vettes, we often think of the old big-blocks or the exotic ZR-1. Those big-blocks were pricey, however, and not always easy to live with. And while the ZR-1 was a jewel, it cost nearly twice as much as the base car. All that changed in '01, with the arrival of the Z06, a genuine performance bargain, with numbers to prove it.

The Z06 could sprint from 0-to-60 in just 4.0-seconds and run the

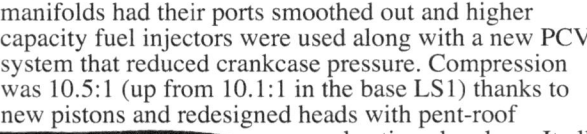

quarter-mile in 12.6 seconds @ 114 mph. Top speed was just over 170 mph. Fuel mileage was 18 mpg in the city and 28 mpg on the highway. The best part was that this kind of performance could be ordered from your local Chevy dealer for just $25 more than the price of the base Corvette!

The hardtop version of the C5 was the perfect platform for the Z06 because it was the stiffest of all three body styles. Since another 35 hp was added to the car with the new LS6, the chassis and body had to be a rigid as possible. The name "Z06" was borrowed from an obscure "off road" racer kit option for the '63 Sting Ray. For an additional $1,818 a buyer got a great foundation for a race car. A loaded Z06 '63 Corvette cost almost $6,700. That's 58% more than the stock Vette in 1963 and was not an easy car to live with on the street.

To sweeten the deal in '01, Dave Hill and his gang used basic hot-rodding tricks - add more power and take out weight. The new Z06 weighed 100 pounds less than the coupe and convertible with the use of lighter glass, a smaller backlight, a titanium exhaust system, and lighter Goodyear Eagle F1 tires.

The new LS6 used a new block casting that was shared with the LS1. The air cleaner and intake and exhaust manifolds had their ports smoothed out and higher capacity fuel injectors were used along with a new PCV system that reduced crankcase pressure. Compression was 10.5:1 (up from 10.1:1 in the base LS1) thanks to new pistons and redesigned heads with pent-roof combustion chambers. It all added up to 385 hp and 385 ft-lb of torque @ 4,800 rpm. The transaxle was stock, except for the more aggressive ratios and a 3.42:1 axle.

The suspension was already in great shape, so only larger stabilizer bars and stiffer springs were needed. The front and rear camber settings were also adjusted for improved stability.

The interior was available in all-black or black-and-red leather, with extra side bolsters, Z06 embroidery on the headrests, and a 6,500-rpm tachometer. The shifter feel was improved by eliminating the rubber bushings and a transmission temperature sensor was also added. Electronic dual-zone air conditioning was also standard.

Unlike the ZR-1, the Z06 was impossible to miss on the street. The car's model-specific wheels had the same diameters as the stockers but were an

inch wider. In front of the rear wheels were mesh-covered brake ducts. And to finish things off, there were the Z06 badges on the front fenders.

Costing just under $48,000, 5,773 buyers signed on the dotted line. This was the first performance package option since the '95 ZR-1. The official Chevy disclaimer read, "The Z06 is for the extreme Corvette enthusiasts." No argument about that!

THE ILLUSTRATED CORVETTE SERIES

2003 50th Anniversary Corvette
"50 Years of Plastic Fantastic Fun"

By the end of '53, no one in GM imagined that the Corvette would still be in production 50 years later. It's amazing that the parts bin car even lasted a few years, let alone 50-plus. The Corvette was GM Chief of Styling Harley Earl's answer for the many GIs who had just returned from the duty with a taste for European sports cars. There wasn't a single American-made sports car in 1953, and frankly, most Americans just didn't understand the little Chevy.

Were it not for fiberglass, the Corvette would never have been more than a color rendering. While more labor intensive to hand-build all of the body parts from fiberglass, it was much less costly than making tooling for a steel body. Even if the car was a flop, GM's investment in the project amounted to little more than some wooden molds and a few improved off-the-shelf Chevy parts. What initially looked like a big gamble for GM was really a low-risk wager.

Not everyone inside GM liked the Corvette and many wanted to see it go away. Fortunately, a passionate Russian engineer was hired to put his skills into the car. Almost overnight, Duntov whipped the Corvette into shape and issued a resounding call to action: "Let's go racing!" In a few short years, the Corvette went from being a beauty queen to a street and track tough guy.

Thanks to his passion for road racing, Duntov was able to cast the Corvette as GM's performance flagship. By the time the '63 Sting Ray arrived, sales were in the 20,000-per-year range, more than enough to ensure the Corvette's continued existence at GM. The Mako Shark-inspired '68 to '82 Corvette was the longest-running of the five generations, and the '79 model sold an all-time record of 53,807 units. The C4 cars were the ultimate comeback Vettes. Their domination of showroom-stock racing was so complete that they were forced to run in their own series, the Corvette Challenge. In 1990 we saw one of the most awesome production Vettes ever, the ZR-1. Costing over $68,000, it was also the most expensive Vette to that date.

When the fifth-generation Vette arrived in '97, it was like the '60s all over again. The lightweight, 345-hp C5 was as quick as a '66 427 model, faster, got much better gas mileage, was more refined, and a lot quieter. Incredibly, the design of the C5 used some 1,200 fewer parts than the C4. Unlike the '86 C4 convertible, the C5 was designed from the beginning to be a convertible, making the topless car as rigid as the coupe version. Road testers were astounded at the solid C5 roadster. The '99 hardtop started out as the "affordable" Vette became the high-performance Z06 in '01. Corvettes had never been quicker, faster, or better.

The $5,000 '03 50th Anniversary option was available on all coupes and convertibles, but not on the Z06. You couldn't miss the special Anniversary Red paint, which was designed to glow, rather than sparkle. The exterior included unique front-fender emblems and champagne-color painted wheels. Included was GM's active-suspension option, the $1,695 Magnetic Selective Ride Control System, and the 1SB Preferred Equipment Group. This sub-package included the heads-up display, power telescoping steering column, electro-chromic mirrors, memory package, and Twilight Sentinel.

From the driver's seat, you couldn't miss the Anniversary package's interior trim. The shale-colored cabin featured lighter gray-beige seats and carpeting along with a darker gray-beige console, instrument panel, and upper door panels. Also included were special embroidered logos on the seat headrests and floor mats. All '03 Corvettes had the 50th Anniversary emblems on their hood, rear deck, manual, and key blanks, as well as on the tachometer and speedometer.

Despite the steep price tag, 11,632 50th Anniversary specials were sold. That's 32 percent of all '03 Corvettes. A loaded coupe cost just over $52,600, while the roadster went for just over $58,700. Clearly, buyers felt that the extra cost was more than worth it. The 50th Anniversary Corvette may not have been the baddest Vette ever made, but it had top-shelf trim, 350 horses under the hood, and a genuine racing heritage to stand upon. Sweet!

CHAPTER 5: SPECIAL EDITIONS AND TUNER CORVETTES

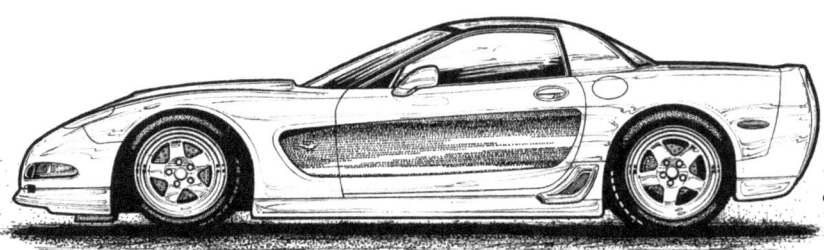

2003 Guldstrand 50th Anniversary 427 Corvette
"Guldstrand-Style 427 Corvette"

Specialty-car builders have been building on the well engineered Corvette for years. Some specialty Vettes, including certain Callaway models, are so heavily modified that they bear little resemblance to the car on which they're based. Then there are others that take a more basic approach.

The factory-built 50th Anniversary Corvette was a beautiful car, but many Vette fans were hoping for more, much more. For those insatiable few, with deep pockets, the Guldstrand version offered an easy fix.

The factory option was available on the '03 coupe and convertible - but not the Z06 - for $5,000 over the base price of the car ($43,895 for the coupe and $50,370 for the convertible). The package included special Red "Xirallic crystal" paint, special interior and exterior decoration, Magnetic Selective Ride Control, and the 1SB option, which bundled various creature comfort upgrades. There was no extra power and, aside from the active suspension option, no additional performance.

It's no surprise that a Dick Guldstrand–designed 50th Anniversary Vette would be different. Guldstrand started his road-racing career in the late '50s and is one of the few to have actually raced a '63 Grand Sport. "Goldie" has competed and won at Sebring, the 24 Hours of Daytona, and the 24 Hours of Le Mans. It stands to reason, then, that Guldstrand knows how to coax a lot of extra oomph from a relatively unmodified production Corvette.

Obtaining a Guldstrand Signature Edition 50th Anniversary Corvette was an easy process. First, you purchased a new $51,155 '03 Z06 Corvette. After signing contracts and payment of an additional $49,330 is made, your Z06 was sent to the Guldstrand Motor Products in Troy, Michigan, for the 8 to 16 weeks build process.

The engine is bored and stroked to 427-ci by Katech for power and durability. The bottom end received a 4340 forged crankshaft connected to Katech pistons and Carrillo rods, yielding a 10.8:1 compression ratio. Billet steel was used for the main caps as well as the head and main-bearing studs. The heads were ported and refitted with the stock rocker arms. A special performance camshaft with higher lift and longer duration orchestrates valve action. A ported throttle body and a pair of Flowmaster mufflers with new tailpipes rounded complete the engine mods.

The Z06 suspension is stock except for an overall lowering of one-inch and the addition of larger, front and rear stabilizer bars. The wheel/tire combination was also upgraded and enlarged, with gummy Michelin Pilot Sport rubber (275/35ZR-18 front and 295/35ZR-19 rear) mounted on Fikse forged rims.

The first thing you'll notice is its brilliant Anniversary Gold paint and Cobalt Blue side decoration. A closer look reveals some very interesting bodywork. The front chin spoiler and side skirts are toned-down versions of the C5-R pieces, while the rear features a mild spoiler and small flares behind the wheels. The hood accentuates the stock twin "humps" and adds a set of vents towards the front. The Z06's signature rear fender scoops remain.

Magazine reviewers who appreciated Corvettes loved the car, praising its race-inspired edginess and distinctive good looks. They really liked the 500 hp and 520 lb-ft of torque, which were sufficient to push the Vette through the quarter mile in just 12.4 seconds.

Guldstrand's goal was to commemorate the Corvette's golden anniversary with a limited run of 50 cars. Only a handful were built, making them quite rare. Was the Signature Edition the fastest, baddest specialty Corvette ever made? Probably not, but it's still an exceptional car.

2004 Limited Edition Corvette
"Salute to the C5-R"

It all goes back to one man's passion for racing. Zora Arkus-Duntov had the kind of expertise that only comes from putting it all on the line in a four-wheel drift. Throughout the Corvette's development, he always had racing on his mind. Bill Mitchell called this quality "having gasoline in your veins," and in Duntov's case, it showed: No sooner had he stuffed

the new 265 small-block into the '55 Vette than secret plans were hatched to build the first Corvette Le Mans racer, the Corvette SS.

Zora kept the program quiet, but when the Corvette SS went public in '57, management pulled the plug. Fortunately the parts escaped the crusher. In '59, Bill Mitchell used the running gear for his Sting Ray racer that won the SCCA C/Modified Championship in '60..

As much as Duntov wanted to build racing Vettes, he was relegated to making parts for independent racers. In 1960, with backdoor help from Duntov, privateer Briggs Cunningham built three Corvettes to race at Le Mans. He won First in his class and Eighth overall.

Then, in '63, Duntov built his last Vette racer, the Grand Sport Corvettes. When word of the project leaked out, plans for a production Grand Sport were shelved indefinitely. Zora spent the rest of his career improving the Vette and providing material support to private race teams.

In '67 Dick Guldstrand and Bob Bondurant took an L88 Corvette to Le Mans. The team ultimately dropped out with mechanical problems, but not before hitting a top speed of 171 mph. Then, in '72, John Greenwood and Dick Smothers raced the BFGoodrich L88 Corvette at Le Mans, dropping out after 10 hours. Greenwood was back at Le Mans in 1976 with his wild, "Batmobile"

wide-body Corvette; he was sidelined after five hours.

There wasn't another major Corvette effort at Le Mans until 1995, when Reeves Callaway's cars grabbed Second and Third Place class wins. With the C5 selling well, and a new attitude towards racing inside GM, Corvette fans saw the first factory-supported Corvette racer in 1999 - the C5-R. After two years of sorting out the car, the team won Le Mans in '01. The C5-R repeated the feat in '02 and '04. For the '04 season, the team won 10 First Place wins in 10 races!

To celebrate the success of the C5-Rs, Chevrolet offered the Commemorative Edition option on all '04 Corvettes - coupes, convertibles, and the Z06. The paint scheme and stripes were based on the '03 C5-R cars, and every available performance and luxury feature was included. This was a $3,700 option for the coupe and convertible, and a $4,335 option on the Z06. A total of 6,899 units were built, accounting for 20 percent of all '04 Vettes.

All Commemorative Edition cars had the special Le Mans blue paint with silver stripes and red piping that started on the hood, went over the roof and on to the rear deck, crossed-flags embroidery on the headrests, polished Z06 wheels with unique centers, and special emblems. The Z06 version also had a carbon-fiber hood that saved 10.6 pounds. The coupe and convertible had a two-tone shale interior, while the Z06 cars had a black interior.

Commemorative Edition Corvettes often are parked together at Corvette shows making for an impressive display. It may have taken 48 years to win at Le Mans, but it was worth the wait. We owe it all to one man's vision, many years ago.

CHAPTER 5: SPECIAL EDITIONS AND TUNER CORVETTES

Mallett Corvettes
"Tweaking the C6 Into a Supercar"

Every generation seems to have its own crop of enthusiasts who aren't satisfied with the status quo. Carroll Shelby was the first tuner to make his mark in the muscle car era. What Shelby did for the Mustang, Joel Rosen did with his Phase III Supercars. In the mid-'80s, Reeves Callaway provided tuner Corvettes for monied enthusiasts.

Then, in the late '90s, two new names surfaced in the Corvette tuner arena: Chuck and Lance Mallett.

The '84 C4 ushered in a new era of racing Corvettes that dominated the competition. The Vettes were so fast they were booted out of the SCCA Showroom Stock Series after the '88 season. The car came back for '89 in the exclusive Corvette Challenge. Chuck Mallett worked as crew chief on several of the Challenge cars and developed an intimate knowledge of the C4. Chuck also built the full tube frame and roll cage for Tommy Morrison's '91 Daytona 24-Hour EDS ZR-1. When the C5 was released in '97, the Mallett brothers were ready to take the hot Vette to new levels.

The introduction of the LS1 engine essentially leveled the playing field for small-block Chevy engine builders. The engines are known to respond well to modifications, and the LS1 was just the same. With a new chassis and engine to work with, the Mallett brothers and Dave Sarafian, founded Mallett Cars, Ltd., and started plans for their specialty Corvette. Mercedes had their Hammer; the Corvette world would have a Mallett!

Specialty-car builders can do things the big car makers would never even try. It took a year for the Mallett team to sort out its first Mallett package - the 435. Due to the LS1's tight bore spacing, the engine could not be bored out to 427 ci. But the stroke was increased to bumped by 26 to yield 372 ci. Compression was raised to 11:0:1 and the LS1 heads only needed minor porting and stiffer springs. A K&N air filter, and stock exhaust manifolds were used with barrel-type mufflers wrapped in carbon fiber. The modified LS1 made 435 hp and 450-ft-lb or torque—increases of 90 hp and 100 ft-lb over stock. The transaxle was stock, but the shifter's rubber bushings were eliminated for improved action.

The Z51 suspension option was used because of its power-steering-fluid cooler and a larger rear sway bar. The car was lowered 1.25-inches, but the stock springs were kept. A larger front anti-roll bar was installed, along with Penske adjustable shocks. Mallett-designed alloy wheels on Goodyear Eagle ZR-S tires and fade-resistant brake pads completed the mechanical mods. "Mallett 435" emblems on the front fenders and headrests completed the package.

Performance of the 435 was very impressive. Zero-to-60 times were a second quicker than stock, at 4.1 seconds. Quarter-mile times went from 13.6 seconds at 106 mph to 12.5 @ 116 mpg. Top speed saw a 17-mph increase over stock, up to 188 mph.

The company went on to offer a line of C5 and C6 performance packages and are also planning a custom-bodied C6. Recently they took delivery of a black '09 ZR1 that will get the full Mallett treatment. Could a Mallett ZR1 be in the offing? We'll see.

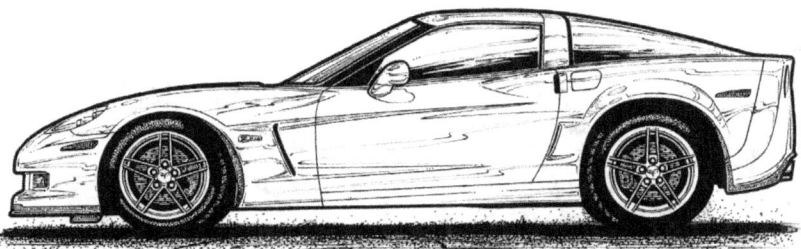

2006 Z06 Corvette
"Semi-Civilized High-Performance"

The Z06 option dates back to '63 as an understated racer kit. Compared with today's 400-horsepower base Vette, the 250 hp '63 entry model was pretty tame. The further up the performance ladder you went, the less streetable the cars became. The solid-lifter big-blocks were tricky to live with, and hot performance options (such as the L88) were ill-suited for street use. If you wanted a really fast Vette with eye-popping braking performance, you had to endure harsh,

race-car driving characteristics. No one ever imagined that one day in the distant future, a production Corvette would perform like the '06 Z06.

Dave Hill and his team took the '01-'04 Z06 cars as far as they could. When the C6 Z06 arrived, it catapulted all aspects of the Corvette's performance into supercar territory. Vette followers hadn't seen a performance leap of this magnitude since the arrival of the '90 ZR-1. Sixteen years later, the Z06 could outperform the ZR-1 in every respect, for almost the same price.

If ever there was an example of a performance car receiving the fruits of racing, it was the '06 Z06. Many of the lessons learned in the C5-R program were poured

wheels, tires, brakes, and other heavy-duty parts is relatively easy, but it adds weight to the car. To counter the additional poundage these parts brought, many advanced weight-saving parts were created, including an aluminum body substructure, a magnesium engine cradle, carbon-fiber front fenders and wheelhouses, and hydroformed aluminum frame rails. Exotic, racing-inspired features included a dry-sump oiling system, a hand-built engine; power steering, transmission, and differential coolers; and a rear-mounted battery.

The new LS7 427 engine was a racer's dream. The all-aluminum small-block made 505 hp at 7,000 rpm and 475 ft-lb of torque at 4,800 rpm. Trick parts included titanium connecting rods, pushrods, and valve springs; forged aluminum pistons with 11:1 compression, a forged steel crankshaft, a low-restriction air-intake system, and hydroformed exhaust headers. The car's revised bodywork included a new front fascia with a larger grille opening and a cold-air scoop, a pair of side vents, aggressive rear-wheel flares

directly into the new Z. But perhaps the most significant difference between this high-performance Corvette and the muscle Vettes of old was the livability factor. Even with 505 hp on tap, a new Z06 is a car you can drive and be happy with every day.

Not only did the C6 Z have 105 more hp than the stock '06 Vette, it weighed 50 lbs less as well. Adding bigger

with built-in brake scoops, 10-spoke aluminum wheels, a larger third brake light, and stainless steel exhaust tips. The interior came with every comfort item imaginable, except for an automatic transmission.

It is not an exaggeration to say that the C6 Z06 was a quantum leap for Corvette. It was also a great platform for even more performance.

CHAPTER 5: SPECIAL EDITIONS AND TUNER CORVETTES

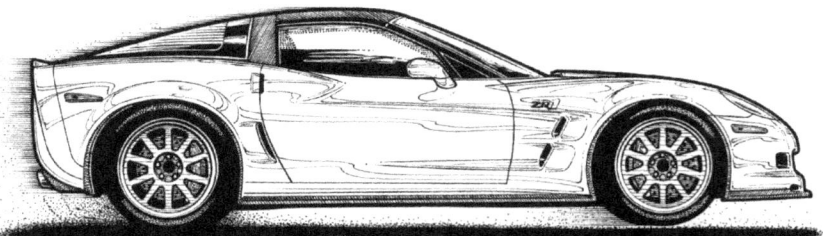

Lingenfelter's 9-Second ZR1 Corvette
"Monster ZR1!"

Chevrolet floored the automotive world with the first-ever supercharged production Corvette. Towards the end of '07, rumors were heating up over a possible supercharged Vette. When the wraps came off, the new Corvette was blown, and its name was ZR1!

It was only a matter of time before someone took apart the 638-hp ZR1 to see if Chevrolet left any untapped power in the 376-ci, all-aluminum LS9 engine. Enter the very

talented team at Lingenfelter Performance Engineering. And oh, they found quite a rich vein of power.

Off the showroom floor with pump gas, the new ZR1 is capable of 0-60 in just 3.5 seconds, the quarter-mile in 11.2 seconds, and a restricted top speed of 205 mph. The LPE team established their parameters: how much quicker can we make the ZR1 using only bolt-on parts? Keep this in mind: No weight was taken out of the car, and none of the ZR1's creature comforts were disabled. Aside from a TR6060 Z06 gearset, the entire drivetrain is stock, including the ZR1's dual-disc clutch setup.

The basic ZR1 engine and drivetrain are so stout that there wasn't anything to change. About 95 percent of the project focused on stuffing more frigid, compressed air into the LS9. The only change to the exhaust system was the addition of a "mild to wild" device that holds the flappers on the exhaust tips open. Even the rear differential gearing is stock. The dramatic increase in power came mostly forward of the Eaton 2-rotor, 4-lobe supercharger.

LPE installed an 8.5-inch-diameter harmonic balancer and a 2.60-inch supercharger pulley to increase the huffer's speed. The stock supercharger's air-intake snout has a bend in its inner port. LPE designed a new casting that straightens out the bend that's worth an extra 60 hp along with the other special parts. A Lingenfelter S&B air filter and a ported stock throttle body complete the intake setup. The intercooler is a major part of the LS9 system. LPE doubled the capacity of the cooler and increased its reservoir capacity. The intercooler's supercharger inlet was also modified. With everything in place, and 109-octane racing gas, the LS9 netted 739 rwhp and 739 rwtq. Talk about finding horsepower!

Running 345/35R1-8 Mickey Thompson ET Street Radials on the rear and M&H Racemaster 185/50R-18 front tires mounted on CCW aluminum wheels, the car was ready for testing. On July 3, 2009, at Muncie Dragway, the ZR1 ran a 10.03 at 141.50 mph. Then, on December 9, 2009, the car made a best-ever run of 9.813 at 145.74 mph!

LPE proved what an astonishing car the ZR1 really is. I'm certain that other tuners will follow. LPE also hinted that a standing-mile top-speed test might be in the works. Lastly, all of the parts used on this car are available - that is, if your ZR1 isn't quick enough for you.

2008 427 Limited Edition Corvette
"Pace & Present"

The next time you're admiring one of those '66-'69 427 Corvette beauties, give a big thank-you to NASCAR. "What?" you ask. "Corvettes never raced in NASCAR." True, the big block was indeed designed for NASCAR, but in the process Chevrolet created a new legend that Corvette fans would never forget.

After watching Impalas try to keep up with the competition, Chevy created the Z11 427 - a stroked 409 truck engine, but it really wasn't enough to win races. What we all know as the Chevy big-block began in July '62 as a project helmed by engineer Dick Keinath. Known inside Chevrolet as the Mark II, the auto press called it "Chevy's Mystery Motor." The bottom end was similar to that of the 409, but it was the cylinder heads that made the mojo. The free-flowing heads had staggered valves that seemed to be pointing in all directions, hence the nickname, "The Porcupine." The Mark II produced over 500 hp, more than enough for Smokey Yunick's Impala to shatter speed records and gather a lot of attention at Daytona in '63.

Then GM proclaimed, "We don't race" and canceled the racing project, but they kept the engine. The new motor was a runner, and Corvette product planners were looking for an easier way to make power than the fuel-injected 327. Zora Arkus-Duntov didn't like the new engine because the package added 150 pounds to the front end. Zora lost this battle, but buyers won a big boost under the hood.

Creating a big-block Corvette involved more than just dropping in a new engine. Needed new parts included: a new hood, a wider radiator, a larger fan and radiator shroud, a revised crossmember, stiffer front springs and a larger sway bar, a stronger clutch, heavy-duty rear axle shafts and universal joints, an improved differential, a new rear anti-sway bar, and host of smaller details.

The $292 L78 production big-block started out as a 396, under rated at 425 hp. With the new side pipes option, the '65 big-block Vette had lots of bark and bite. Then the following year, GM boosted the big-block's displacement to 427 ci. To prove that the engine could be civilized, the hydraulic-lifter L36 provided 390 hp without the solid-lifter hassle.

In '67, Chevy created the legendary 435 hp L71, topped with three 2-barrel carburetors and a large, triangular air cleaner. Racers could order the aluminum-headed L88 and L89 and in '69 there was the famous all-aluminum ZL1.

Now let's fast-forward to the '06 LS7-powered Z06. Although considered a small-block engine, the high-tech LS7 shares nothing with its SBC predecessors. Packing 505 net hp (at least 600 horses by the old "gross" rating system) the C6 Z06 can click off high 11s in the quarter-mile all day long, with the air conditioning and CD player running.

The '08 Corvette 427 Special Edition Z06 is a trim-only package that uses the same hardware as a regular Z06. The $12,920 option comes with Crystal Red Tintcoat paint, "stinger" hood graphics and 427 badge, exclusive 10-spoke chrome wheels, a body-colored rear spoiler and door handles, "427" embroidery on the seats and floormats, and Z06 door plates.

Additionally, every car is signed and numbered by recently retired Corvette plant manager Wil Cooksey. The production run is limited to 427 units domestically and 78 imports, for a total of 505 - the same as the LS7's output rating. Corvettes have a long history of being bold, fast, and uniquely American. The 427 Special Edition Z06 fits right into that tradition.

CHAPTER 5: SPECIAL EDITIONS AND TUNER CORVETTES

2008 Pace Car Corvette
"Twins Pace the '08 Indy 500"

In 1978, VETTE magazine was a bi-monthly publication, and I was a contributing artist and writer. I was talking with then-editor Marty Schorr about my next illustrated article when he asked, "Did you hear the good news? A Corvette is going to pace the Indy 500, and they're going to offer replicas!"

Although many muscle cars had paced the 500, the Corvette just didn't seem like the right fit for Indy cars. Nevertheless, the '78 Pace Car edition was a gorgeous model. Initially, Chevy was going to make just 300 Pace Cars, but dealers and customers howled. By the end of '78, 6,502 copies had been built.

Now, let's fast-forward to '86, when General Chuck Yeager drove a yellow Corvette Pace Car convertible at Indy. Chevy decided that all '86 Corvette convertibles would be "pace car replicas." A total of 7,315 were built, and each a set of Indy 500 Pace Car decals the customer or dealer could apply if he or she so chose. But very few decal sets ending up adorning the sides of '86 roadsters.

The '08 model year marks an important milestone for the Corvette and its relationship with The Indy 500. 2008 was the 30th anniversary of the first Indy 500 Pace Car Corvette, and a record the tenth time the Corvette has paced the race.

A Corvette has paced the 500 in '78, '86, '95, '98, '02, '04, '05, '06, '07, and '08. Replicas of the Vette Pace Cars, meanwhile, were offered in '78, '86, '95, '98, '07, and '08, and these models have proved to be some of the most valued of the special editions. But wait, for '08 Chevy had two Corvette Pace Cars on hand. The black-and-silver version was an available option, and the greenish-gold, E85-powered Z06 was for track use only.

The publicly offered '08 Pace Car was available in both coupe and convertible form, for $59,090 or $68,160, with the base LS3, six-speed manual or optional ($1,250) paddle-shift automatic transmission and five-spoke aluminum wheels. The package included the special two-tone paint, Indy 500 logos on the front fenders and seats, and a Z06 rear spoiler. The 3LT option package included Heads Up Display, Power Telescoping Steering Column, Auto Dimming Mirrors, Memory Package, Heated Seats, and the US9 Bose Sound System. Convertibles got the Power Roof option as standard. For a little extra grunt and grip, the Dual Mode Exhaust and the Z51 Performance Package were included. The only other options were the $1,750 Navigation and the $1,400 Dual Removable Roof Panels. Emerson Fittipaldi, who drove the E85 pace car in the race, signed all 500 cars.

The actual Z06 Pace Car was a one-of-a-kind Corvette built to show that high performance could also be green. Decoration aside, the car was a stock Z06 with modifications to the fuel system and powertrain controller that allowed it to run on E85. The Gold Rush Green paint scheme was stunning, fluctuating between metallic gold and green depending on the level and angle of the light. The subtle checker pattern on the sides was similar to that used on the production pace car.

There's factoid about E85 and Fittipaldi: The two-time Indy 500 winner is in the ethanol-refining business in his native Brazil, which happens to be the leader for ethanol usage in cars.

2008 represents the fifth year in a row that a Corvette has paced the Indy 500 and the second year in a row they dished up two special edition Vettes. In '07 we saw the Ron Fellows Special Edition Z06 and another Pace Car Special. This year we have the Special Edition 427 Z06 and the Pace Car Special. I think that Chevy is liking this "special edition" thing.

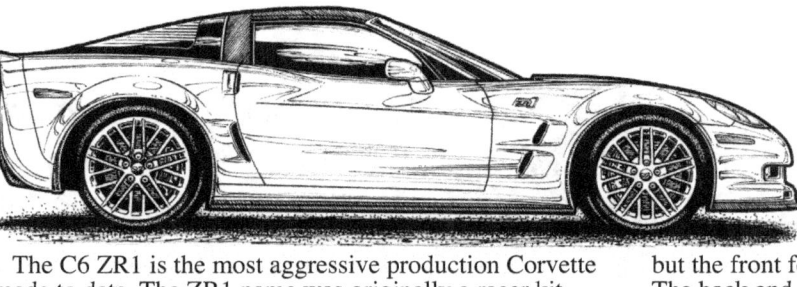

2009 ZR1 Corvette
"Chevy's World-Class Supercar"

The C6 ZR1 is the most aggressive production Corvette made to date. The ZR1 name was originally a racer kit option from '70-1/2 to '72. The C4 ZR-1, with its jewel-like LT5 engine, was a terrific machine, but it didn't look that much different from a regular Corvette. Not since the '65-'69 big-blocks, with those loud sidepipes, have we has so much visual testosterone. The '09 ZR1 bears a strong resemblance to the L88 Corvettes, with their flared fenders, but unlike the earlier super-Vettes, this is a mega-muscle machine you can live with everyday.

Forty years after the L88 and ZL1, we now have a Corvette that delivers unimagined performance in every area. Let's draw some comparisons.

The new ZR1 packs a net 638 hp and 604 ft-lb of torque. The L88 and ZL1 engines never received accurate published power ratings, but output was estimated to be close to 550 gross hp. The new ZR1's LS9 engine also passes emissions tests and is capable of over 20 mpg on the highway. The beasts of old got 8-10 mpg and had no emissions controls whatsoever. The new ZR1 also has a suspension that won't hammer out your fillings and brakes that don't have to be hot to work. Yes, 40 years of development have paid off big-time.

The ZR1 looks tough from every angle. While the Z06 is a very aggressive-looking, the ZR1 takes things to the next level. The entire front end and the roof section are made of carbon fiber. Chevy decided to show off the exotic material by using a $60,000-a-gallon clearcoat over the new chin spoiler, rocker panels, front fenders, and roof. The new hood is one-inch taller than a regular Vette's, bears a slight resemblance to the C3 big-block hoods, and features a Plexiglas window that shows off the LS9's engine cover. The front and rear fender flares are the same as the Z06's, but the front fenders have larger, more aggressive vents. The back end has a short, full-width spoiler, and ZR1 badges adorn the front fenders and rear bumper cover. The ZR1 is loaded with exotic hardware. The all-aluminum LS9 engine is not only supercharged, it has an intercooler, port fuel injection, and a 10.75-quart dry-sump oil system. The TR6060 six-speed transmission has been beefed up, uses a LUK dual-disc clutch. and the gear ratios are closer than those in the Z06.

The ZR1 rides on Speedline forged-aluminum wheels that measure 19x10 inches in the front and 20x12 inches in the rear. The Michelin Pilot Sports measure 285/30-19 on the front and 335/25-20 on the rear. The brake system uses Brembo carbon-ceramic rotors that are vented and cross-drilled, and measure 15.5x1.6 and 15x1.4 inches fore and aft, respectively. Six-piston calipers are employed in the front, and four-piston units are used in the back. The brake pads are twice the size as those used on the Z06 and will last the car's lifetime in street use.

The ZR1's rock-solid chassis and frame are derived from the Z06, but the suspension is modified with next-generation Delphi Magnetorheological (MR) variable shocks, softer springs, larger sway bars, and revised rear-suspension geometry.

The interior has only slight additions. The seatbacks feature "ZR1" embroidery, a boost gauge and "ZR1" tach face plate spruce up the instrument cluster, and the door-sill plates also bear the car's model designation. And so you don't forget how fast the ZR1 can take you, the speedometer goes up to 220 mph!

Now the rumor mill is buzzing with talk about where Chevy will go with the ZR1. All-wheel-drive and a new interior could be added, but we'll have to wait and see!

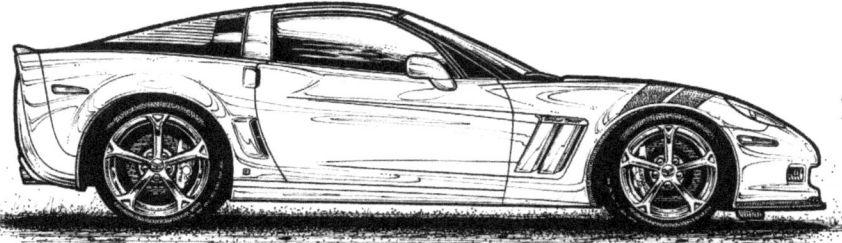

2010 Grand Sport Corvette
"The Grand Sport Is Back!"

There's nothing quite like a surprise at a birthday party. On April 24, 2009, at the National Corvette Museum's C5/C6 Registry Birthday Bash, GM officials floored the audience with the unveiling of the '10 Grand Sport Corvette. The last time we saw a Grand Sport was more than 14 years ago, in '96. Times were very different then, as the C4 was making its last appearance. The Admiral Blue Grand Sport - with its 330-hp LT4 engine, white center stripes, red hash marks, black wheels, and other assorted details - was an instant classic. Production was limited to 1,000 units, priced at $40,475 for the coupe and $48,310 for the roadster, and was the most expensive of the '96 Corvettes.

Of course, the story goes back to '63 when Mr. Duntov just wouldn't stop building Corvette race cars. It was all very simple; Zora just couldn't accept being beaten by the 2,000-lb Cobra. To give the new Sting Ray a chance, he built five 2,000-lb racing versions of the street Vette. But it wasn't meant to be and we're lucky the Grand Sports weren't sent to the crusher as punishment. Let's fast-forward 47 years to the '10 Grand Sport.

The C6 Grand Sport is a completely different animal. The base LS3 engine produces 430 hp — 100 more than the C4 GS. The new option fits neatly between the base Corvette and the Z06, and is available on both coupe and convertible models, in all color combinations. The signature fender hash marks are optional. Perhaps most notable are the Z06 body panels, which include front and rear flared fenders, a front air-splitter, and a rear spoiler. The rear brake-cooling scoops are functional, but the front nose scoop is not. Visually separating the Grand Sport from the Z06 are a set of revised front-fender vents, with their '67-inspired vertical slats. Model-specific five-spoke wheels are available in silver, Competition Gray, or chrome. The fronts measure 9.5 x 18 inches and are shod with Goodyear F1 run-flat tires sized 275/35ZR-18. The 12 x 19-inch rears, meanwhile, get massive 325/30ZR-19s. The front brakes have cross-drilled 14-inch front rotors and six-piston calipers, while the rears boast 13.5-inch rotors with four-piston binders. All four calipers are painted silver and wear red "Corvette" lettering.

Since the Grand Sport replaces the Z51 Performance Option, all of the Z51 goodies - heavy-duty springs, shocks, and stabilizer bars, along with coolers for the engine oil, transmission fluid, and steering fluid - are included. Additionally, all six-speed manual cars come with the Z52 option, which adds a dry-sump oil system, a rear-mounted battery, and a differential cooler. Manual cars also receive a new launch-control system. This system allows the driver to simply floor the gas, at which point the computer automatically selects the optimum launch rpm. All that's left for the driver to do is drop the clutch and start shifting. All of the standard Corvette options are available on the Grand Sport, including four trim packages and the Dual Mode Exhaust System. Priced at $55,720 for the coupe and $59,530 for the convertible, the new Grand Sport is still around $15,000 less than a Z06. Zero-to-60 times clock in at 4 seconds flat, with quarter-miles in the low 13s or better. The car generates 1.0g on the skidpad and has an EPA rating of 26 mpg on the highway. Top speed is between 185 and 190 mph, making the latest Grand Sport faster than even the old racing versions.

It's ironic that a moniker that had slipped into the mists of racing legend, is now a reasonably priced, beautiful, full-fledged production car. Thanks to legions of fans that kept the faith, the C6 Grand Sport can take its place among the greats of Corvette history.

The Future of the Corvette

It seems that a few years into every generation Corvette, designers start thinking about a replacement car. In the Summer of '08 we got a glimpse of a possible C6 replacement in the form of the *Transformers* movie-concept car. Speculation over future Corvettes has been "sport" for automotive journalists for decades, and with all of the turmoil inside GM and everything being up in the air, C7 *and* C8 speculation is as juicy as can be.

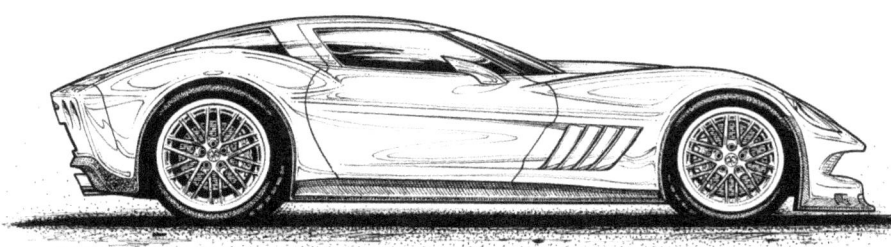

C7 Corvette
"Return of the Split-Window Coupe Sting Ray?"

Let me say at the outset that I have no inside connections to the Corvette design group and even if I did, I'm certain that they're not about to spill the beans. Two recent developments have stoked the flames to a fever pitch. First was the worst Corvette sales year since '61. Sales went from 35,310 in '08 to 13,934 in '09 - a 60 percent drop! The only good part was that sales of sports car across the board were similarly off. Second was the reaction of GM's new upper management.

According the BusinessWeek, ten of GM's 12 member board of directors have no car experience and have reacted the the Corvette's sales drop by calling upon GM design centers from around the world to submit new designs for the C7. While that strategy might "make sense" if you have no car design background, from this writer's position, the Corvette could lose its essence for the sake of "let's do something different." So far, we have not seen any of the "world designs." Three design parameters have been drawn. First, to attract more customers in Europe. Second, to attract younger buyers. And third, to make the car smaller. Let's take these concerns apart. First, although Europeans like seeing the booming Corvettes at Le Mans, they don't and probably never will buy very many. Corvettes are, and have always been, the antithesis of European design. Second, Corvettes have always cost twice as much as a regular Chevy. A $50,000 base Corvette is much more than most young people today can afford And third, the "Corvettes are too big" complaint is a visual issue. The current 911 Porsche Turbo and the Nissan GT-R Premium weigh 362 and 1,105-pounds more than the Z06 Vette respectively and don't get heat for their size. So, does the Corvette have a weight problem?

The latest news is that the C7 will be an interim car while the "world-class" mid-engine C8 is being developed for a possible '18 release. It's all completely up in the air. Seven or eight years out is an eternity in the car business.

The proportions of my illustrations are the same as the Centennial concept car and since the design draws on the C2 as a start, I took the shape even closer to the C2 Sting Ray configuration.

The side-view of the nose is definitely "Shark" and the grille, side marker-signals, and air splitter are definitely C6 ZR1. I liked the forward-leaning front fender vents on the Centennial but borrowed the four-louver side-vents from the '67, incorporated into the C6-like side coves. The Centennial car has vertical doors, which seem gimmicky to me. I made the doors shorter and cut them into the roof.

The front air-splitter, side skirts, and rear valance bring the car up to date. When covered headlights were illegal, the pop-up design made sense, but the faired in, covered lights add character. I tried a few different hood domes and felt that this one worked best. The '67 Singer-style seemed forced. While the grille on the Centennial was sort of interesting, I saw too much Cadillac and not enough Corvette. The pointedness of the Centennial is good, but the gills and grille just lost me.

Since the arrival of the C5s, Corvettes have been criticized for having a big butt. The rear fenders of the Centennial's rear fenders are unnecessarily bulky and help to complicate the back-end design. By eliminating the large rear fenders I was able to slim down the back end - no more big butt. Tail lights are classic Corvette.

If a Sting Ray-like roof comes back, the first year should be a split-window and subsequent versions a full window, as a salute to the original. While it was interesting to see the homage to the split-window on the Centennial, I didn't like the center indent on the roof that runs back to the center end point of the leading back edge.

Why did I reach so obviously into the C2 design. The C6 has a gentle Sting Ray flavor on its front and rear fender humps. The Centennial makes that more obvious. By removing the cartoon front and rear gills, I was able to slim down the back end and hold on to the excellent nose design of the C6. The fender humps are almost Mako Shark II-like, yet keep touch with the C2-style front fender humps. The back end is classic corvette, updated with a center brake-light and ground effects rear valance. Blog responses have been very positive towards the four center-mounted exhaust tips. Side-pipes and rear brake vents were so tempting, perhaps on the ZR1 version.

Running gear for the next Vette is not yet known, so lets speculate a little. Since the chassis of the C6 ZR1 is completely sorted out, it would make an excellent base for the C7. GM recently announced that the next generation small-block engine would be E85 compatable. However, looming on the horizon are much tougher CAFE standards, so it's possible we'll see the 427 LS7 go away. Direct-port injection allows for higher compression, so maybe a smaller DPI engine will deliver equal performance as the LS3. Let's hope that they come up with a world-class interior. I do not see the C7 being much smaller, as the current car has a lot stuffed into it. The Z06 might be supercharged and AWD in the C7 ZR1 would be astinishing.

Talk of an interim car leaves me flat. Why bother, just make the current car better. Designing a new Corvette is the hardest styling job in Detroit - it has to look new, yet familiar. I hope that the Corvette stylists are able to draw on the car's rich styling background and don't lose their way chasing a "world car" concept. The Corvette is uniquely America and should stay that way.

THE FUTURE OF THE CORVETTE

More Great Titles From CarTech®

HOW TO REBUILD THE BIG-BLOCK CHEVROLET by Tony E. Huntimer. This book covers the basics of any engine rebuild with more than 450 color photos and step-by-step instruction. Subjects covered include the history of the big-block Chevy, preparation and tool requirements, engine removal and teardown, first inspection, parts, machine work and clean-up, final engine assembly, and start-up. Softbound, 8.5 x 11 inches, 160 pages, approx. 450 color photos. *Item #SA142*

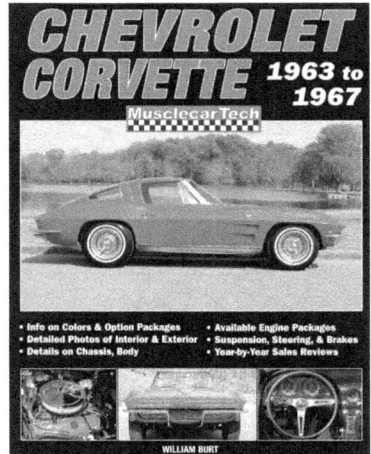

CHEVROLET CORVETTE: 1963–1967 by William Burt. When the 1963 Corvette first appeared, it was obvious that the engineers had cut many of the car's ties to the past — the new Corvette had its own identity. No one can mistake any Corvette produced in 1962 or earlier for a 1963 model. This book uses more than 250 color photos to demonstrate the striking beauty of the Sting Ray 'Vette. Burt covers the available engines, transmissions, suspension, interiors, body styles, colors, and option packages, giving you an all-in-one source for 1963–1967 Corvette information. Softbound, 8.5 x 11 inches, 112 pages, 200 color & 50 b/w photos. *Item #SP101*

How to Rebuild GM LS-Series Engines by Christopher Werner. With the increasing popularity of GM's LS-series engine family, many enthusiasts are ready to rebuild. The first of its kind, How to Rebuild GM LS-Series Engines, tells you exactly how to do that. The book explains variations between the various LS-series engines and elaborates up on the features that make this engine family such an excellent design. As with all Workbench titles, this book details and highlights special components, tools, chemicals, and other accessories needed to get the job done right, the first time. Appendices are packed full of valuable reference information, and the book includes a Work-Along Sheet to help you record vital statistics and measurements along the way. Softbound, 8.5 x 11 inches, 152 pages, 450 color photos. *Item #SA147*

HOW TO REBUILD THE SMALL-BLOCK CHEVROLET REVISED AND UPDATED EDITION by Larry Atherton & Larry Schreib. How to build a street or racing small-block Chevy in your garage. A step-by-step approach explains every procedure used to build or rebuild a small-block engine from crankshaft to carburetor. Includes disassembly, parts inspection, required tools, how to avoid costly mistakes, plus hundreds of performance tips. This book is a completely revised and updated edition. Softbound, 8.5 x 11 inches, 160 pages, over 600 color photos. *Item #SA26*

YENKO by Bob McClurg. A wide range of Chevrolet cars received the YENKO treatment, starting with the Stinger Corvairs and finishing with turbocharged Camaros and even Vegas. Author Bob McClurg tells the fascinating story of how Don Yenko worked his magic on Novas, Chevelles, and, of course, the legendary first-generation Camaros. While many enthusiasts are aware of the cars, few know much about the man behind them, or how he was able to catapult his small-town Pennsylvania dealership to national prominence. Maybe even more amazingly, he accomplished all of this while being a dedicated family man too. This is the complete history. Hardbound, 8.5 x 11 inches, 208 pages, 350 color & 100 b/w photos. *Item #CT485*

FUELIES: FUEL INJECTED CORVETTES 1957-1965 by Robert. Genat Fuelies: Fuel Injected Corvettes 1957-1965 celebrates the nine years of production of the Corvette, the Corvette engines, and the fuel injection units that transformed the car into a performance icon. In that era, "Fuelie" was the slang term used to describe any fuel injected Corvette. And at that time the fuel injected Corvettes were the fastest cars on the street, road course, and drag strip. In addition to the rough exhaust note created by the high compression ratio and long-duration camshaft, gearheads could identify Corvettes with the fuel injection units by the distinctive hiss they produced at idle. The book also covers passenger car installations (Chevrolets from 1957 to 1959, Pontiacs, and Chryslers) and other fuel injection oddities. Softbound, 9x9 inches, 192 pages, 305 color photos. *Item #CT452*

CarTech®, Inc.
39966 Grand Avenue, North Branch, MN 55056
Telephone: (651) 277-1200 or (800) 551-4754 Fax: (651) 277-1203
www.cartechbooks.com

More great titles available from CarTech®...

S-A DESIGN

...per Tuning & Modifying Holley Carburetors — Perf, street and off-road applications. (SA08)

...stom Painting — Gives you an overview of the broad spectrum of custom painting types and techniques. (SA10)

...eet Supercharging, A Complete Guide to — Bolt-on buying, installing and tuning blowers. (SA17)

...gine Blueprinting — Using tools, block selection & prep, crank mods, pistons, heads, cams & more! (SA21)

...vid Vizard's How to Build Horsepower — Building horsepower in any engine. (SA24)

...evrolet Small-Block Parts Interchange Manual — Selecting & s wapping high-perf. small-block parts. (SA55)

...gh-Performance Ford Engine Parts Interchange — Selecting & swapping big- and small-block Ford parts. (SA56)

...w To Build Max Perf Chevy Small-Blocks on a Budget — Would you believe 600 hp for $3000? (SA57)

...w To Build Max Performance Ford V-8s on a Budget — Dyno-tested engine builds for big- & small-blocks. (SA69)

...w To Build Max-Perf Pontiac V8s — Mild perf apps to all-out performance build-ups. (SA78)

...w To Build High-Performance Ignition Systems — Guide to understanding auto ignition systems. (SA79)

...w To Build Max Perf 4.6 Liter Ford Engines — Building & modifying Ford's 2- & 4-valve 4.6/5.4 liter engines. (SA82)

...w To Build Big-Inch Ford Small-Blocks — Add cubic inches without the hassle of switching to a big-block. (SA85)

...w To Build High-Perf Chevy LS1/LS6 Engines — Modifying and tuning Gen-III engines for GM cars and trucks. (SA86)

...w To Build Big-Inch Chevy Small-Blocks — Get the additional torque & horsepower of a big-block. (SA87)

...nda Engine Swaps — Step-by-step instructions for all major tasks involved in engine swapping. (SA93)

...w To Build High-Performance Chevy Small-Block Cams/Valvetrains — Camshaft & valvetrain function, selection, performance, and design. (SA105)

...gh-Performance Jeep Cherokee XJ Builder's Guide 1984–2001 — Build a useful Cherokee for mountains, the mud, the desert, the street, and more. (SA109)

...w to Build and Modify Rochester Quadrajet Carburetors — Selecting, rebuilding, and modifying the Quadrajet Carburetors. (SA113)

...building the Small-Block Chevy: Step-by-Step Videobook — 160-pg book plus 2-hour DVD show you how to build a street or racing small-block Chevy. (SA116)

...w to Paint Your Car on a Budget — Everything you need to know to get a great-looking coat of paint and save money. (SA117)

...w to Drift: The Art of Oversteer — This comprehensive guide to drifting covers both driving techniques and car setup. (SA118)

...rbo: Real World High-Performance Turbocharger Systems — Turbo is the most practical book for enthusiasts who want to make more horsepower. Foreword by Gale Banks. (SA123)

...gh-Performance Chevy Small-Block Cylinder Heads — Learn how to make the most power with this popular modification on your small-block Chevy. (SA125)

...gh Performance Brake Systems — Design, selection, and installation of brake systems for Musclecars, Hot Rods, Imports, Modern Era cars and more. (SA126)

...gh Performance C5 Corvette Builder's Guide — Improve the looks, handling and performance of your Corvette C5. (SA127)

...gh Performance Diesel Builder's Guide — The definitive guide to getting maximum performance out of your diesel engine. (SA129)

...w to Rebuild & Modify Carter/Edelbrock Carbs — The only source for information on rebuilding and tuning these popular carburetors. (SA130)

...ilding Honda K-Series Engine Performance — The first book on the market dedicated exclusively to the Honda K series engine. (SA134)

Engine Management-Advanced Tuning — Take your fuel injection and tuning knowledge to the next level. (SA135)

How to Drag Race — Car setup, beginning and advanced techniques for bracket racing and pro classes, and racing science and math, and more. (SA136)

4x4 Suspension Handbook — Includes suspension basics & theory, advanced/high-performance suspension and lift systems, axles, how-to installations, and more. (SA137)

GM Automatic Overdrive Transmission Builder's and Swapper's Guide — Learn to build a bulletproof tranny and how to swap it into an older chassis as well. (SA140)

High-Performance Subaru Builder's Guide — Subarus are the hottest compacts on the street. Make yours even hotter. (SA141)

How to Build Max-Performance Mitsubishi 4G63t Engines — Covers every system and component of the engine, including a complete history. (SA148)

How to Swap GM LS-Series Engines Into Almost Anything — Includes a historical review and detailed information so you can select and fit the best LS engine. (SA156)

How to Autocross — Covers basic to more advanced modifications that go beyond the stock classes. (SA158)

Designing & Tuning High-Performance Fuel Injection Systems — Complete guide to tuning aftermarket standalone systems. (SA161)

Design & Install In Car Entertainment Systems — The latest and greatest electronic systems, both audio and video. (SA163)

How to Build Max-Performance Hemi Engines — Build the biggest baddest vintage Hemi. (SA164)

How to Digitally Photograph Cars — Learn all the modern techniques and post processing too. (SA168)

High-Performance Differentials, Axles, & Drivelines — Must have book for anyone thinking about setting up a performance differential. (SA170)

How To Build Max-Performance Mopar Big Blocks — Build the baddest wedge Mopar on the block. (SA171)

How to Build Max-Performance Oldsmobile V-8s — Make your Oldsmobile keep up with the pack. (SA172)

Automotive Diagnostic Systems: Understanding OBD-I & OBD II — Learn how modern diagnostic systems work. (SA174)

How to Make Your Muscle Car Handle — Upgrade your muscle car suspension to modern standards. (SA175)

Full-Size Fords 1955–1970 — A complete color history of full-sized fords. (SA176)

Rebuilding Any Automotive Engine: Step-by-Step Videobook — Rebuild any engine with this book DVD combo. DVD is over 3 hours long! (SA179)

How to Supercharge & Turbocharge GM LS-Series Engines — Boost the power of today's most popular engine. (SA180)

The New Mini Performance Handbook — All the performance tricks for your new Mini. (SA182)

How to Build Max-Performance Ford FE Engines — Finally, performance tricks for the FE junkie. (SA183)

Builder's Guide to Hot Rod Chassis & Suspension — Ultimate guide to Hot Rod Suspensions. (SA185)

How to Build Altered Wheelbase Cars — Build a wild altered car. Complete history too! (SA189)

How to Build Period Correct Hot Rods — Build a hot rod true to your favorite period. (SA192)

Automotive Sheet Metal Forming & Fabrication — Create and fabricate your own metalwork. (SA196)

How to Build Max-Performance Chevy Big Block on a Budget — New big-block book from the master, David Vizard. (SA198)

How to Build Big-Inch GM LS-Series Engines — Get more power through displacement from your LS. (SA203)

Performance Automotive Engine Math — All the formulas and facts you will ever need. (SA204)

How to Design, Build & Equip Your Automotive Workshop on a Budget — Working man's guide to building a great work space. (SA207)

Automotive Electrical Performance Projects — Featuring the most popular electrical mods today. (SA209)

How to Port Cylinder Heads — Vizard shares his cylinder head secrets. (SA215)

S-A DESIGN RESTORATION SERIES

How to Restore Your Mustang 1964 1/2–1973 — Step-by-step restoration for your classic Mustang. (SA165)

Muscle Car Interior Restoration Guide — Make your interior look and smell new again. Includes dash restoration. (SA167)

How to Restore Your Camaro 1967–1969 — Step-by-step restoration of your 1st gen Camaro. (SA178)

S-A DESIGN WORKBENCH® SERIES

Workbench® Series books feature step by step instruction with hundreds of color photos for stock rebuilds and automotive repair.

How To Rebuild the Small-Block Chevrolet — (SA26)
How to Rebuild the Small-Block Ford — (SA102)
How to Rebuild & Modify High-Performance Manual Transmissions — (SA103)
How to Rebuild the Big-Block Chevrolet — (SA142)
How to Rebuild the Small-Block Mopar — (SA143)
How to Rebuild GM LS-Series Engines — (SA147)
How to Rebuild Any Automotive Engine — (SA151)
How to Rebuild Honda B-Series Engines — (SA154)
How to Rebuild the 4.6/5.4 Liter Ford — (SA155)
Automotive Welding: A Practical Guide — (SA159)
Automotive Wiring and Electrical Systems — (SA160)
How to Rebuild Big-Block Ford Engines — (SA162)
Automotive Bodywork & Rust Repair — (SA166)
How To Rebuild & Modify GM Turbo 400 Transmissions — (SA186)
How to Rebuild Pontiac V-8s — (SA200)

HISTORIES AND PERSONALITIES

Quarter-Mile Chaos — Rare & stunning photos of terrifying fires, explosions, and crashes in drag racing's golden age. (CT425)

Fuelies: Fuel Injected Corvettes 1957–1965 — The first Corvette book to focus specifically on the fuel injected cars, which are among the most collectible. (CT452)

Slingshot Spectacular: Front-Engine Dragster Era — Relive the golden age of front engine dragsters in this photo packed trip down memory lane. (CT464)

Chrysler Concept Cars 1940–1970 — Fascinating look at the concept cars created by Chrysler during this golden age of the automotive industry. (CT470)

Fuel Altereds Forever — Includes more than 250 photos of the most popular drivers and racecars from the Fuel Altered class. (CT475)

Yenko — Complete and thorough story of the man, his business and his legendary cars. (CT485)

Lost Hot Rods — Great Hot Rods from the past rediscovered. (CT487)

Grumpy's Toys — A collection of Grumpy's greats. (CT489)

Woodward Avenue: Cruising the Legendary — Revisit the glory days of Woodward! (CT491)

Rusted Muscle — A collection of junkyard muscle cars. (CT492)

America's Coolest Station Wagons — Wagons are cooler than they ever have been. (CT493)

Super Stock — A paperback version of a classic best seller. (CT495)

Rusty Pickups: American Workhorses Put to Pasture — Cool collection of old trucks and ads too! (CT496)

Jerry Heasley's Rare Finds — Great collection of Heasley's best finds. (CT497)

Street Sleepers: The Art of the Deceptively Fast Car — Stealth, horsepower, what's not to love? (CT498)

Ed 'Big Daddy' Roth — Paperback reprint of a classic best seller. (CT500)

Car Spy: Secret Cars Exposed by the Industry's Most Notorious Photographer — Cool behind-the-scenes stories spanning 40 years. (CT502)

...Tech®, Inc. 39966 Grand Ave., North Branch, MN 55056. Ph: 800-551-4754 or 651-277-1200 • Fax: 651-277-1203
...ooklands Books Ltd., PO Box 146 Cobham, Surrey KT11 1LG, England. Ph: 01932 865051 • Fax 01932 868803
...ooklands Books Aus., 3/37-39 Green Street, Banksmeadow, NSW 2019, Australia. Ph: 2 9695 7055 • Fax 2 9695 7355

Visit us online at www.cartechbooks.com for more info!

More Information for Your Project ...

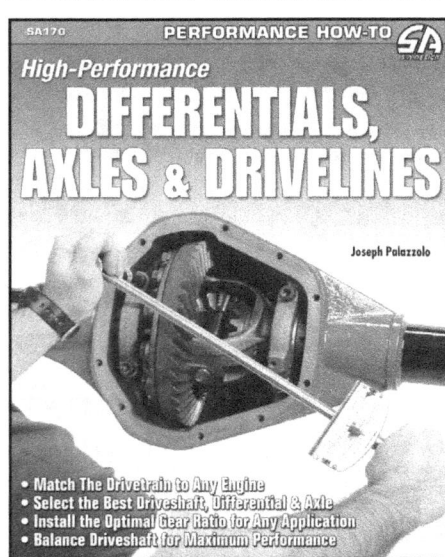

HIGH-PERFORMANCE DIFFERENTIALS, AXELS & DRIVELINES *by Joseph Palazzolo* This book covers everything you need to know about selecting the most desirable gear ratio, rebuilding differentials and other driveline components, and matching driveline components to engine power output. Learn how to set up a limited-slip differential, install high-performance axle shafts, swap out differential gears, and select products for the driveline. This book explains rear differential basics, rear differential housings, rebuilding open rear differentials, limited-slip differentials, and factory differentials. Ring and pinion gears, axle housings, axle shafts, driveshafts, and U-joints are also covered. Softbound, 8-1/2 x 11 inches, 144 pages, approx. 400 color photos. ***Item #SA170***

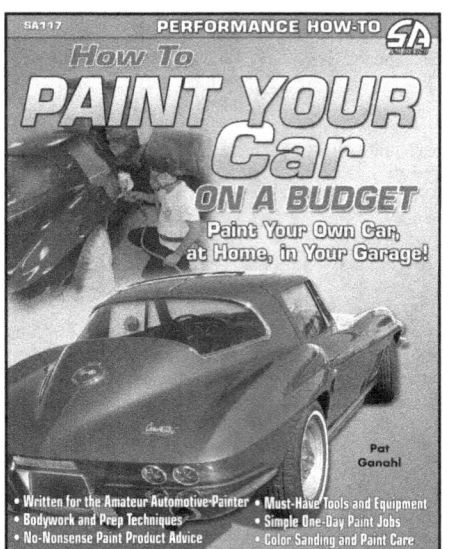

HOW TO PAINT YOUR CAR ON A BUDGET *by Pat Ganahl* If your car needs new paint, or even just a touch-up, the cost involved in getting a professional job can be more than you bargained for. In this book, author Pat Ganahl unveils dozens of secrets that will help anyone paint their own car. From simple scuff-and-squirt jobs to full-on, door-jambs-and-everything paint jobs, Ganahl covers everything you need to know to get a great-looking coat of paint on your car and save lots of money in the process. Covers painting equipment, the ins and outs of prep, masking, painting and sanding products and techniques, and real-world advice on how to budget wisely when painting your own car. Softbound, 8-1/2 x 11 inches, 128 pages, approx. 400 color photos. ***Item #SA117***

THE STEP-BY-STEP GUIDE TO ENGINE BLUEPRINTING *by Rick Voegelin* this book is simply the best book available on basic engine preparation for street or racing. Rick Voegelin's writing and wrenching skills put this book in a class by itself. Includes pro's secrets of using tools, selecting and preparing blocks, cranks, rods, pistons, cylinder heads, selecting cams and valvetrain components, balancing and assembly tips, plus worksheets for your engine projects, and much more! Softbound, 8-1/2 x 11 inches, 128 pages, over 400 b/w photos. ***Item #SA21***

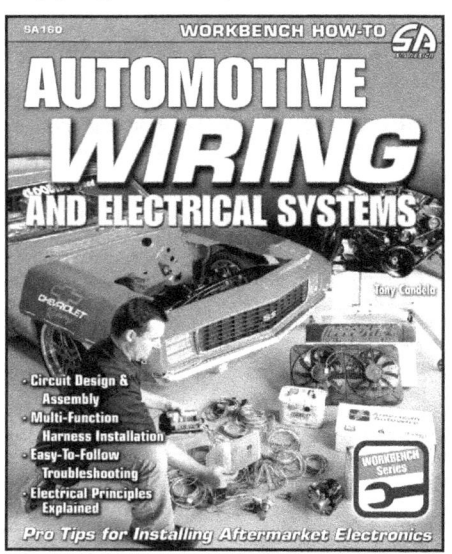

AUTOMOTIVE WIRING AND ELECTRICAL SYSTEMS *by Tony Candela* This book is the perfect book to unshroud the mysteries of automotive electrics and electronic systems. The basics of electrical principles, including voltage, amperage, resistance, and Ohm's law, are revealed in clear and concise detail, so the enthusiast understands what these mean in the construction and repair of automotive electrical circuits. Softbound, 8-1/2 x 11 inches, 144 pages, approx. 350 color photos. ***Item #SA160***

AUTOMOTIVE BODYWORK AND RUST REPAIR *by Matt Joseph* This book shows you the ins and outs of tackling both simple and difficult rust and metalwork projects. This book teaches you how to select the proper tools for the job, common-sense approaches to the task ahead of you, preparing and cleaning sheet metal, section fabrications and repair patches, welding options such as gas and electric, forming, fitting and smoothing, cutting metal, final metal finishing including filling and sanding, the secrets of lead filling, making panels fit properly, and more. Softbound, 8-1/2 x 11 inches, 160 pages, 400 color photos. ***Item #SA166***

PERFORMANCE AUTOMOTIVE ENGINE MATH *by John Baechtel* When designing or building an automotive engine for improved performance, it's all about the math. From measuring the engine's internal capacities to determine compression ratio to developing the optimal camshaft lift, duration, and overlap specifications, the use of proven math is the only way to design an effective high performance automotive powerplant. This book walks readers through the wide range of dimensions to be measured and formulas used to design and develop powerful engines. Includes reviews the proper tools and measurement techniques, and carefully defines the procedures and equations used in engineering high efficiency and high rpm engines. Softbound, 8.5 x 11 inches, 160 pages, 350 photos. ***Item #SA204***

www.cartechbooks.com or 1-800-551-4754

www.ingramcontent.com/pod-product-compliance
Lightning Source LLC
Chambersburg PA
CBHW051413070526
44584CB00023B/3409